M000287397

Interanimations

# Interanimations

*Receiving Modern German Philosophy*

Robert B. Pippin

The University of Chicago Press
Chicago and London

**Robert B. Pippin** is the Evelyn Stefansson Nef Distinguished Service Professor in the John U. Nef Committee on Social Thought, the Department of Philosophy, and the College at the University of Chicago. He is the author of several books, including *After the Beautiful* and *Nietzsche, Psychology, and First Philosophy*, both also published by the University of Chicago Press.

The University of Chicago Press, Chicago 60637
The University of Chicago Press, Ltd., London

Printed in the United States of America

24 23 22 21 20 19 18 17 16 15    1 2 3 4 5

ISBN-13: 978-0-226-25965-9 (cloth)
ISBN-13: 978-0-226-25979-6 (e-book)

DOI: 10.7208/chicago/9780226259796.0001

Library of Congress Cataloging-in-Publication Data

Pippin, Robert B., 1948– author.
Interanimations : receiving modern German philosophy / Robert B. Pippin.
pages cm
Includes bibliographical references and index.
ISBN 978-0-226-25965-9 (cloth : alk. paper)
ISBN 978-0-226-25979-6 (e-book)
1. Philosophy, German—19th century. 2. Philosophy, German—20th century. 3. Hegel, Georg Wilhelm Friedrich, 1770–1831. 4. Nietzsche, Friedrich Wilhelm, 1844–1900. I. Title.
B2741.P57 2015
193—dc23

2014044794

♾ This paper meets the requirements of ANSI/NISO Z39.48-1992 (Permanence of Paper).

# Contents

# Introduction

> Philosophy without the history of philosophy,
> if not empty or blind, is at least dumb.
> —Wilfrid Sellars, *Science and Metaphysics*

## I

"The history of philosophy," along with its various subdivisions ("ancient," "early modern," "nineteenth-century German," and so forth), is now a standard category in academic philosophy. But it means different things to different people. In particular it means two different things.

For one group, the primary job of "the historian" is to state as clearly as possible what a philosopher meant to say by writing what he did. The goal is straightforward: *explication de texte*. For some in this group, this means locating the writing in its proper historical context, both social and philosophical, identifying the philosopher's likely interlocutors, and understanding the influences on the position as well as the way the ideas were taken up by the philosopher's successors. The history of philosophy, in other words, is intellectual history, not philosophy.

For another, smaller group of "historians" in this first group, this localization and context setting is useful but not so important. Their guiding assumption is a kind of perennialism. The greatest questions—How ought one to live? What is forever forbidden and why? How can a many also be a one? Are we just atoms in the void?—are eternal and must reappear and must be faced by every age. The assumption is that attending to what the greatest philosophers have thought and written about these questions is the best way to think about them—the best way to learn *how* to think about these questions—for oneself. The assumption is often that interpreting what the philosopher meant to say can be extremely difficult, and that such a difficulty is not eased by attention to inheritances, influences, or contexts. One must, every age must, simply grapple with the classic text, engaging in very careful "close reading." The relation to the text can sometimes be more pious than critical, rather as if one's job is to understand and revere.

Scholars in philosophy departments engaged in recovery of the past can be motivated by a belief in the inherent "preservationist" value of correctly capturing the meaning of a text or the transmission of ideas. They might differ from the professional historian of ideas only on the assumption that a thorough training in philosophy is necessary to formulate the ideas properly. Or they might argue, as Sellars claimed, that the history of philosophy is the lingua franca of philosophy itself.[1] Without a proper education in such a history, it could be argued, we can lose sight of why some contemporary problem is a problem, can fail to appreciate either the depth or the triviality of some current formulation, will not fully appreciate the varieties of ways philosophy can go about its business, or can be busily reinventing the wheel, unaware of how much work had already been done, how many dead ends already discovered. But, again, for anyone in this first group: the history of philosophy is not philosophy. It is at best preparatory or ancillary to, or a kind of reenactment of, philosophy, not a way of, as it is said, "doing philosophy."

For a second group, writing about historical figures can indeed be a way of "doing philosophy." To understand such an idea, and to understand the dangers of such an approach, we should first recall the striking remark by Ulrich von Wilamowitz-Moellendorff in his famous lecture at Oxford in 1908, "Greek Historical Writing." Wilamowitz said something of relevance to the authors discussed here. He said that

> our task is to revivify life that has passed away. We know that ghosts cannot speak until they have drunk blood, and the spirits we evoke demand the blood of our hearts.[2]

1. Sellars, *Science and Metaphysics*, 1. The whole paragraph is a fine statement, and it is the source of the chapter epigraph.

2. Wilamowitz-Moellendorff, *Greek Historical Writing and Apollo*, trans. G. Murray, 25.

I understand this gory metaphor to mean the following. While most with any interest in a historical figure would concede the necessity of a thorough scholarly preparation, and acknowledge that it is necessary to know the original language and what a philosopher would mean by writing *that, then,* and *for whom,* this preparation is not the end of the story. The simple question driving this version of writing about great figures in the philosophical past is: *Is what the philosopher wrote true,* or at least philosophically valuable for us today, comprised of ideas we can actually learn from? In fact, for many in this group the historical/hermeneutical and philosophical/evaluative cannot be separated. We cannot understand what a philosopher meant to say without understanding why the philosopher felt entitled to claim what he claimed. They are not separate questions. In approaching works of philosophy, there is no separation between assessment and understanding. This involves trying to reconstruct a philosopher's arguments with some charity and respect (often very hard to do, perhaps because one might have to fill in gaps in an argument when they are seen to occur), or in effect "philosophizing along with" the philosopher. The German Romantics, especially Friedrich Schlegel in his *Gespräch über die Poesie,* even invoked a kind of term of art for this and argued it was essential for philosophy, not just explicative: *symphilosophieren,* philosophizing with or together.[3] This could be one meaning of providing "the blood of our hearts": to treat the philosophers as living interlocutors in philosophy (or to bring them back to life), not as dead figures of mere historical interest, the way a chemist might treat the history of chemistry. These ghosts of the past will not speak to us unless we "revivify" them with such a genuinely philosophical mode of address. We must be so invested in this encounter that we are willing to admit that some of our most deeply held philosophical convictions can be challenged by these ghosts.

Wilamowitz was well aware of the dangers of such an approach. It is after all *our* blood that we are supplying. He went on to say that, if such ghosts drink, then "something from us has entered into them; something alien, that must be cast out."[4] And it is true that some approach the history of philosophy as "plunderers," or pirates, taking what they can use for their own purposes, ventriloquizing their own ideas in the historical figure's, importing an alien, incompatible framework, and contorting the historical

3. Schlegel, *Kritische Ausgabe seiner Werke: Charakteristiken und Kritiken I,* 2:285–86.

4. Wilamowitz-Moellendorf, *Greek Historical Writing and Apollo,* 25.

figure's ideas until they fit ours. But with a thorough historical and scholarly preparation we can ask these figures "our" questions, not merely try to understand "theirs" (perhaps even questions that the original philosophers would not be able to recognize as such), or can provide them our blood, in a way that genuinely revivifies the dead figure, rather than infects them with something alien.

There is of course one other possible attitude toward the history of philosophy besides these two, and anyone who works on historical figures has no doubt heard some version of the attitude. No one, it is argued, who is working on chemistry or physics or a sociological study feels any need to prepare for such work by understanding the history of chemistry or physics or sociology. There are plenty of philosophical problems to work on, whether they have been treated by past figures or not. We should just get to work on them. Such sentiments are animated by a concern one sees at its clearest, if less polemically, in Kant. Philosophy has a very long history, so long, and with contributions by so many indisputable world-historical geniuses, that anyone serious about philosophy has to ask: Why no progress? We have instead, still, after two thousand years, no consensus, various camps and schools, and extremely unusual geographical categorizations ("European" or "Continental" versus "Anglo-American") more appropriate to food than to any common and distinctive search for knowledge.

An understandably impatient reaction to this situation would be: Doesn't this suggest that there is something profoundly wrong with philosophy itself? So wrong that the only good reason to work on issues in philosophy is to free ourselves from the delusion that there are such things as distinctly philosophical problems? A less radical response, equally understandable, would be: with the full development of modern natural science, we are now in position to start philosophizing properly for the first time, and all such philosophy should begin with the assumption that the proper account of nature and human nature is science. This is essentially Kant's position, and in one way or another all philosophy after Kant has had to deal with such a challenge. For these reasons, the history of philosophy is not important to Kant; it is mostly a history of uncritical dogmatism and errors. Kant liberated us from dogmatic metaphysics; Frege, from psychologism in logic, and he "invented" the quantifier. There *has* been progress.

There is no way to settle all such issues here. Formulated in the right way, each of the positions noted above has merit, even the last. We *should* think seriously about why (if it is the case!) there has been no "progress" in philosophy. We might argue that this is not because of something inherently deluded within philosophy, but because the question itself betrays a misunderstanding of philosophy. Perhaps philosophy is not the sort of human enterprise that could "progress." (Perhaps at its core, it is not doctrinal at all, but a "way of life.") No one, no one credible, could claim that our default assumption should be that Ibsen must be a better playwright than Shakespeare because he wrote later, or that Shakespeare must be better than Sophocles, and if we do not see such progress, there must be something wrong with playwriting. Not many philosophers accept such an analogy, arguing instead that what makes great literature in any genre is great writing, not great thinking (already a somewhat crude and implausible division of labor), akin to what makes for great sculpture or great music. If we pursued that issue we would have to try to understand the neighboring relations between philosophy and art and literature, on the one hand, and between philosophy and mathematics and science on the other, something like the twin sources of inspiration for, or even twin sides of, philosophy. The question of the historicity of philosophy would have to arise as well, its location both in and beyond its age (in a way not dissimilar to Homer or Shakespeare).

Some examples of what the second group above hold — that interpreting (and even criticizing) a historical figure can be a way of advancing, working through, coming to understand better, and defending a philosophical position — are presented in the following as evidence that the project is possible without anachronism, on the basis of sound scholarship and solid textual knowledge, but animated by more philosophical than historical intentions. None of them seems to me at all guilty of the reproach one hears about such a philosophical aspiration — "treating Plato as if he wrote for an Anglophone philosophy journal published yesterday." In fact the examples are of reflections (mine) on other philosophers' reflections on historical figures in the hope that such a dialogic interchange can also be philosophically valuable. There is a larger assumption behind such an aspiration.

That assumption concerns whatever "success conditions" there might be for philosophy. On the assumption that philosophy is not a form of empirical knowledge (although the widespread appeal to "intuitions" in philosophy has exposed those who make such an appeal to "experimental" philosophical results and counters) and that mathematics-like forms of proof are only as valuable as the nonmathematical premises that must first be assumed and defended before any notion of proof can get any grip, then there can be no general, methodologically secure way to know when a defense of a philosophical position has been successful. There is in philosophy nothing remotely analogous to the relationship between theoretical and experimental physics, and there is no sense in hoping there is or will be. ("Experimental" philosophy has to count as something like an objection to philosophy, not an elaboration of it.) Of course, the gold standard in any serious attempt at knowledge would be to know that the position was true, but philosophical questions are often questions about meaning and value asked in ways such that strict truth conditions in the normal sense do not apply. We might want to make sense of the wide variations in what human beings in the Western tradition have valued, or how a person can undergo many radical psychological transformations and still be the same person, or make sense of the possibility of consciousness on the assumption that the only relevant explananda are neurological. In these and many other cases, the success conditions for such interrogations, *when sense has finally been made*, seem impossible to fix in any general way. Make sense to whom? How did one get from the absence of full sense or intelligibility to its presence? How *could* one? What would explain that success?

It is not the case, of course, that the mere fact of being able to convince as many people as possible that your version is the satisfying one ensures that it is in fact successful. You may simply be a good, clever, powerful rhetorician. Not for nothing was the earliest "life-threatening" attack on philosophy the charge that it is indistinguishable from sophistry, mere success in argument. But while not a sufficient condition (persuasive ability), at least the engagement with interlocutors and critics is a necessary and unavoidable condition of *some* satisfaction that one might have made more sense than before one's attempt. *Philosophy is thus essentially and not incidentally dialogic.* Every philosophical position must start out as a proffer; it "lives" (remains a live possibility, attracts attention, criticism, defense) or is animated, only *in* such interanimated exchanges, even exchanges with dead people whom we must revivify.

It is conceivable that such a dialogic condition can be created within a single mind. Encouraging beginning philosophy students to "write dialectically," not just espousing views, but anticipating and responding to objections and then imagining counters to such responses, is to encourage the creation of such an internal dialogic situation. But human imaginations are limited, and opportunities for personal fruitful encounters quite finite. One publishes and hopes for reaction; one travels to colloquia and conferences and does not merely report one's results in the manner of the scientist. One presents one's proffers. And one especially hopes for instruction from great agenda-setting figures from the past who have interests similar to one's own. In interrogating such figures, and imagining their responses to contemporary formulations of their questions, even formulations they might not be able to recognize as such, one is simply seeking the best interlocutor possible on the issues that interest one: say, a priori knowledge, acting under the guise of the good, the nature of organic unity, or the purpose of art, and so forth. Or one might come to believe that we have been led astray on some issue or other because of the enormous influence of some historical figure and might want to use that figure as a foil, a way of setting things straight. This all, again, presupposes as a condition of its possibility that the "way in" to a philosophical text from the past requires the appropriate scholarly preparation and sensitivity to historical context. And it concedes that there is no reason to believe engagement with one aspect of a position requires acceptance of all of it.

In response to all this, philosophers uninterested in philosophy's history will argue that anyone interested in the possibility of a priori knowledge or whatever should just try to work out systematically his or her own answer. Historians interested in past texts as historical documents will argue that a philosophical interrogation of these texts from a contemporary position is necessarily anachronistic. The advice that follows from both positions is oddly the same: no *philosophical* engagement with figures in the history of philosophy is worth the effort. My hope is that everything that follows will count as at least an indirect answer to such objections.

## II

In the eleven essays that follow, I consider a number of philosophers, mostly contemporary, in two cases (Heidegger and Strauss) themselves now historical figures, and try to explore the nature of this philosophical interanimation, the effective rejection of the advice from both camps just cited. That is, I try to present and explore what I think of as excellent examples of fruitful, genuinely philosophical engagements with historical figures. In each case I express some disagreement, not, I hope, in the manner of "correcting" "mistakes" in interpretation, but in a like-minded attempt to find what remains philosophically valuable in the philosopher under question.

Given my own interests, the historical figures in question are Hegel and Nietzsche, introduced by an initial discussion of the contemporary revisionist readings of Kant's moral theory. This Hegel-Nietzsche duality comes burdened with some momentous claims. Hegel is often called the last systematic, speculative metaphysician in the European tradition, and is characterized as a triumphalist about such an ending. The love of wisdom finally ended in wisdom in his systematic account of the partiality and interconnectedness of all the basic positions in the history of philosophy. Whether that is true or not, his work has to count as the most sustained philosophical reflection on the fact that philosophy has a history, and the most ambitious attempt to make some overall sense of that history. Although it is a bit of an exaggeration, it is not far off to say that Hegel is the last representative of philosophy in the grand style, a systematic philosophy. (Others take Hegel at his word and interpret it ironically. Hegel *did* succeed in bringing traditional philosophy to an end, but by revealing its inner impossibility.) And Nietzsche is sometimes claimed as the first postphilosophical thinker, the first to imagine what reflective thought must be, now that philosophy has failed. While there is something right about both characterizations, much more patient work still needs to be done on both, especially on the details of their various claims and the contemporary resonance of such detailed explorations, before any such sweeping generalities are even thinkable. Partly this is because there are by now as many "Hegels" as there are "Nietzsches" in the literature, and there a great many of both, something not surprising if the "animation by interanimation" claim above is roughly accurate. In fact, people citing some claim supposedly made by Plato or Hegel are very likely citing some interpreter's version of Plato or Hegel, often unknowingly, and that means without any sense of the alternative possibilities. (The myth of "the" text is as misleading as the Myth of the Given.) *Considering these figures as they have been considered* thus also helps to highlight what in the thinkers has attracted contemporary interest and, because the commentators at issue are all astute readers as well as philosophers, what of philosophical value there might be in such interests.

Considering first "Kant as he has been philosophically considered" involves considering rejoinders to one of the two most persistent criticisms of Kant's moral theory. Those are known as the "formalism" objection (Kant's moral law is too abstract and formal to be actually action-guiding) and the "rigorism" objection (Kant reserves attribution of moral worth to a kind of motivation, acting from duty alone, that is too narrow and far too strict to capture what we want to approve of in attributing moral value to some actions). Philosophers like Barbara Herman, Marcia Baron, Allen Wood, and

Tom Hill want to say not only that these objections attack a straw man, not the real Kant, but also that a proper consideration of Kant's actual account reveals a philosophically deeper and more persuasive moral theory. We can see that working out a proper response to the objections is thus a way of working out a more adequate moral theory and moral psychology. Likewise, objecting to such defenses (as I briefly do) is a way of worrying not only that something essential in Kant's theory is thereby left out but that, having left it out, the revisionist positions do not achieve a more adequate moral theory and moral psychology.

The four chapters on Hegel and Hegel interpretation cover the main areas of revived Hegelianism in the last thirty years: what has been called "Sellarsian" or "Pittsburgh" neo-Hegelianism, the continuing importance of Hegel in the "critical theory" tradition, and the resonance of Hegelian ideas in postmodernist discussions. None of the "Hegels" on offer by these philosophers would be recognizable to, say, an early twentieth-century Hegelian theologian or a so-called British idealist Hegelian, but all, I want to say, are exploring genuinely Hegelian philosophical claims in ways that rightly and carefully bring Hegel into the center of many contemporary debates. Again, disagreeing with aspects of these interpretations (as I do) is also a way of arguing that the philosophical value and relevance of Hegel's position are weakened if interpreted in the ways on offer. (This needn't be the case, of course. One could certainly argue that with regard to the particular questions at issue Hegel's position is otherwise than that attributed and, even so, worse off philosophically. There are plenty of examples of that out and about. But those are not the issues I am concentrating on in these rejoinders.)

The same strategy is employed in the discussion of the five Nietzsche interpretations. In two cases, those of Heidegger and Strauss, the issue is complicated because those two philosophers are much more explicitly working out their own positions, in their own distinctive way, in such an "encounter," or *Auseinandersetzung*, with Nietzsche. Just what they are trying to say about Nietzsche can be elusive. In one instance, "The Expressivist Nietzsche," I am responding to objections to my own reading of Nietzsche in my book *Nietzsche, Psychology, and First Philosophy*. Such an iteration in a discussion (an interpretation, responses, a response to the responses) does not seem to me unusual, but what we ought to expect about the uniquely interanimated nature of the life of philosophical concepts.

In the final case, that of MacIntyre, "Nietzsche" comes to stand for a whole host of modern philosophical positions that MacIntyre wants to object to in his influential book *After Virtue*. This represents yet another way in which engaging with figures in the history of philosophy can be a way of "doing philosophy," in this case rejecting a modern line of thought that MacIntyre traces back to Nietzsche, and supporting another, an Aristotelian. In this discussion, it is what is absent that is relevant to such a genealogy—Hegel's position, but, yet again, only if properly interpreted.

# 1

# Rigorism and the New Kant

## I

According to Kant, pure reason can be practical: it can determine unconditionally what persons ought to do or refrain from doing, and such persons can act solely upon acknowledgment of such a rational law, "solely from duty." Hegel argued against Kant that the institution of morality cannot be understood as a product of the exercise of pure practical reason, a matter of rational law acknowledged as unconditionally binding by individuals conceived as distinct, self-determining rational beings. Instead, while the content of the claims of morality (the claims of universally binding obligations, of an equal entitlement to moral respect, and of a necessary link between the worth of actions and the intentions of the agent) is quite real and unavoidable according to Hegel, that content is not the result of purely rational self-legislation, and so not to be understood as unconditionally binding. Instead, such normative considerations are aspects of a certain sort of social and historical institution, and have a limited role to play in assessing conduct and holding each other to account. Moral considerations are, but are only, components in a specific, historical form of a common "ethical life" (*Sittlichkeit*).

Said another way, while both Hegel and Kant agree that morality involves the right sort of respect for and realization of human freedom, and while both agree that such freedom involves the exercise of, and appeal to, reason, Hegel does not agree that this exercise of reason involves the application of a formal criterion, a "test" for, primarily, permissibility. Rather, practical rationality, or acting reasonably, involves a social practice of giving and asking for justifications in a certain way, a way that cannot be specified formally. Hegel also claimed that, viewed collectively, we were in effect getting "better" at such justifyings and appealings over historical time.

Hegel also objected to what he took to be Kant's picture of moral life as fundamentally a kind of battle between what pure practical reason legislates and what a radically evil sensible nature always inclines us to do. Hegel did not deny that there could be such conflicts, but he did object to giving this form of moral struggle a paradigmatic status. Doing so reveals flaws, Hegel argued, that are typical of all the basic and unresolvable dualisms that make up Kantian philosophy, especially that between reason and sensibility.

A good deal of the argument for these claims rests on two well-known, more specific criticisms of the moral point of view: the formalism and the rigorism objections. The first claims that Kant's supreme moral principle, the Categorical Imperative, cannot be effectively applied so as to rule in or rule out specific courses of action; it is so "formal" that it cannot be action-guiding.[1] This sort of criticism has appeared throughout the history of Kant literature, and a recent version by MacIntyre prompted several spirited responses, especially by O'Neill.[2]

The second takes note of the fact that Kant in the *Groundwork* ties the evaluation of the moral worth of an action to the psychological motives of the agent, and that Kant appears to limit the bestowal of any moral approval to what he himself admits to be an extremely rare state: that wherein the agent "acted on duty *alone*." In his *Phenomenology of Spirit,* Hegel disputed the very possibility of such a motive, and tried to show that attempting to meet such a standard would have to insure what he called "dissembling" (*Verstellen*), a kind of artificial, ad hoc reformulation of maxims so that one could technically and narrowly claim moral worth. Hegel went on to claim that the most likely result of attempting to act from the motive of duty alone would be hypocrisy, not moral worth.

In a better-known version of the rigorism objection, due originally to Schiller, Kant is taken to mean that the presence of any motivating sensible

1. The most often cited (and philosophically, the weakest) expression of this criticism occurs in the *Philosophy of Right,* where Hegel claims that the principle only amounts to a practically useless insistence on avoiding contradiction. Since there can be many mutually inconsistent policies, each of which itself avoids contradiction (like a policy allowing private property and a policy banning private property), such a rule is of no practical use.

2. MacIntyre, *After Virtue: A Study in Moral Theory*; O'Neill, "Kant after Virtue."

interest, even if accompanying an additional commitment by an agent to do the right thing just because it is right, completely excludes moral worth. This would be quite counterintuitive, as if a great sacrifice for another, performed out of sympathy and love, is of no moral value, but a grudging acknowledgment of a duty to aid, accompanied by no sympathy or even by a great distaste at having to compromise my self-interest, is morally more worthy. (Bernard Williams's "one thought too many" objection has sparked much of the recent exchange about this issue, as has an interest in moral "particularism," and so a worry that moral rules ask us only to look at what is common and shared about cases, thus ignoring that our actual reasons to act seem always tied to particular persons and contexts of concern.)[3]

Responses to these charges have taken a number of forms. In recent years an approach that concentrates on issues of Kant interpretation has become particularly influential, and it is that approach I propose to discuss here.[4] The Kant charged with formalism and rigorism is not defended; we hear instead that the Kant charged with these failings is not the real Kant but, in case after case, a straw man. Critics who attack the rigoristic notion of "acting on duty alone" as the criterion of moral worth have not understood the function of that passage in the *Groundwork*. Critics who wonder about the motivational source for an overriding allegiance to a formal principle need not do so, since they have misdescribed Kant's position. The claim in defense is that allegiance to such a principle is only an introductory aspect of Kant's position and that the full position involves a much better account of what is at stake for us when we try to conform to a universalizability requirement. (What is supposed really to be at stake, as we shall see, is a fundamental value, humanity as an end in itself.) Other critics who caricature Kant as an ascetic who formulates a moral theory with no attention to the emotional, anthropological, and historical details of human life are also attacking that straw man. On the contrary, once again our basic allegiance in Kant's theory is not to "conformity to a rule" (how could it be?)

3. Cf. Bernard Williams, "Persons, Character, and Morality," and Barbara Herman's discussion in "The Practice of Moral Judgment," 74 ff.

4. This is in itself quite interesting. What used to be qualified defenses of the purity and rigor of Kantian morality against objections that sought to understand morality within and not above a variety of inescapable human concerns and historical and social limitations (objections that risked the specter of accommodationism and conformism to make their point) have become instead a "me too" strategy, an attempt to present Kant as having already and properly taken account of various facts about human nature, history, and the nature of human sociality.

but to a substantive value, and once we understand this properly we can see that Kant hardly ignored or dismissed the anthropological and historical issues raised by his critics. (These concerns turn out to be indispensable in a Kantian theory of moral judgment, in determining what commitment to such a value requires in some place at some time.) If it's sociality, character, virtue, emotions, or historical change you are worried about and you believe Kant has neglected or misunderstood the issues, think again. They are quite central to Kant too, if his full position is understood.

It is this latter sort of "anything you can do, I can do better" defense, especially against Schiller- and Hegel-type rigorism objections, that I want to discuss. I will concentrate on two main issues here as a way of suggesting that Kant's defenders have ceded too much to the objections, or too much for Kant to remain a consistent Kantian. The first concerns the duty and moral motivation/moral worth problem. My claim here will be that the clarifications offered by such commentators as Barbara Herman, Marcia Baron, and Allen Wood do not escape the deeper point of the rigorism objection, especially as it bears on Kant's theory of freedom. The second concerns the role of practical reason in action and the Kantian doctrine of value. Construing Kant as a substantive value theorist (as Hill, Wood, and Herman do) might help avoid many of the standard objections, and others against deontology made famous by Anscombe,[5] but there is no internal Kantian reason, I want to argue, for regarding our capacity to set and pursue material ends as a fundamental value that must always be respected in all our activity.

## II

It is not difficult to understand why readers like Schiller worried about Kantian rigorism. Consider this passage from the *Second Critique.*

> What is essential in the moral worth of actions is that the moral law should directly determine the will. If the determination of the will occurs in accordance with the moral law but only by means of a feeling of any kind whatsoever, which must be presupposed in order that the law may become a determining ground of the will, and if the action does not occur for the sake of the law, it has legality but not morality.[6]

5. G. E. M. Anscombe, "Modern Moral Philosophy."
6. Kant, *Kritik der praktischen Vernunft,* 71; *Critique of Practical Reason,* trans. Beck, 75.

And, as a famous, nearly unbelievable passage in the *Groundwork* puts it:

> The inclinations themselves as sources of needs, however, are so lacking in absolute worth that the universal wish of every rational being must be indeed to free himself completely from them.[7]

The fact that Kant seems to be saying that *only* actions done "from duty alone" deserve moral praise, or our "esteem" (*Hochschätzung*), and that he seems to claim that since all inclinations lack absolute worth, they lack all worth, has led some to conclude that Kant must therefore also be saying that acts not done from duty alone have no worth or moral significance at all, or that an act with any sort of nonmoral motive is immediately disqualified from having moral worth.[8] If this were true, it might indeed be subject to Schiller's criticism.

When the objection is understood this way, the literature has not lacked for Kantian rejoinders. Many of these (especially the best and most influential version, Barbara Herman's) take the form of showing through textual analysis that Kant's worry in the *Groundwork* was not about the mere presence of sensible motives, but rather concerned actions that were otherwise appropriate morally (actions that happened to conform to duty) but, in his very specific examples, were done *only* because of reliance on such sensible motives and would not have been done otherwise.[9] A person who acts beneficently *only* to satisfy feelings of sympathy, without any regard for what is morally right, simply cannot be counted on to do the right thing when such feelings are absent, and so deserves no moral praise. And when we imagine such a person suddenly without those inclinations and instead consumed by misanthropic aversions to aid, we will "see" more clearly in the example what motivation by duty alone is, and we can thus better see

7. Kant, *Grundlegung zur Metaphysik der Sitten*, 428; *Foundations of the Metaphysics of Morals*, trans. Beck, 45.

8. Indeed, given an extremely narrow interpretation of what Kant says in the *Religion* book about rigorism, he might be taken to mean that any action not based on doing one's duty is thereby evil, contrary to duty. Cf. *Die Religion innerhalb der Grenzen der bloßen Vernunft*, 29–30; *Religion within the Limits of Reason Alone*, trans. Greene and Hudson, 25.

9. Herman, "On the Motive of Acting from Duty" and "Mutual Aid and Respect for Persons." This interpretation corresponds nicely with the passage from the *Second Critique* quoted above, since he does not there address a case of simply wanting to do what duty also requires and which I so acknowledge, but, much more carefully, a case where the sensible interest *must* be present for me to act.

that it is possible and that it merits moral praise. So, there is nothing morally second-class in someone saving a loved one when motivated in that case only by love and sympathy. The point is that (a) when all we know is that that particular act was motivated by such a desire, there is no basis for any ascription of moral worth, even as an evaluation of character. (For all we know our supposed subject would also be just as inclined to render aid by buying drugs for or lying to protect the loved one.) And (b) if we do know that the act would only have been performed if such a feeling of sympathy were present, then we know enough to know that the act is disqualified from moral worth. (Indeed it thereby qualifies as a kind of evil, according to Kant's classification.)

So Herman's solution leaves us without Schiller's problem, and is a valuable qualification, but it only clarifies a few aspects of the problem of a good will: i.e., what, for Kant, cannot be a case of moral worth, and the rejoinder makes clear that Kant did not believe we deserve moral worth only if we dislike doing what we ought to do. But since there are hardly any cases where we can definitively say a person "would not have acted" except to satisfy an inclination, or "would have acted" from duty no matter what contrary inclination or aversion, we are left with a virtually unusable positive criterion of moral worth. Surely the much more common, perhaps universal cases are those where there is always some sensible inclination to act (such as to be thought well of), or some aversion to acting (fear of being found out), along with some sort of accompanying moral motivation (and thus, unavoidably and necessarily, some uncertainty about what the "strength" of the moral resolve would be if unaccompanied).

There are basically three interesting interpretive solutions at this point, and none of them seems to me adequate.

(i) The restrictiveness would be loosened somewhat if we could show (as Marcia Baron tries to show) that the criterion of "acting from duty" could still be satisfied even if "what duty demands" is not our "primary" but only a "secondary" motive.[10] This would be the case for a very wide range of permissible actions if we could claim that even though in particular cases I acted to satisfy some need or inclination, some sort of check or constraint always functioned as a real "regulative" condition on all my action; that is, if

10. Baron, *Kantian Ethics Almost without Apology*, esp. chap. 4, "Is Acting from Duty Morally Repugnant?," 117–26. This is a distinction borrowed and modified from Herman (see 129).

my conduct is always and everywhere "governed by a commitment to doing what is morally right"[11] and thus it is true that I *would* never have performed any of these actions if any *were* contrary to duty, I can know that I only perform them if they are permissible.

Kant does of course speak of "imperfect duties" like this, as duties of wide latitude, where no particular action is required, and beneficence would be a good example. I must have a policy of some beneficence, but how much and what sort of aid and with respect to whom is not thereby determined. I can save my wife first just because she is my wife, and still merit moral approval if it is also the case that I really do have a policy of beneficence and would have also saved someone if my wife were not a potential victim in this case.

But it also seems highly counterintuitive to suggest that *in a particular case* an agent deserves what amounts to Kant's gold standard of approval, esteem, if she were primarily motivated only by a burning desire for respectability, just in case we can also claim something so speculative and hard to demonstrate as that "she would also have so acted if that desire had not been present." This seems quite an attenuated way to interpret acting "*from* duty." It is consistent with the issue of duty never consciously arising, and consistent with morally worthy actions done from the most venal and egoistic (but not immoral) motives imaginable, as long I can be said to have a general commitment to conforming to the moral law. Whatever such a commitment amounts to, it does not seem relevant to the appraisal of a particular action. (It might be relevant to an appraisal of character, as we shall see below.) Moreover, it seems a particularly indeterminate and so virtually inapplicable criterion. Its truth conditions are very hard to state clearly, and it is most unlikely that experience would ever provide us with a clear test case, since, even if it might be plausible to imagine that a person could acknowledge and act on a duty to aid without any of the previously motivating sensible interests, in any real-life instance there would still most likely be *other* sensible interests at work, no matter the sincerity of the additional moral motive.

(ii) Other commentators (like Richard Henson) claim something very similar: that an individual action could satisfy our self-interest as much as possible and still deserve moral praise if it could also be claimed that in the

11. Ibid., 113.

specific case of a so-called overdetermined action, if the sensible motive were not present, I still would have performed *that deed* (or perhaps, somewhat more strongly, if it could also be said that even if a sensible *aversion* to the required deed were present, I still would have acted). (His analogy of a "fitness report" is like this.)[12]

This is close to a point that Herman also concedes, although it means both end up with the same problem, and in a related way, as does Baron. Herman wants to cleave closer to the *Groundwork* text and insist that Kant *really* did mean to restrict moral esteem (*Hochschätzung*), that particular sort of moral evaluation, to actions *actually* performed out of duty in the absence of any cooperating interest, but that he fully realized that such occurrences are very rare, and he did not simply ignore considerations of what the agent would do in other circumstances. The counterfactual questions that we raise in order to disentangle why, primarily, I did what I did are, she claims, answers to different questions, questions of moral strength or Kantian virtue, and relevant only to assessments of *character*. That is, Herman admits that if we are able to claim that the subject really would have acted rightly without such an inclination, we can praise as morally worthy the subject's *character*, even if not this particular action.

But again, it is hard to see though how we would ever successfully get out of this bewildering counterfactual jungle. Once we must start seriously worrying about what a person would do in order to specify whether she has a good will or not, we open the door to all sorts of counterfactual speculation, and what we hold constant and what we vary can seem arbitrary. If Kant is going to tie moral worth to a good will, he must be able to specify generally what having such a good will amounts to. The counterfactual speculation is supposed to help out in that task, but then we have no way to limit the scope of counterfactual speculation and it is therefore always possible to consider such a possession a result of moral luck. All we have to do is hold some aspects of the putative life history steady and imagine quite possible variations that make such an attainment much less plausible. If we think we have evidence that in other circumstances the subject would have acted without that interest, but he just avoided as a matter of luck another experience that *would* have certainly so disinclined him to act that he would not have, does the introduction of this uncertainty then disqualify his moral

12. Cf. Richard Henson on the "fitness report" issue in "What Kant Might Have Said: Moral Worth and the Over-Determination of Dutiful Actions."

character from praise? If we can still claim that he would have acted anyway, even in the face of this weighty aversion, but we can show that his capacity to do so was the result of privileged training and education, which, were it to be experienced by someone who had morally failed, would very likely have made *that* failure much more unlikely, can we then really congratulate our agent on his moral fortitude, etc.? (As with Baron's argument earlier, any speculation about what a subject "really is committed to"—or would do in various situations—opens a door to an endless series of complex counterfactual claims about what someone would do, none of which could settle anything, since each of these could easily be imagined to obtain as a matter of mere "moral luck.")[13]

Shifting attention from actually, in some specific action, "acting from duty" as our gold standard of moral worthiness to "being committed, as a general policy, to what duty requires" does not, I conclude, help matters much.[14]

13. Baron also tries to deal with the putative "repugnance" of acting solely dutifully, especially in cases of beneficence where some agent fulfills a duty to visit a sick friend but goes grudgingly and with irritation. She notes that someone so motivated wholly by duty to visit is not objectionable because he is doing only his duty with no sympathy, but because he is *not* really doing his duty, which is to visit and *benefit* the sick, and this requires right attitudes and affective states. These can be said to be aspects of his duty because the agent has (has had before this instance) a duty to cultivate the right attitudes. (See *Kantian Ethics*, 122.) But that just pushes the problem back a step. We might easily imagine reacting with the same repugnance to attitudes and emotional responses to others that are the result of such careful and especially dutiful cultivation. One is reminded of Kant's own example of someone visiting the sick in order to develop in himself the right feelings of sympathy and sadness at the misery of others so as to be able to call on such emotions when he needs them. What could be more "alienating" than such a picture?

This problem reveals another important one too large to discuss here. One might think this moral luck problem attends every theory of character, but there are important special problems in Kant's case. His theory of freedom requires such a strict notion of individual accountability (the central moral issue often is blame) that all these dialectical gymnastics are necessary in order to draw some sort of causal line between one agent and the deed performed. Aristotle and Hegel, for several reasons, do not require such a line. This is of course one reason people worry about their positions on individual moral accountability, but at least they do not face these Kantian positions.

14. Although stated differently, Baron's and Henson's positions amount to the same thing. If, in Baron's argument, I am acting from duty as a "secondary" motive, this means that although I am strongly inclined to perform an action, it is true to say that, given my regulative, overall commitment to duty, I would have done so even if there were no such motive. The issue of whether I get credit for moral worth with respect to my character is not all that important. The common problem is what it means to say something about what I would do, and especially how I got to be that "I." See the following footnote.

(iii) Still others, like Allen Wood in his 1999 book,[15] satisfied that Kant did not mean we must be unhappy in order to do what is required, and that it is clear why Kant insisted that anyone acting *only* out of sensible interest is morally unworthy, conclude that, beyond that, Kant himself never seemed to attach much importance to whether this merit badge of moral worth could actually ever be assigned, and that he never describes it as a possible desideratum from the agent's point of view (especially because I can never know my own motives that thoroughly anyway). He therefore concludes that Kant himself is basically uninterested in these complex questions of "overdetermination" of motives, as if they are issues that would have to be disentangled if the evaluation were to be applied and the theory of good will to be defended.[16]

Of course, we can't go too far in this direction, since Kant certainly wanted to tie the worth of actions to the motives of agents. But what Wood wants us to do is to look beyond the putatively minor issue of "acting from duty" (which Kant uses only to make a point in an epistemologically clear way) and concentrate more on the general issues involved in having a good will. That is, Wood wants to clear away all of these counterfactual puzzles by claiming that Kant did not mean to equate the "good will" he so values with, strictly, acting from duty. (The example of the holy will already shows this much.) After all, Kant's theories of virtue and education all aim at creating, not avoiding, cooperating sensible inclinations to do the right thing, and he is perfectly willing to offer praise for nondutiful cases of patriotism and sympathy, even if not "esteem." Generous, sympathetic souls can still be said to have good wills in that their acts conform to, are according to, duty and do not aim at base ends. The ideal that character formation aims at, being strong enough to do the right thing *just* because it's right, remains a general orienting ideal and need be nothing more.

However, Wood does not say why, in his cases of "good will, but not acting from duty," this sort of approval should be anywhere in the "moral" neighborhood.[17] He suggests that it is praiseworthy because at least what is

15. Wood, *Kant's Ethical Thought.* I discuss at length Wood's interpretation of Kant in "Kant's Theory of Value: On Allen Wood's *Kant's Ethical Thought.*"

16. A point made by Baron is important here. "Kant's pragmatic concern in discussing moral motivation is not primarily with evaluating acts retrospectively as morally worthy or lacking in moral worth, but with the cultivation of character, and, more specifically, the cultivation of a good will" (*Kantian Ethics,* 153).

17. Cf. in the *Groundwork,* "For, in morals the proper and inestimable worth of an absolutely

"according to duty" was done.[18] But this "approval" could just amount to: since we find it so difficult to act from duty, it is *better* to rely on education to create inclinations that lead us to act according to duty. That is certainly better than acting against duty and is in that (extremely miserly) sense praiseworthy; it is better than evil. But any stronger sort of approval will lead us toward the counterfactuals that Wood and others want to avoid, or too far away from the foundation of Kant's moral theory—the link between the worthiness of the actions and the subject's intentions. If, in our socialization and education, we have come to anticipate with pleasure a good reputation and are therewith strongly inclined always to do the right thing so as to be thought well of, there is of course an attenuated sense in which we can call such actions "good." They are in accordance with duty. But in *that* sense, so are the same actions even when motivated by egoism, or a desire to seem righteous, and the minimal character of such approval ("not evil") is much clearer. If Kant is going to reintroduce some *morally* relevant sense of worthiness beyond just acting from duty alone, the only criterion would seem to be, again, something like "would have also acted thus *without* such cooperating inclinations," returning us to the subjunctive world Wood wants to avoid. Again, there might be all sorts of pragmatic reasons to praise an instance of patriotism that happens not to be done out of duty, but it is, ironically, when the rewards of nonmoral praise and approbation become *effective* that a Kantian must start to worry about whether the subject could perform the acts without *these* inclinations, just as Kant does in fretting about fanaticism in what he regards as Schiller's sentimentalism, if not "checked by duty."

So, on the one hand, these counterfactual speculations are unavoidable if Kant wants to maintain that overall moral worth must be linked to what an individual subject did or would elect to act on in various circumstances. Given that Kant has an "uncaused cause," or incompatibilist "spontaneity" theory of freedom, in order to avoid Schiller's parody, we have to be able in our assessments to imagine various circumstances, and to specu-

*good will* consists in the freedom from *all* influences from contingent grounds which only experience can furnish" (*Grundlegung*, 426; *Foundations*, 43, my emphasis). It is true that in this passage Kant is talking about what is "prejudicial" to the purity of moral practice, but it would take quite a stretch to read this passage as only about rhetorically effective ways of praising action. It appears to mean just what it says: that moral worth is *exhausted* by acting strictly ("freedom from *all* influences") according to duty.

18. Cf. Wood, *Kant's Ethical Thought*, 31, and 32 on "moral approval" again.

late about whether the subject has sufficient strength of resolve to act righteously. We are always looking to that subject and that subject's possession of an effective power to act. However, on the other hand, it is impossible to get any reliable results out of such speculation, subject as they always are to the vicissitudes of moral luck. The basic difficulty here is that Kant's theory of freedom requires him to hold a subject wholly "responsible" for her character, or that strength of resolve, as an individual agent. If this sort of individual, noumenal responsibility were not at the center of our theory of freedom, the situation would look very different.[19] Such a debate about the nature of freedom is at the heart of Hegel's criticism of Kant's attempt to tie normative assessment to what single maxim produced or was in some noumenally causal way responsible for the deed. But that is a vast, different story.

## III

The following passage in the *Groundwork* has assumed a great deal of importance in the most influential attempts to answer the formalism objection.

> But suppose that there were something the existence of which in itself had absolute worth, something which, as an end in itself, could be a ground of definite laws. . . . Now I say man, and, in general, every rational being exists as an end in himself, and not merely as a means to be arbitrarily used by this or that will. The practical imperative, therefore, is the following: Act so that you treat humanity, whether in your own person or in that of another, always as an end and never as a means only.[20]

If this and many similar passages mean that Kant is treating the capacity of human beings to set their own ends on the basis of reason as itself a fun-

19. So, when Herman introduces here "rules of moral salience," or some prior-to-moral-judgment moral knowledge, we end up so relativizing moral assessment to a subject's dependent relation to that community's moral awareness, that we effectively shift attention to the quality of that community's self-knowledge, and away from the "strength" of will in the individual subject. That is a shift, I would agree, that should be made, but it is unclear to me how we can do so in a way consistent with Kant's theory of freedom. See Herman, "The Practice of Moral Judgment," 90 ff.

20. Kant, *Grundlegung*, 428–29; *Foundations*, 45.

damental, substantive value, the human good, and is claiming that moral righteousness consists not in bringing about ends or simply conforming to rules, but in always respecting and expressing the proper reverence for such a "self-subsistent end" (*selbständiger Zweck*), then the traditional characterization of Kant as a "deontologist" would be inaccurate, and the famous formalism objections would be irrelevant.

Such an approach would make somewhat clearer Kant's own view of the complete expression of his moral theory, and not one limited just to the first two formulations of the Categorical Imperative, the Formula of Universal Law, and the Formula of a Law of Nature. It would make it possible to follow more closely Kant's own exposition in the *Groundwork*, his claim that up until the discussions of the Formula of Humanity and the Formula of Autonomy and the Realm of Ends, he had only meant to describe a necessary condition of the morally good, the form a maxim must be able to assume if it is to count objectively as morally appropriate. He had not yet, as he puts it himself, "connected" such a principle with a "rational will," and had not intended to claim a complete picture of what is involved in our adherence to a moral principle. The fact that the maxims must be able to take this form was only meant to be the preliminary to a wider argument about what "subjectively," for the agent, counts as a reason to adhere to such a restriction. What the agent must be presumed to be "positively" striving for, what value she is keeping faith with, requires a deeper and fuller account of "ends." What is important in such an extension is brought out clearly in the distinction Kant draws between "the ground of legislation" as lying "objectively [in] the form of universality" *and* "subjectively in the end" (i.e., the end in itself).[21] The full concept of an action always requires this introduction of an end in order to account for the subjective motivation of any agent acting in a morally permissible or obligatory way. In the case of moral motivation, this is not an end to be produced, or a material end that gives us a reason to act because of the desires that the attainment of that end would satisfy, but, as already noted, it is unique, a "self-subsistent end," respectful adherence to which "produces" desires and aversions in anyone so adhering to such a policy, just by virtue of the fact that the agent has committed herself to that principle. Thus, when we try to universalize the maxim of an action, what we are trying to do is to answer the question of whether ratio-

21. Kant, *Grundlegung,* 431; *Foundations,* 48.

nal nature would be respected under this maxim. We want to see if a principle could be "a principle of rational agency."[22]

Moreover, as Herman points out, such a notion allows us to explain something that Kant must be able to, but cannot on the old deontologist reading: how, if several courses of action are morally required, one might be said to be "more" morally required. We have to be able to count something as more or less morally valuable, and we can only see that by attention to Kant's *value theory*, his view about the human ability to conform to practical rationality as the fundamental value. (At least this is how Herman and Wood and several others put it. It might be more perspicacious to add that the exercise of practical rationality is constitutive of freedom for Kant, and a free life is, for him, the absolute value.)

It is true that Kant writes as if he wanted to identify human nature essentially with "the capacity to set ends." The ends we pursue, especially the comprehensive general ends that emerge as the result of pragmatic reflection, organization, and hierarchical ordering, are not set for humans by nature, in a purely instinctual way, and in *that* sense we can say that "*we* set such ends." We have no naturally determined niche in the world and must set our own. In order to have general goals, we must deliberate and resolve on some to the exclusion of others. But we are also finite creatures and set any such end in a quite limited context, always—and this is the crucial point—in response to, and in the service of, some sort of material inclination, a concern not itself a possible product of practical reflection because it is already that without which there is nothing to reflect about.

That is, the claim about "rational end-setting" as an "absolute value" might make some Kantian sense if it could be established not just that pragmatic and instrumental end-setting require, in general, *reasoning*, but that *reason itself* establishes or determines the final end to be pursued, and that holding to a policy set in this manner is a conformity to such practical reasons. (To use Herman's formulation: "Separateness—being a source of reasons *all the way down*—is a constitutive feature of rational agency.")[23] And if reason is to determine the end, then the object of such deliberation must be some sort of objective good, some criterion available to reason, by virtue of which rational distinctions between better and worse could be objectively

22. Herman, "Leaving Deontology Behind," 228.

23. Ibid., 231 (my emphasis). My point could be put by saying: reason could not possibly be a "source" "all the way down."

made. But these conditions are impossible to meet in Kant's terms. Being the source of what turns out *for me* to be compelling reasons, and relying on reason itself to determine an objective good, are very different things.

The simplest way to make that point would be to note that the practical activity of reasoning goes on in a human condition so limited as to render any true self-determination (rational end-setting) by a pragmatic reason impossible. Our talents, capacities, needs, desires, weaknesses, and so forth form the background without which we would have no pragmatic decisions to make. It would be far too unfair to Kant to take this point about finitude to imply (as his claims sometimes seem to) a simplistic, egoistic hedonism in such nonmoral deliberation and action, as if I am always acting directly "for the sake of my pleasure" in the formulation of any policy. Of course I do not care for my children in order to receive the pleasure and satisfaction such attention brings *me*. I care for them because I am concerned with *their* welfare as my end, not mine. But it is also misleading to infer that their well-being is thereby an "intrinsic" value or a good in itself that reason alone can "set." I do not reason out that their welfare is an objective good. I cannot help the needs and feelings I have in a family life, and I formulate my pragmatic plans about my children not because of any rational reflection on "why one ought to have children and do things for children" (there is no objective measure of possible material ends, according to Kant), but because of the needs, emotional ties, and love that I experience as requiring a plan in the first place, and in the service of which I act. And I don't have to be *experiencing* an emotion like great sympathy for their suffering to be able to say that many of my actions are intended to alleviate their suffering, all because of my inextricable attachment to them. So, my holding through thick and thin, and through the temptations of egoism, to a plan for the well-being of my children surely does not manifest an end "set" purely by reason, and "what holds me" to my plan is surely not how attached I am to my worth as a rational end-setter—all even though a lot of "reasoning" is going on as I determine what to do. And in the same sense, when I fail to hold to this end that I have set for myself, that failure cannot be described as a "failure of practical rationality." It is my love for my children, pursued in as rationally reflected a way as possible, that must ultimately be counted as decisive in what I do, and my keeping faith with such ends has to do with their matter-of-fact importance to me, not any ultimate sense of my own worth. And none of this need mean that a desire or inclination somehow pushes or causally determines what I do. Of course, I have to count such a need as worth acting on, but for Kant, reasoning "runs out" very quickly in any attempt to determine what is objectively better or worse to do.

Or at least, it "runs out" if we assume, as I think we should, that if reason is truly to set an end, it can do so only by discriminating objectively better from objectively worse, or by determining the objective good. I take it that it is uncontroversial that Kant does not think reason alone can reach such absolute material results on its own. But the situation is not much helped if we qualify the goal and try to have reason determining something like the objectively good "for me." Reason is just not doing the lion's share of the work in such limited circumstances. What makes a career like police work, say, objectively "better" for me than philosophy must be completely relativized to what I regard as more important in life (fame, the truth, the will of God), and then, even my reflective determination of what should be the most important in *that* sense must again be relativized to considerations that I already count as weighty in this sense, and so on.

Moreover, the role that such a claim about "objective value" can play has to be very different in Kant's theory. The idea that something's being an objective end-in-itself, our rational nature, gives us thereby reasons to act suggests a familiar teleological structure. A certain state of being or of mind is better, and so gives us stronger reasons to pursue it, just because it can be said to further or promote what it must be assumed we are all seeking to realize or fulfill: our essential natures. I take it as also uncontroversial that Kant cannot accept this sort of link between having a nature and thereby having a reason to act. The reason-giving character of such an end for him does not come to some overall objective benefit (e.g., happiness, contentment). His claim is that we are obligated to respect such an end unconditionally, apart from any reason connected to benefit. And (here we have reached both the deepest and most controversial aspect of Kant's theory) we are so obligated because we must be assumed to *have obligated ourselves*. The law demanding such respect is "*self-legislated*." The end gets its value because we give it to such an end. Whatever this means, its invocation at this point at least demonstrates how far we are from the kind of appeal made in teleological accounts of practical reasons. There is no way Kant could count "being rational end-setters" as providing reasons to act without contradicting his most important claim in moral theory: that we are only bound to what we bind ourselves to.

And it is at least clear why it is so important to the "substantive value Kantians" nevertheless to try to claim that "it is reason that ultimately sets all our ends on the basis of a determination of objective goodness of those ends." This is so important because it is the heart of the claim that reason is the absolute and sole *source* of all human value, and that claim is the heart of an argument about why I "have a reason" (am bound) to respect unconditionally the rational capacity in all others to set ends. If, as maintained above, "reasoning" (about means or relations among ends) is just one of the factors involved in ends getting set, the consistency claim could just show that I cannot coherently attribute such a role to reasoning in my own case (whatever role it has, however great or small) and that I then deny it to others. If, on the other hand, reason is the absolute condition of all value, there is no such variance possible. Reason in all of us must have the status of an absolute value, in order for anything else to have a value. But, as I have tried to show, that argument is not available to Kant.

# 2

# Robert Brandom's Hegel

Bob Brandom's marvelous *Tales of the Mighty Dead* is an essay in "reconstructive metaphysics," especially the metaphysics of intentionality. Not surprisingly, he is drawn to early, implicit manifestations of his own account of the essential elements of a successful explanation of intentionality: that it be functionalist, inferentialist, holist, normative, social pragmatist, and, we now see more clearly, historically inflected. Brandom himself wants to claim that intentionality is not the primordial phenomenon in human mindedness; it is derivative, depending on normativity, that is, the achievement of socially recognized normative statuses constituted by normative attitudes, and in such a context, Brandom's Hegel has to qualify as the most promising Brandomian, *avant la lettre*. "Making it explicit" is as important to Hegel as to Brandom. Hegel's notions of being-for-self and being-for-others, and their inseparability; the contrast between certainty and truth; the attack on any logical or empiricist atomism; the insistence on holism; the rejection of any Cartesian dualism between body and mind in favor of a compatible and systematically connected distinction between the factual and the normative;[1] the achievement of socially recognitive statuses as essential to

1. Brandom is, I think, profoundly right to say that for Hegel the realm of the *geistig*, the spiritual, is "the normative order" ("Reason, Expression, and the Philosophic Enterprise," 94). See also Pippin, "Naturalness and Mindedness: Hegel's Compatibilism," and Brandom, *Making It Explicit: Reasoning, Representing, and Discursive Commitment*, 30 ff. and 624 ff.

the possibility of intelligibility and understanding—all these and more have strong roles to play in Brandom's theory too.

I want to raise a number of questions about Brandom's Hegel, but I should admit at the outset that the relevance of those questions will depend on just what Brandom means by the *de re* method of interpretation he defends at the beginning of *TMD*.[2] I note that on the one hand, Brandom admits that his methodology involves "selection, supplementation and approximation,"[3] "selection" being the source of potential controversy since it is easy to imagine it functioning as a Get Out of Jail Free Card whenever questions about textual fidelity arise. This "selection" issue is especially critical because, as Brandom of course knows, Hegel's theory of normativity in his *Phenomenology* is much, much broader in scope than the issues in Hegel about which Brandom has, up to this point at least, commented. Hegel's theory ranges over religion, art, burial practices, the Crusades, slavery, phrenology, hedonism, morality, and forgiveness. Indeed, Hegel's version of the theory seems to do, in effect, exactly what Noam Chomsky worried about when criticizing Donald Davidson (past winner of the international Hegel Prize). When Chomsky accused Davidson of "erasing the boundary between knowing a language and knowing our way around the world generally" and complained that this would push a study of language (conceived in either a Davidsonean or a Brandomian/Hegelian, holist way) into a "theory of everything," Hegel would simply nod and agree and wait

2. Brandom, *Tales of the Mighty Dead* (hereafter referred to in the text as *TMD*). Brandom understands philosophical texts in a way consistent with his way of understanding understanding: the meaning of these texts is a matter of inferentially articulated commitments; we understand what a concept in a particular text means by seeing how it is used by an author, what moves it licenses and what it prescribes, and how it would be understood (used) in the community at the time. Or, in a different approach, we can try to understand how an original concept would be used in a later context, such as ours. In this latter case, one is concerned not with what the author took to follow from her premises but with what really *does* follow. One can focus on what the conceptual content is *about*; what the author must be committed to if truth is to be preserved, given what one now knows, or given what logical expressive resources one now has. This is roughly what Brandom means by the difference between interpretations or "specifications of conceptual content" and "discursive scorekeeping," *de dicto* and *de re*, and his importation here of his own semantic arsenal, with its core distinction between undertaking and attributing commitments, serves his hermeneutical purposes very well. As the magisterial chapter 8 of *Making It Explicit* argues, these two specifications are not ascriptions of different beliefs, beliefs with different contents. They "specify the single conceptual content of a single belief in two different ways, from two different perspectives, in two different contexts of auxiliary commitments" (*TMD*, 102).

3. Ibid., 111.

for what he would recognize as some sort of criticism to appear.[4] *Das Wahre ist das Ganze,* after all. While it is of course possible to "select out" most of Hegel's account in order to concentrate on "*what in Hegel's idealist, pragmatist, historicist holism might be relevant to a theory of conceptual content,*"[5] that possibility at least raises the question of whether those elements in Hegel's thought are isolatable in this way, whether, seen in the light of Hegel's full *theory of normativity and especially normative change* (in effect what Hegel understood as his philosophical "theory of everything"),[6] even the role of such notions in an account of conceptual content will have to look different.

So there is some danger that the somewhat broader questions I want to raise could look irrelevant to the specific purpose to which Brandom wants to put Hegel's "objective idealism," or that they can be treated as topics for further study, once the nature of conceptuality is clear. But I don't think that the tasks can be divided like this, and I take my bearings on the issue from Brandom's own self-imposed requirements, as when he asks questions like: "Do the notions of objective idealism and conceptual determinations that result from the two Hegel chapters [in *TMD*] fit well with other things Hegel says?"[7] This is just the question I want to pose,[8] especially because

4. Chomsky, *New Horizons in the Study of Language and Mind,* 146. See also Richard Rorty's very valuable (non-Hegelian) response to such worries in "The Brain as Hardware, Culture as Software."

5. *TMD,* 111.

6. Chomsky of course means that holist, conceptual-role linguists would have to be committed to a natural-scientific theory of everything; their version of language would not leave a discrete research program for modern neurolinguists.

7. Brandom, *TMD,* 114.

8. This question of "responsibility" to the text is a tricky problem to raise since however one raises it, one can seem to be insisting on some kind of *priority* for *de dicto* interpretation, and that is not, I think, what Brandom means. This assumption would take us back to thinking of original or core meaning as locked up inside a text, instead of in the process-like, inferential way proposed by Brandom. *De re* interpetation is something *else,* something different, and equally respectable philosophically. Once Strawson, say, has discarded the problem of the justification of synthetic a priori judgments and Kant's idealism claim that we only know appearances, there is not much in his *de re* reconstruction that Kant could have acknowledged as a commitment. But there is *something* of Kant left after the "selection" and "supplementation," something of what *Kant* really looks like *in* the new context of Strawsonean descriptive metaphysics. What is left is the distinction between concepts and intuitions, the discursivity of the human intellect, and the idea of there being "bounds" to any experience we could make sense of. *De re* interpretation is a process, a way of navigating in *our* territory, but guided by *some* insight of a historical author. So even within interpretation understood this way, there must *be* this guidance, this responsiveness to, say, *Hegel's* understanding of conceptual content, even when expressed throughout in a non-Hegelian, new "logical expressive" vocabulary. (This is already a version of a common and

I am not sure that Brandom can get what he wants out of Hegel without something like Hegelian, comprehensive "theory of everything" questions inevitably arising. (I have also not found it possible to deal with Brandom's Hegel without importing a good deal of Brandom's Brandom, in *Making It Explicit*.[9])

There are several examples of how that problem arises. I only have time to discuss four well-known Hegelian claims and Brandom's take on them (or the absence of a take), and, as is common in these encounters, no time at all to describe how much I have learned from these extraordinary and inspiring essays. (i) Hegel's philosophy is an idealism. (ii) This idealism is a holism. (iii) Rational norms must be understood as *socially* instituted over time. This means that their binding force comes from our having subjected ourselves to them (they are "self-legislated") and that later norms can be understood as the *result* of various breakdowns and crises in earlier institutions. Indeed, in Hegel's account our being able to understand them as such responses is a crucial feature in the claim that later norms are more developed, a more successful actualization of the appeal to reason in human affairs, and so that they make possible a greater realization of freedom. At the very least one important aspect of this development must involve, Hegel thinks, some sort of social "struggle for recognition," sometimes violent, resolvable at all only in a state of true mutuality. (iv) Finally, philosophy is historical, fundamentally, and always "of its time," where that means several controversial things. The most controversial was just mentioned: human history should be understood as the progressive realization of freedom, and this because reason is more and more "actual" in human affairs and freedom is self-rule according to laws of reason.

In each of these four cases, not only are Hegel's broader ambitions curtailed by Brandom, but the absence of these broader goals means that questions have to arise for Brandom's project that cannot be answered with the resources developed by it.

---

very sweeping intuitive reaction to Brandom's inferentalism: that understanding the content of a concept cannot be exclusively understanding its inferential articulations since those material implications and incompatibilities must themselves be already guided by [are legitimated by appeal to] a grasp of something which directs such inferential processes. He has several ways of responding to this, and the issue will come up frequently below.)

9. Brandom, *Making It Explicit: Reasoning, Representing, and Discursive Commitment* (hereafter referred to in the text as *MIE*).

# I

The first issue is *idealism*, a term Hegel uses in a wide variety of ways.[10] But whatever else he means, he certainly also means to signal an attack on at least one dogma of empiricism. The first three chapters in the *Phenomenology of Spirit* are clearly out to argue that no story about the origin of concepts, and no use of such a story to defend the objectivity of concepts, can rely on appeal to any putatively immediately given or noninferentially warranted content, sensory or otherwise, as foundational or as tribunal. The unavailability of *any* sort of directly intuited item, even in concept realism or rationalist theories of *noesis*, means that we will need a different sort of story to justify the normative constraints imposed on the origination and explanation of judgmental claims, where they can be justified. This does not mean that one of those constraints cannot be something like "what experience won't let us say about it," but the nature and workings of that constraint will have to be different from any appeal to immediacy, the given, etc.

This can fairly be called an idealism since it seems to make the possibility of experience, experiential knowledge, and explanatory success *dependent* on conceptual rules that are not themselves empirically derived, given that the possibility of empirical experience already depends on such discriminating capacities. Thus it can be said that such required discriminatory capacities and processes are "contributed by us," and are contentful only by virtue of their role in our practices, not by virtue of some story that can be traced back to something directly available in experience.[11] Since many people for many years understood Kant's version of this claim to be saying that such a dependence meant we could not be said to be experiencing external objects in the normal sense but only mind-dependent entities, appearances, or *Erscheinungen*, and since whatever else he is saying, Hegel is clearly not saying *that*, at least in Hegel's case we will have to be careful about what such dependence amounts to.

10. Sometimes idealism is simply another word for philosophy; sometimes (it is claimed) it is invoked to attack any ontological commitment to finite particulars (cf. Hegel, *Wissenschaft der Logik* 1:145; *Science of Logic*, trans. Miller, 154–55); sometimes (it is claimed) it means a Platonic claim that all of reality is actually a manifestation of "the Absolute Idea."

11. In Hegel's radical language, concepts are "self-determining." He is forever saying that the Concept gives itself its own content. See Pippin, "Die Begriffslogik als die Logik der Freiheit."

Brandom proposes a helpful distinction at this point. He suggests that we should distinguish between sense-dependence and reference-dependence and that doing so helps us see there is no evidence that Hegel understood his own claim of dependence as anything but sense-dependence; that is, that he did not believe all finite particulars were existentially dependent on concepts that could pick them out, or that such objects could only exist when and for as long as they were thought by a human or a divine mind. Rather, in the examples used by Brandom, "the concepts of singular term and object are reciprocally sense-dependent. One cannot understand either without at least implicitly understanding the other and the basic relations between them."[12] Likewise with the concept "fact" and "what is assertable in a proposition"; likewise law and necessity on the one hand, and counterfactually robust inference on the other.[13] Reciprocal sense-dependence like this—essentially between modally robust material exclusions in reality and subjective processes for identifying such exclusions and trying to avoid incompatible commitments—thus helps one interpret some of the well-known battle cries in Hegel's assertion of his idealism, such as, in his *Differenzschrift*, "The principle of speculation is the identity of subject and object,"[14] i.e., the principle of speculative idealism is the reciprocal sense-dependence of subjective processes and meaningful claims about objects.[15]

This interpretation of "objective idealism," the claim that the intelligibility of the notion of an objective world is dependent on, and is only intelligible in terms of, the subjective process of acknowledging error in experience, or rejecting incompatible commitments, is clearly a variation, albeit a weak variation, on Kant's radical Transcendental Turn, such that all "object talk" could amount to (the only determinate experiential content that could be given the notion) is rule-governed synthetic unity, that the object *is* just "that in the concept of which the manifold is united." But this Kantian

12. Brandom, *TMD*, 197.

13. For a much fuller defense of such views, especially with regard to the role of singular terms, see chapter 6 of *MIE*. The great advantage of Brandom's way of formulating the issue of idealism is that it demystifies the notion of a normative fact. See *MIE*, 625, and especially Habermas, "From Kant to Hegel: On Robert Brandom's Pragmatic Philosophy of Language," and Brandom's reply, "Facts, Norms, and Normative Facts: A Reply to Habermas."

14. Hegel, *The Difference between Fichte's and Schelling's Systems of Philosophy*, trans. Harris and Cerf, 80; *Differenz des Fichte'schen und Scelling'schen Systems der Philosophie*, 6.

15. There is a form of reference-dependence in Brandom's fuller account, but it is, as he says, "asymmetrical." There could not be concept-wielding, judging subjects unless reality were conceptually articulated in the way Brandom proposes; but not vice versa.

heritage would also seem to raise inevitably the Kantian question of just how robust Brandom's version of this dependence is, what I called his weak Kantian variation.[16]

That is, when Kant claimed that there is a "sense-dependence" between a notion like "*event*" and "*capacity to distinguish a succession of representations from a representation of succession*," and that this discrimination must itself be possible because otherwise there could not be a unity of apperception, and that it *is* only possible on the condition that all elements intuited successively in a manifold follow from another (some other) according to a rule (with necessity), he was not making the rather anodyne observation that the meaning of any claim to discrimination and unity in our experience is dependent on what could count as discriminable to us, given whatever capacities to discriminate we possess, and so whatever discriminatory capacities we do have constitute in some way what intelligible claims about discriminable objects could meaningfully amount to. *That* sort of observation only gets its bite in positions like psychologism, or the positivist notion of verificationism, or in Kant's transcendental "necessary conditions for the possibility of experience" project, with its accompanying need for a deduction, or Wittgenstein's *Tractatus* idealism in which the limits of language *are* the limits of the world, and I do not yet see where Brandom thinks his version gets its bite or is more than anodyne. Moreover, for Kant, because object talk is sense-dependent on our epistemic conditions, Kant feels he has to raise the question: "Granted, this is the only way we could make experiential sense out of 'event,' but what of events in themselves, considered apart from *our* conditions for meaningful claims about events?" This sort of question may already be a mistake (and Hegel certainly thought it was), but it is not clear why or in what sense it is on Brandom's account. It is only the great generality of the claims about objects, facts, and laws that makes such a question otiose for Brandom; that is, who could disagree with the claim that the way one *understands* facts is tied to what one *understands* by the content of assertions?[17]

16. These terms are all relative. Brandom's version is much stronger than Kant's in another sense, since he understands the inferential practices on which object talk (symmetrically) depends to be social in nature, to involve commitments undertaken and attributed to one by others. That is how he interprets Hegel's sweeping remarks linking the structure of the subject with the structure of *der Begriff* (*TMD*, 216 ff.).

17. Put in a strictly Kantian way, on Brandom's account it would seem that we could get by with an "empirical deduction" (indeed a somewhat historically open-ended account, with-

This is important in a Hegelian context because Hegel believed in radical conceptual change, at what Kant would regard (in horror) as the categorical or constitutive, empirically unchallengeable level. This means that it must be possible that a kind of gap can seem to open up in some sense-making practice, the appearance of a gap between what Hegel calls (subjective) certainty and what he calls "truth," which for now we can just mark as the beginning of some sort of insufficiency in that heretofore smoothly running practice. This gap is *internal* to a practice; it is not an empirical insufficiency, or a skeptical doubt about objects as they would be in themselves, and if we follow Brandom's reformulations, this must be understood as a kind of "meaning breakdown." This all suggests that at the very least we should say that whatever subjective capacity or process we *try* to identify as "all that an object or objective structure or value claim or obligation claim *could* mean for us" will have to be *provisional* (it will always be indexed to a historical time and historical community) and that some account of the nature of this provisionality is called for. Emphasizing Hegel's interest in basic historical change in constitutive normative commitments is not necessarily inconsistent with Brandom's take on Hegel, but I take it as significant that Hegel wants to make this point by discussing the relationship between "the This" and sense certainty, "the thing and many properties" and perception, "force" and the understanding, "life" and self-consciousness, reason and itself, and so on, and does not make a case for a general dependence between discriminable and discriminating capacity. That is, there is a determinate account of what this sense-dependence could actually amount to and what these covariations could look like, and it is especially significant that he tells the story of these putative dependencies and the "experience" of their insufficiency in a kind of idealized *narrative*. And in order eventually to get real historical development into Hegel's story of objective idealism, the constitutive (and socially instituted) dependence at issue will have to start out with more substantial claims just so that various specific historical failures (especially failures not due to empirical discovery) can be accounted for.

This issue of normative change will return a few more times. For now,

---

out a firm distinction between pure and empirical concepts), and not require a "transcendental deduction." And when Hegel calls the *Phenomenology* a "deduction" of the standpoint of philosophical science he seems to have more in mind than this general dependence claim.

we can note simply that for all that Brandom has helped us see how Kant changed the subject—from the character and quality of our grip on concepts to the question of the concepts' normative hold or grip on us—we also need to see how Hegel refocused the issue *yet again*, how he emphasized as of the greatest importance how a concept can come to lose that normative grip. In typical Hegelian fashion, it is only by understanding *that* that we understand what such a grip amounts to in the first place.[18]

The point is also important when we are talking about thick normative concepts and the sort of binding force they can be said to have in Hegel's account. For the basic ethical notions Hegel is interested in also function as instituted (made more than found) and constitutive. One becomes a citizen by being taken to be one, recognized as one; there *are* citizens only insofar as there *are* these rules applied in discriminating social roles, and yet it is still possible for such a practice to begin to fail in some way not at all tied to something essential in citizenship-in-itself that a former practice had simply "missed" (as, for example, in Hegel's account of the failures of Roman or Jacobin citizenship), nor (to anticipate again) tied simply to what a later community in fact "reconstituted" as citizen. Of course, since Brandom sides with Quine against Carnap, he is happy enough to admit even radical meaning change "within" experience, and he has his own common-law analogy to explain it and its progressive character. More on that in the last section below.

## II

Brandom's holism has already been manifest. It is paradigmatically what it is by virtue of its "material exclusions": excluded are any strict concept-intuition, or conceptual scheme versus content dualism, or any conceptual content atomism. He gives us several formulations of the position, many quite illuminating about historical changes in the modern notion of representation. (As in the dawning realization that "the vertical relations between thoughts and things depend crucially on the horizontal relations between thoughts and thoughts.")[19] This theme in Hegel brings us to the heart of Brandom's own theory of inferentialist rationality, his account of double-

18. Hegel, *Die Phänomenologie des Geistes*, 57; *The Phenomenology of Spirit*, trans. Miller, 51.
19. Brandom, *TMD*, 26.

book deontic scorekeeping, and his rich account of the variety of material inferential relations.[20] There is no way to do any justice to the details of what he takes to be manifestations of that theory in Hegel, or how extraordinarily illuminating much of that discussion is. I need to concentrate on the main potential problem Brandom detects in Hegel's version of holism.[21]

It is this. Brandom distinguishes between "weak individuational holism" and "strong individuational holism." The former holds that a necessary condition for the possibility of the determinate contentfulness of concepts is "articulation by relations of material incompatibility" (where, given his dependence claim, he means by such relations both those for properties and states of affairs, and for propositions and predicates). Strong holism claims that articulations by material incompatibility are *sufficient* for determinateness.[22] Since Hegel does not seem to start off with an antecedent set of possibilities, such that knowing what a concept excludes helps establish something like the location in logical space for such a concept (as in a disjunctive syllogism, say), and holds that immediacy as immediacy (such as direct receptive immediacy) is indeterminate (and this is the notion Brandom will want to "supplement" or alter), Hegel can seem to understand determinacy as *wholly* a matter of these relations of material exclusion, or what Brandom calls "symmetric relative individuation." But if *everything* is determined by relations of material exclusion, then "the relata are in a sense dissolved into the relations between them," and we have the obvious problem: "Relations between *what*, exactly?"[23] (This is actually an old problem in discussions of Hegel. The earlier and very important manifestation of Hegel as a strong individuational holist was the British "internal relations" monist version of Hegel's metaphysics.)

20. See his introductory chapter in *TMD*, "Five Conceptions of Rationality," for a lapidary summary, as well as Brandom, *Articulating Reasons: An Introduction to Inferentialism*.

21. A qualification here that introduces an issue too large for this context. Many times what Hegel means by "Das Wahre ist das Ganze" is not holism in Brandom's sense but completeness, what the German literature discusses as the *Abgeschlossenheit* of Hegel's system. This involves the claim that for a kind of concept (let us say, whatever sort is the subject of the *Science of Logic*), full determinacy (and we can never be satisfied with anything else) requires understanding the *complete* inferential articulations of any concept in a system that is itself complete or closed. (See Hegel, *Wissenschaft der Logik* 2:486; *Science of Logic*, 826). Brandom has (wisely, I think) relaxed that requirement, but as noted at the outset, there is still some sense in which Hegel ties a theory of linguistic meaning to a "theory of everything."

22. Brandom, *TMD*, 183.

23. Ibid., 187.

However, there is an assumption in this question that seems to me un-Hegelian, a kind of misleading either/or exclusive disjunction. It seems plausible to assume that in coming to understand more and more about a concept's content, in the course either of empirical discovery or changing normative practices, we can just make do with some provisional, fixed designation of the relata, either a provisional definition or paradigm-case locator, which itself is subject to change in the light of broader inferential articulation, perhaps even very extensive alteration. We could even isolate and treat as privileged a small set of clear inferential articulations, holding in place what we are treating as relata so that we can explore various other inferential articulations (of *it*, that relatum, so loosely but effectively defined). We could do this just pragmatically, without any commitment to essentialism or analyticity or there really *being* a privileged set of inferential relations. For example, ultimately the notion of human subjectivity, marked originally by simple consciousness—in Hegel the possibility of a subject having a take on an object—comes to have over the course of the *Phenomenology* a "content" that is a function of very many various reflective and social and ethical capacities that Hegel (mirabile dictu) argues are ultimately necessary conditions even for the possibility of a simple take on an object. I see no reason to think that in order to present a theory like this, once we understand this array of capabilities, Hegel also owes us an answer to the question: Yes, but what is the relatum here, what is *that which* has these capacities or contains these inferential possibilities? There are always provisional ways of picking out designata in order to introduce a more extensive capability, but only a grammatical illusion (a "paralogism," as Kant put it in this particular case) created by this "that which" locution would lead us to think we need a fixed relatum all the way through. (Even Kant's own *Merkmale* theory of concept determinacy allows *great* flexibility in the settling of such determinacy.)[24]

I suspect that Brandom introduces this question and tries to solve it because he is worried about making Hegelian objective idealism compatible with some sort of direct constraint by the sensible world (a way to fix the relata in inferential relations in a way that does not involve representing, claim making, or content, but that ties our concept application to a deliverance of

24. See the discussion of empirical concepts in the second half of chapter 4 of Pippin, *Kant's Theory of Form: An Essay on the "Critique of Pure Reason."* See also John McDowell's criticism of Brandom on concept determinacy in McDowell, "Comment on Robert Brandom's 'Some Pragmatist Themes in Hegel's Idealism.'"

sensibility), because he wants to preserve in some strongly intuitive way a strict covariation between subjective processes and objective facts and objects (relations with no fixed relata are obviously counterintuitive in this regard) and because he is thinking of what he takes to be a Sellarsian picture of how that happens. What Brandom often refers to as "the Harman" point is supposed to help, a distinction between inferential *relations* and inferential *processes*.[25] As he puts it: "Inference is a process; implication is a relation."[26] This distinction will allow us to be more careful in understanding what we mean when we link conceptual content to "relations" of material exclusion. In Hegel's account that means that we should not be trapped into seeing material exclusion everywhere as relata simply *standing* in relations (or as, *per impossibile*, standing in nothing but relations). Objective relations of incompatibility can only be made sense of, in Brandom's sense-dependence claim, as processes of resolving and avoiding subjective incompatibilities of commitment, and fixed concept determinacy must be explicable under these "objective idealist" conditions. Once we understand that the relations in question count as implication relations just by constraining rational belief change, by playing that role in an ongoing inferential process, and we understand how that process works, then our earlier worry about Hegel's strong holism will not look so suspicious.

For, according to Brandom, we always, in our discursive practices, have to start with some sort of *antecedently* differentiated datum—he suggests *signs* like proposition letters. (This is supposed to satisfy our intuitions on the "object side.") This analogy trades on "orthodox mathematical abstraction by the formation of equivalence classes." His point is clearer, I think, in his summary of Hegel on perception.

In his Hegelian example of property determinacy, Brandom tries to make more concrete this model of holistic role abstraction by going over the supposed "stages" in Hegel's account, where properties are first thought of atomistically, determinate apart from any relation to another, and then, given the indeterminacy of these results, thought of wholly in terms of excluding incompatible material relations, a stage that according to Brandom threatens the dissolution of relata mentioned before. *These* relations among

25. That is, to use Brandom's illustration: *Modus ponens* does not instruct you that from "If *p*, then *q*; and *p*" you should conclude *q*. You might have better reasons for not concluding *q*. *Modus ponens* only expresses a logical relation that constrains what we should do (never: all of *p*; if *p*, then *q*; and ~ *q*).

26. Brandom, *TMD*, 192.

roles can now be thought of as consisting wholly in relations because "immediacy," marking as a kind of sign the content of experience responded to differentially, has already made it possible to track a class or set of such markers, even though on their own they remain a je ne sais quoi. The key is (and it is impossible to stress it too much) that this immediacy is not *representational,* a sign of something else. Our ability simply to respond differentially and noninferentially is making a contribution to the process of determination of content (to that which is in relation) but initially only in our differential responsiveness and by such items expressing *potentially* a higher-order inferential discrimination implicit in the discriminability of the item but not directly apprehendable as such. *We* must do that work of determination in this process. "One must build the holistic roles in stages, starting with something construed as immediate, and then investigating the mediation implicit in taking it to be determinate."[27]

This view of the relation between immediacy and mediation (and the insistence that immediacy play some sort of role like this in experience) strikes me as quite Sellarsian (at least as Brandom interprets him) and suggests the same problem one finds in (Brandom's) Sellars. The problem is the un-Hegelian language of "stages" rather than "moments" (in the German sense of elements, *das Moment,* instead of the notion of temporal stages, *der Moment*), and this way of linking us to the sensible world by merely causally elicited "responses." Brandom's Sellars chapter is called "The Centrality of Sellars' Two-Ply Account of Observation," and the "twoness" involved is similar to what was just summarized. The first ply is what results from a "reliable differential responsive disposition" (or RDRD). We share with nonhuman animals, some machines, and even some normal objects the ability to respond differentially and reliably to distinct environmental stimuli. But these responses, even if they involve the uttering of a word, are not representational, do not yet have content, and for Sellars this is primarily because no *commitment* to anything has been established. That happens only with concept application, and attribution of commitment by others. (There are several ambiguous formulations about this issue. In the second Hegel chapter, Brandom says, with respect to immediately elicited responses, that in these cases particulars exercise an "authority over the universals or concepts that apply to them."[28] But since these responses are merely elicited, or

27. Ibid, 206. "Construed as immediate" already begins to give the game away.

28. Ibid., 224.

"wrung" from us, the question of authority should not arise. According to Brandom, authority, or a normative claim in general, is something *granted*, not elicited.)

The greater problem comes when one tries to establish a connection between these two dimensions, since the first is a matter of what is simply causally elicited and the second involves a normative commitment not presumably simply provoked, caused, or directly elicited by the RDRDs. These responses thus do not seem to be doing any "guiding," and when considered *just* as RDRDs, they appear to be normatively inert with respect to what I end up committed to.[29] If even perception is "normative all the way down" (and "reliable" already indicates that), then these causal episodes of elicited responses look like window-dressing designed to comfort a potential reliabilist or externalist or cognitivist. Brandom claims that while some of that might be true, there could not be a *global* independence of observational response from concept use, and he notes that "purely theoretical concepts do not form an autonomous language game, a game one could play though one played no other."[30] But the reason he immediately gives is that "one must be able to respond conceptually to the utterance of others to be talking at all."[31] This almost concedes that what counts as *reliable* responsiveness (something that must be established for there to be any relation between these two "plies") is itself mediated by the social normativity Brandom is elsewhere eager to stress. If others in the discursive community administer such things as the "reliability" ascription, something of the content of such a norm will eventually begin functioning for individuals as norms, internal to the discrimination process itself, as a constituent of the sensible uptake itself. Brandom thus concedes that our very dispositions can be said to change as a result of systematic sources of error.[32] And Brandom himself also concedes that for thick moral concepts it is hard to imagine two such separate strands, such that one could differentially respond to instances of courage or cruelty, in a way that was just causally elicited.[33] Since whatever else it is, Hegel's philosophy is systematic, it is hard to imagine that the inapplicability to this case of the "build in stages" picture of the immediacy-

29. There is such an account in Sellars, but it depends on two notions that are best worked out in his *Science and Metaphysics: Variations on Kantian Themes*: picturing and analogy.

30. Brandom, *TMD*, 366.

31. Ibid.

32. Ibid., 366–67.

33. Ibid., 367.

mediation relation that Brandom proposes would not mean that something is wrong with the core picture.

The moral here seems to me to redound back to Brandom's account of Hegel on immediacy. Rather than having "stages," all in some way or other modeled after the Sellarsian two-ply, reliable-responder/normatively-committing observer, Hegel's position seems to me to be a more thoroughly "processual" holism. His position on the mediate character of even direct sensory experience is not poised to collapse everything into a "strong individuational holism," nor to adopt Brandom's building stages model, but to deny the separability of immediate and mediate elements, even while insisting on the contribution of both. In Hegel's account, I am suggesting, and in full Brandomese: The failure of atomistically conceived property determinacy is meant to signal not that our immediately elicited perceptual responses should therefore be construed as nonrepresentational, signlike discriminable items that will form something like the basis of an abstraction to roles that *are* inferentially articulated but that a fuller, more adequate picture of this one-ply but complexly and inseparably structured dimension of experience is required.[34] To be sure, this will seem to give us a much less robust picture of answerability to the world and a more important role for answerability to each other, but since in Brandom's account any immediate element in experience does not cause or on its own constrain concept application, he has that problem anyway. In the Sellars chapter, after noting the very basic theme of his inferentialism, that "grasping any concept requires grasping many concepts," he also has to ask a question that is not helped by his elaborate account of holistic role abstraction. The question is: "*How* good must one be at discriminating . . . in order to count as grasping the concept?" He answers that it is a matter wholly of how one is treated by the other members of the linguistic community, a matter of having achieved a "social status" by having been recognized as having achieved it. This, it seems to me, both undermines the real role any appeal to our immediate re-

34. Cf. Hegel's remark: "Die Kantischen Formen der Anschauung und die Formen des Denkens gar nicht als besondere isolirte Vermögen auseinanderliegen, wie man es sich gewöhnlich vorstellt. Eine und eben diesselbe synethetische Einheit . . . ist das Princip des Anschauens und des Verstandes" (*Wissenschaft der Logik* 2:327). An obvious concession here: this—"a fuller, more adequate picture, etc."—is easy to say, harder to do. Brandom has made clearer than anyone else has just how tricky and complicated are the issues in perceptual knowledge, singular reference, and modality that have to be faced in an inferentialist, rationalist, social pragmatist position, whether it be Hegel's or Brandom's.

sponsiveness to the world plays in discursive practices and reraises the problem of an inferential positivism. Our common sense and somewhat realist intuitions still require *some* response here: *What* is the community relying on when such a status is granted? Merely what future communities might, probably, decide? What constrains the granting of such status?[35] Isn't the basic question just pushed back a stage? Hegel has an answer to this, but it involves that ambitious theory of the realization of freedom and "meaning breakdowns" noted earlier and about to arise again.

## III

This last issue—our collective responsibility for our norms—obviously raises the question of the nature of the "Brandomian socialism," what he calls the semantic pragmatism, crucial to his theory of normativity and therewith of possible conceptual content, and the way he accounts for the historicity of norms and normative change. In neither case, I want to argue, is there "enough" of a Hegelian notion of sociality or historicity at work. Here is a summary formulation of the sociality-of-norms claim.

> What is needed is one of the most basic Hegelian emendations to Kant's normative rationalism: an understanding of normative statuses such as commitment, responsibility, and authority as social achievements. Hegel construes having bound oneself by applying a concept as occupying a certain sort of social position, having a certain sort of social standing.[36]

All of this seems to me quite right and a substantial and extremely valuable reformulation of the Kant-Hegel relation. It is when Brandom goes on to discuss the nature of this social status that his account seems to me not so

35. This is roughly the kind of issue that arises in the exchanges between Brandom and John McDowell. McDowell typically challenges the notion of self-legislation by claiming, "There is indeed a sense in which the source of the norms is in us. But what that idea comes to is not that we confer authority on the norms in an act of legislation that brings them into being as authoritative, but just that they are constitutive of the practice of thinking, an activity in which we realize potentialities that are our own" ("Self-Determining Subjectivity and External Constraint," 106). But the complaint that any legislator is guided by the very norms of rationality that supposedly first have to be "conferred" can arise from any number of directions. Thus Habermas, "From Kant to Hegel," 24. I do not believe that Hegel is subject to this charge of paradox. See my *Hegel's Practical Philosophy*, chap. 3.

36. Brandom, *TMD*, 32.

much wrong as critically incomplete. In Brandom's account (as well as in his account of Hegel's position), what commitments you undertake are up to you, but the content of those commitments, just *what* you are committing yourself to by committing yourself to claim P, is not; that is "administered" by others. ("I commit myself, but then *they* hold me to it.")[37] These other scorekeepers also resolve questions about what commitments you are in fact *entitled* to make, independently of what you claim to be entitled to. As we saw earlier, what it is to have achieved the social status of a competent concept applier is and is only a matter of being recognized as such by other scorekeepers.

Brandom's language of normative commitment being a matter of "having bound oneself" is quite true to the deeply Kantian position on normativity, as necessarily self-legislated, which Hegel took up and vastly expanded, himself following many of Fichte's crucial emendations of the notion. I could not agree more that this is the heart of the heartland, what distinguishes the rationalism of the Kantian and post-Kantian German tradition from its rationalist predecessors.[38] Kant's notion that we are only bound to what we bind ourselves to shows up everywhere in what we call German Idealism, reappearing in Fichte's notion of self-positing and clearly manifest in Hegel's otherwise mysterious claims that *Geist* is a "product of itself," or that the Concept "gives itself its own actuality." It is, however, a *highly* metaphorical notion in all three thinkers; there is no original moment of self-obligation, any more than there is a Fichtean I that initiates experience *de novo* by positing a not-I. The metaphor is also very hard to interpret discursively; it can seem, as McDowell has put it, that Brandom is committed to a position "that brings norms into existence out of a normative void."[39]

However, because Hegel formulates the claim in the first person plural, and as something that occurs over time, any worry about a transition from a normless to a normative situation is much less relevant to him. There is no original normless situation, only an ongoing, continuous historical process of initiation or socialization into a community's normative practices, demanding allegiance in all sorts of practical, engaged and largely implicit

37. Ibid., 220.

38. I have defended this interpretation of post-Kantian philosophy in several papers since the later 1990s, and in *Hegel's Practical Philosophy: Rational Agency as Ethical Life*. See also Pinkard, *German Philosophy*, for a narrative of German philosophy that tracks developments in and responses to such an issue.

39. Smith, *Reading McDowell*, 277.

ways, and receiving it in an equally various number of practices of consent, affirmation, or sustenance, and in a variety of modalities of self-legislation and self-obligation.[40] Hegel thinks that art, for example, is one of these modalities. As noted above, though, if the "autonomy thesis" is "what makes them [norms] binding is that one takes them to be binding,"[41] it is *extremely hard* to present a nonmetaphorical notion of this self-imposition. As soon as we move beyond explicit assertoric judgments ("That metal is molybdenum")[42] and explicit performatives ("I promise to drive you to the airport tomorrow morning"),[43] more practical and implicit modes of "commitment" are much more difficult to discern, both for an individual and for any potential scorekeeper. (We can tell *something* by what a person does and what he is willing to say or has said, but the situation gets immediately very complicated once we venture beyond assertions about molybdenum or promises about driving.) Moreover, equally important, just because such practices are rarely explicit or well defined with respect to their scope, there is also an ongoing unavoidable *contestation* about the claims made on behalf of such rules over historical time, about attribution and entitlement claims and denials, as the context of application changes and strains the original understanding. The issue Hegel is most interested in is one we would now call the basic difference (if there is one) between the *matter-of-historical-fact normalizing practices of the scorekeeping police* and some sort of *progressive normative development*. And this still leaves a lot metaphorical since, in the phrase of Haugeland's that Brandom borrows and makes use of—"transcendental constitution" is always "social institution"[44]—there is no clear nonmetaphorical reading of just *how* "societies" can be said to "institute" anything (or, especially, try and yet fail to do so, ending up with mere coercive enforcement of some against many or many against some, rather than something that can be understood as a self-obligation to a self-legislated rule). There is at least no reason to think this occurs at something like a constitutional convention of original, basic rule making and pledges of allegiance, and there is plenty of reason to think it is a problem that re-

40. This is one reason why Brandom's invocation of Pufendorf and the strong "imposition" metaphor, like a "cloak thrown over its [the natural world's] nakedness," is, from a Hegelian point of view, misleadingly subjectivist (see *MIE*, 48).

41. Brandom, *TMD*, 219.

42. Ibid., 221.

43. Ibid.

44. Haugeland, "Heidegger on Being a Person," 18.

quires some answer if we are talking about genuinely normative social engagements, and not just "carrots and sticks" success at socialization.

Indeed, Hegel believes that a kind of systematic sense can be made of the continuities and crises in attempts at institution and maintenance of allegiance—"wholesale," not just "retail," to invoke a Brandomean turn of phrase—and that without this systematic story we are left with no way to distinguish later normative improvements from later reconfigurations of social power in enforcing a new regime.[45] Without this more ambitious enterprise, a social pragmatist inferentialist holism like Brandom's is indistinguishable from a kind of "inferentialist positivism." I mean by this that while Brandom can avoid what he calls regularism or can justify attributing an original intentionality to a community and not just note regularities in behavior (that is, he can justify the claim that its participants are playing the normative game of giving and asking for reasons and therewith both undertaking as well as attributing and assessing commitments of others), this does not yet explain *how* either an external interpreter or internal participant can properly challenge the authority of the norms on the basis of which the attributions and assessments are made, or how those norms can fail to meet those challenges. Brandom can describe *what happens* when such a challenge occurs, but he wants to stay out of the question of the putative merits of challenges in general. That is for the participants to thrash out, and his (Brandom's) own account remains "phenomenalist."[46] Without that further account, though, we remain mere historical sociologists (or underlaboring explicit-makers); to be sure, makers explicit of what par-

45. Hegel, that is, believes that participants in historical communities can come to suffer in some distinct way from unreason, what Brandom calls incompatible commitments, and that this sort of suffering can explain the most important conceptual-normative change and can explain it as progressive (where it can). He thinks that appeals to reason have a social power that needs to be distinguished from the mere exercise of social power parading as adequate reason, even if philosophers can only do so retrospectively.

46. For Brandom intentionality is derivative; it depends for its explanation on normativity. This normativity is understood as a deontic matter, of normative statuses instituted by deontic attitudes. The dependence of norms on institution or imposition resulting *from such attitudes* is normative phenomenalism. This much—that normative statuses such as commitments are products of social practical attitudes—is not being disputed. The claim is that they cannot *just* be such products, full stop. For the content of the attitudes also needs to be explained, and for Hegel that will lead to a claim about the priority of "objective spirit" over "subjective spirit," or the priority of "institutions of meaning." Something counts as a gift not just because of the attitudes of participants sustaining the institution of gift-giving, since those attitudes already reflect the institutional rules for the practice into which individuals have been socialized.

ticipants count as the *distinctly normative*, and of its history, but resigned to *recording* the sorts of challenges and defenses "they" would regard as appropriate then and there, or scoring them on our current scorecard, but without an account of how "they" got to be "us." While illegitimate claims to normative authority, in other words, are clearly still putative norms, and while, when they are invoked, the game of giving and asking for reasons has begun, unless we can go on to ground the difference between merely putative and genuine claims to authority, the distinction between manipulated or coerced behavior and norm-responsive conduct will be empty. Threatening you offers you in *some* sense a reason to obey me, and you would be obeying in *some* sense in a way responsive to a reason, your interest in your well-being. But it is hard to see how one could describe that as your being responsive to a claim for a distinctively normative authority.[47] ("Positivism" is an apt word for this not only because Brandom's take on idealism can sound a bit like verificationism,[48] but because in normative terms, from his first writings on Christianity and the early Christian community until his last writings on politics, Hegel's self-identified chief problem was what he called "positivity." He meant by this the successful administration of what appear to be norms but, even with actual acknowledgment and the attitudinal support of individuals, still must count as missing some crucial element that would distinguish an alienated from a truly affirmative [self-imposed] relation to the law.)

I do not at all want to give the impression that Brandom is committed to what he calls an "I-We" conception of sociality.[49] He makes crystal clear in chapters 1 and 8 of *MIE* that he does not, that his sociality is of the "I-you" variety. By the "scorekeeping police" I mean here whatever, for most score-

47. It is open to Brandom to concede freely that scorekeeping practices can break down, change, etc. But if that is all we have to say about it, this looks like something that happened *to* the participants, rather than something they did—did to themselves and for an end. The former may be all we can finally say, but the latter is Hegel's narrative ambition.

48. For Brandom's differentiation of himself from verificationism, see Brandom, *MIE*, 121 ff. Making use of Dummett's distinction, Brandom claims that the verificationists are right to tie meaning to circumstances under which a term can be employed, but they neglect that the appropriate consequences of its use are also as relevant.

49. This is another book-length theme with respect to Brandom's Hegel interpretation. Hegel does speak of "an I that has become a we," but he does not mean by this that what a "community" as a matter of fact takes to be true or right or obligatory is thereby the criterion of truth or right or obligatory or good for any individual "I," which is what Brandom is worried about in "I-We" talk.

keepers, when each distinguishes the difference between what another *takes* to be "what ought to be done," say, and "what ought to be done," will end up *determining* how they make that distinction in a way that is shared and thus determining "how the attitudes of those who keep score on each other are answerable to the facts."[50] Again, as just noted, Brandom does not want to go there, or go any farther than this. He thinks the conditions for the success of his theory are satisfied when he explains *what* "objectivity" *will amount to* in his inferentialist semantics (it amounts to being able to make this distinction between normative status [objectively correct] and normative attitude [taken to be correct]; all else is part of the messy contestation that philosophy cannot judge).[51] We need to stop with this understanding of objectivity as "a structural aspect of the social-perspectival *form* of conceptual contents."[52] We should be philosophically satisfied with the claim that "the permanent possibility of a distinction between how things are and how they are taken to be by some interlocutor is built into the social articulation of concepts."[53] This formalism is the most profoundly un-Hegelian aspect of his theory. From Hegel's point of view, we will not really know what being able to make this distinction amounts to (as distinct from, say, what individual perspectival scorekeepers have in various times and places *taken* the distinction to amount to) unless we track the distinction as "realized" concretely and come up with some way to understand if we are getting any better at making it. (If we don't do this, we have what I called inferentialist positivism.)[54] Put in a formula: Brandom believes that meaning or conceptual content is a matter of use, inferential articulations within a social game of giving and asking for reasons. He is right that Hegel agrees with this, but Hegel also claims that the question of the authority of the articulations scored in certain ways at certain times is also indispensable to

50. Brandom, *MIE*, 632.

51. Ibid., 601. See also Rosen, "Who Makes the Rules around Here?" and Brandom's response, "Replies."

52. Brandom, *MIE*, 597.

53. Ibid.

54. Again, I hope it is clear that this does not accuse Brandom of what he has called "regularism," the reduction of norms to mere regularities in a practice. We can understand the difference between appeals to norms and summarizing "how we mostly go on" (for example, the latter can only in very odd circumstances be *offered* to someone as a reason, and, in Brandom's language, commitments must be understood as instituted by proprieties of scorekeeping, not by actual scorekeeping), all while still remaining confused about how to differentiate appealing to an authoritative norm, and merely seeming to.

the question of such content, and that we cannot understand that dimension except insofar as the possible articulations are, as he says everywhere, "actualized," *verwirklicht*. (For example, in Hegel's account, understanding why the basic norms of ancient Greek ethical life failed as they did, began to lose their grip, tells us something we need to know and could have come to know in no other way, about the difference between the purported authority of an appeal to a norm, and actual authority.)[55] As we shall see in a minute, this ties Hegel's notion of philosophy *much* more closely to history than Brandom does.

The claim is that from Hegel's perspective, the problem with Brandom's version is not so much a problem as a gap, a lacuna that Brandom obviously feels comfortable leaving unfilled (cf. the earlier discussion here of the "selection" of only some Hegelian themes), but that seems to me indispensable. This might seem a bit unfair. After all, Brandom has roped Hegel into an extraordinary, impressive project that has accomplished a very great deal in itself and as an illumination of Hegel: a way of understanding scorekeeping practices sufficient to confer various sorts of conceptual content. These include nonlogical propositional content, contents associated with predicates and singular terms, pronouns, demonstratives and proper names, and even the logically expressive content of conditionals, negation, quantifiers and so on. And this is not to mention the ingenuity of the demonstration of how anaphoric chains work in communicative success, how one can secure both coreference and token repeatability "across the different repertoires of commitments that correspond to different interlocutors."[56] Nevertheless, however ungrateful it can sound, there is something crucial to Hegel's project that does not appear in Brandom or Brandom's Hegel. The issue is most obvious in cases where the main problem Brandom tracks—the problem of conceptual determinacy, conceptual content—intersects with the question of conceptual authority; cases where everyone understands what the concept is about, purports to be about (the putative content is determi-

55. There are various ways of cashing out this notion of actualization. One would be the more traditional pragmatist emphasis on a kind of "coping successfully with reality" test, where, armed with various cognitive claims, one fails to achieve practical ends; this is the paradigm case for an empirical learning experience. See Habermas, "From Kant to Hegel," 330. There are a lot of false positives in this approach, but in general it is closer to Hegel's approach than Brandom's, as in Hegel's Jena writings on labor, the account of desire in the *Phenomenology*, and the required transition between observing and practical reason in the Reason chapter there.

56. Brandom, *MIE*, 588.

nate), but where serious disagreement has arisen about whether that clear purport is *fulfilled*, justified, legitimate, whether the concept *really* picks out anything. (Since any application of a concept is a normative claim, a claim not that this is what has been thought to belong together, but this is what ought or even must be thought together, these two dimensions of the problem are obviously inseparable.) This distinction most interests Hegel when the issue is change or a partial breakdown with respect to fundamental, paradigmatic normative principles, *what scorekeepers rely on* when they distinguish between what another takes himself to be authorized to do and what he is really authorized (or forbidden or simply ought) to do, cases like divine and human law, the claims of faith and of Enlightenment, the claims of natural right, moral freedom, revolutionary political authority, or moral purity. (When scorekeepers cut up the normative world in a certain way, such as distinguishing between "the law of the heart" and "the frenzy of self-conceit," their scores *already* mean something: they carry material normative implications, not accessible to the parties in play, often directly contrary to their own intentions, and not dependent simply on how future scorekeepers will as a matter of historical fact extend and supplement and alter the implications of their commitments. It is a limitation of Brandom's account, and a mark of his differences with Hegel, that his theory of "meaning normativity" is reductionist in this way, reducible to the attitudinal states of individuals.)[57]

The most intuitively clear manifestation of this limitation and the positivism that results from it occurs in chapter 3 of part 1 in *MIE*, the "queen's shilling" example. Brandom calls to mind the eighteenth-century practice wherein merely accepting the offer of such a shilling was counted as having enlisted in the queen's navy. The practice was intended to allow a public

57. Many of Hegel's arguments for the priority of sociality are familiar by now. Participation in a certain form of social life is *transformative* as well as instrumentally useful, and so there is too great a contrast between what an individual becomes by such participation, and what he would have been without it, for the preinstitution individual to serve as a standard for the rationality and authority of the institution. Such social institutions are also originally *formative* of individual identities, and so would be conditions for the possible development even of rational egoists and rational egoist "culture," and so cannot be viewed as the product, even ideally, of such individuals. And the institutions necessary instrumentally to protect and guarantee individual egoism or conscience-following cannot *themselves* be sustained effectively without relations of trust and solidarity that cannot be supported on considerations of individualist interest or individual conscience. Cf. Rousseau, *Social Contract*, bk. 1, chap. 8, and Pippin, "Hegel on Institutional Rationality."

sign of acceptance for those illiterates who could not sign a contract, but was widely used by recruiters who essentially tricked drunken victims in taverns into such acceptance. According to Brandom, "Those who accepted found out the significance of what they had done—the commitment *they had undertaken*, and so the alteration of their status—only upon awakening from the resulting stupor."[58] I think most of us would say intuitively that the fact that others attributed such a commitment to an individual did not mean the individual was, in normative fact, truly so committed, that the practice counted an action as a commitment illegitimately, that it does not qualify as a commitment. But for Brandom, to undertake a commitment is *just* for an individual to do something that makes it appropriate for others to attribute a commitment to that individual, where "appropriate" is a matter of a standing actual practice. Brandom's account will allow a distinction between what seemed a commitment but was really not (the recruiter mistakenly used the wrong coin), but not between what others count as a change in status and what really amounts to a change in status. *All* that the latter involves for Brandom is a change in the attitudinal states of others, and this position will not even allow the problem that bothered Hegel his entire career to arise: that problem of "positivity," subjection by others, according to appropriate, public practices, to a status of "undertaken commitments" not recognized as such by the individual. What Hegel takes as deeply problematic is counted by Brandom as a wholly unproblematic example of attributing commitments. (In this regard, the fact that Brandom concedes that "the whole community" may end up wrong in the way they score, even "by their own lights," is an idle concession. As his own theory would have it, unless we know what that concession includes and excludes, how it might actually be used in cases like this one, it is a concession *without content*, and Brandom's own willingness to agree that our poor drunken sailor *is* in fact *normatively* committed to service in the queen's navy—that *he* actually *undertook* this commitment—is not encouraging about what such a content might be.)[59] While Brandom sometimes gives the impression that the

58. Brandom, *MIE*, 163 (my emphasis).

59. See Brandom on Dummett on *Boche* (Brandom, *MIE*, 126ff). Brandom is right that the explicative task of philosophy can help make clear that the consequences implied by the use of a term (like *Boche*) betray materially bad inferences (that all Germans are unusually aggressive and warlike), but he appeals here to an inference that everyone (or most everyone) would agree is simply empirically false. By and large that is not what is "discovered" or what is relevant in a claim that the status of a lord, or the nature of honor, or the private ownership of capital,

position defended in *MIE* or the position attributed to Hegel just leaves open questions about genuine versus illusory claims to normative authority, I would say that it is quite clear that he has already taken positions on normativity, commitment, entitlement, and obligation — the positions apparent in this passage.

What the issue comes down to is how, or to what extent, one can make a certain dimension of human sociality — the institution, sustenance, sanctioning, and administering of normative commitments — essential to one's semantics without offering anything like a much fuller social theory, a comprehensive view of the social bond *or* a full blown normative theory, a theory of what counts as the distinction between "exercise of normative authority" and "exercise of coercive power."[60] To be sure, Brandom considers that he has provided a general account of normativity and a sufficient view of sociality. For the former he often invokes "Kant's distinction between the realm of nature, whose denizens are bound by rules in the form of laws of nature, and the realm of freedom, whose denizens are bound rather by their *conceptions* of rules — that is, by rules that bind them only in virtue of their own acknowledgment of them *as* binding."[61] As noted, this does not help us much in trying to understand what *counts* as doing this ("acknowledging *authority*") and what settles the question of the scope and content of just what I have bound myself to.[62] When Brandom notes that the latter is

---

all involve materially bad inferences, as if the badness of the inference can be discovered in this empirical sense. Even with *Boche*, it is highly unlikely that the use of the term became inappropriate when its empirical falsity was finally displayed.

60. There is a parallel here to a remark Brandom makes in *Articulating Reasons*, that "I have managed to say a lot about conceptual content in this essay, without talking at all about what is represented by such contents" (77). One might say that Brandom has managed to say a lot about the social administration of norms without telling us much about what a norm is (what it materially excludes) or what a society or social administration is.

61. Brandom, *TMD*, 219.

62. There are also passages in *TMD* that give one pause about the firmness of the distinction between nature and norm, fact and ought. In the Sellars essay, he suggests that responsiveness to norms can be assimilated into, are just another manifestation of, reliable differential responsive dispositions, causally elicited, not the acknowledgment of what there is reason to say. See *TMD*, 360: "Besides these language entry moves, the language learner must also master the inferential moves in the vicinity of 'green': that the move to 'colored' is OK, and the move to 'red' is not, and so on. Training in these basic language-language moves consists in acquiring more RDRDs, only now the stimuli, as well as the responses, are utterances." This sounds like Quine at his most behaviorist, not anything to do with Kant or Hegel. But see the bottom of page 626 of *MIE* on irreducible normativity. Does a trained-up language-language move that is essentially triggered by an utterance-stimulus count as a normative commitment?

a matter to be administered by others, it is easy enough to imagine cases where that appeal settles nothing and only invites further controversy (as when actions are taken in my name by a supposedly representative assembly, where commitments are attributed to me by others on the basis of what, given the institutional rules of elections and representation, I can be said to have bound myself to).

Moreover, it is precisely this *indeterminacy* that is important to Hegel. His theory of, especially, practical rationality is such a radically historical bootstrapping theory that essential elements will go missing (such as this unavoidable conflict) if we stay at Brandom's notion of "negotiation" between "those who attribute the commitment and the one who acknowledges it."[63] In a footnote, Brandom makes clear that he is well aware of this problem.

> Talk of negotiation is bound to sound too irenic a rendering for the sort of strife and confrontation of inconsistent demands Hegel depicts. But, though the issue cannot be pursued here, I think there are good reasons to treat the martial, uncompromising language Hegel is fond of as misleading on this point. Nothing is absolutely other, nor are any claims or concepts simply inconsistent for him. It is always material incompatibilities of content (rather than formal inconsistencies) whose mutual confrontation obliges an alteration of commitments.[64]

This passage has an odd ring to it. As Brandom clearly suspects, it *does* have a "Can't we all just get along" meliorism or irenecism that does not at all fit the *Phenomenology*. And it comes close to saying: if Hegel had understood Brandomian inferentialist semantics better (the resources for which are already implicit in other aspects of Hegel's project), and so had not sometimes confused negotiable material incompatibilities with formal inconsistencies or the clash of brute otherness, he would not have indulged such "martial" tendencies. But there is no evidence that I know of, and none provided by Brandom, that Hegel's emphasis on the "violence" that consciousness suffers at its own hands is just a result of such a view about brute other-

63. Brandom, *TMD*, 221.
64. Ibid., 388.

ness or formal inconsistencies. There is plenty of room for what Hegel often treats as tragic conflict if those two points are conceded.[65]

Moreover, Hegel's "slaughter bench of history" formulations are not the result of commitments in a philosophical anthropology (wherein, supposedly, a violent struggle for prestige and ultimately recognition as essential aspects of human nature are invoked as explicans for social and normative change). There is another reason why Hegel is so concerned in any account of the social mediation needed for communicative success, political stability, or ethical life[66] that one never abstract from or in any way ignore that there are never simply human agents or subjects at play, that any such subject must always first be considered either subject to the will of another or able to subject others to his will, either bondsman (*Knecht*) or lord (*Herr*). This is because the status of person or free agent, someone capable of leading one's own life, of seeing oneself in one's deeds, is indeed, as Brandom rightly notes, not an ontological category for Hegel but a historical and social achievement. That achievement, however, has as its central task the problem of distinguishing between what we identified previously here as the difference between the administration of social power (perhaps complete with the "willing" submission of docile subjects) and the achievement of a form of life in which the freedom of one depends on the freedom of all. The whole ball game in Hegel comes down to the question of whether he has in fact discovered a historical, developmental way of making the case that this distinction *can* be made (without any form of moral realism or Kantian "moral law" universalism), and of saying what institutional form of life actually achieves these desiderata, and whether he is able to show that it is the unfinished and still unfolding achievement of modernity to have begun to do all this. Hegel's claim to philosophical immortality rests on this novel attempt to make this distinction between putative claims to normative legitimacy that are in reality exercises of coercive power for the sake of unequal

65. Antigone and Creon both agree that there is a divine law and a human law and that each should stick to its proper place. Their disagreement is both "material" and not one of brute otherness, but it is nonetheless tragic. They are both right, as Hegel reads it. For more on this issue, see Pippin, *Hegel on Self-Consciousness*, chap. 2.

66. The Fred Astaire–Ginger Rogers "dance" of sociality, with entwined, shared commitments, while allowing each his or her own different moves, the particularity of each, is the image Brandom sometimes evokes. See the exchange with Habermas.

advantage (nonreciprocal recognitive statuses) and successful claims to normative legitimacy, to do so by beginning with an image of a situation regulated exclusively by exercises of power, and to show that the ultimate unsustainability of such a relation can be demonstrated "experientially," or "internally," that ultimate achievement of agent status requires a recognitive social status that cannot be achieved by exercises of power alone.[67] The nerve of this internally self-negating developmental process will ultimately amount to Hegel's theory of freedom, both required for successful normative self-regulation but impeded or denied by just those forms of institutional practice that implicitly require that very status (of free subjects).

This turns out to be a long story, and I realize that Brandom thinks his version accommodates most of it. Indeed, in another essay on Hegel not included here, he has developed a rich and challenging reading of Hegel's claims that recognitive relations can be said to "develop" out of erotic ones, that reflexive self-relations depend on being able to attribute normative attitudes toward others, and ultimately that I can be a subject that things can be *for* only by recognizing those who recognize me, by being recognized by all those whom I recognize, and by recognizing all those whom those whom I recognize recognize (including, ingeniously, me). This is the story for him of how one crosses "the crucial boundary between the merely natural and the incipiently normative."[68] But here again, at bottom, the crucial move occurs in attributing to others commitments or normative attitudes in the satisfaction of desire. I take the other to be a subject who *takes* this object to be suitable to satisfy his desire, not a being who merely differentially responds in a reliable way to what elicits such a response. And that again means attributing a possible difference for this other subject between what is taken to be an appropriate satisfier of hunger, say, and "what *is*." And, again, this not only *introduces* us to the basic condition necessary for the attitude to

67. Brandom is certainly willing to state that the entire community may be wrong about what commitments they are entitled to, and that if so, this can only be wrong "by their own lights," "wrong given how they have committed themselves to its being proper to settle such questions and assess the answers." This is in footnote 29 to chapter 3 of *MIE*, on page 674. But Hegel does not treat this as something discoverable by an outside interpreter. He (Hegel) wants to understand what goes wrong *in* the actual game of giving and asking for reasons when things begin to "go wrong by their own lights," how that "going wrong" experience plays a role in the establishment of what going rightly would be.

68. Brandom, "The Structure of Desire and Recognition." For a detailed response, see Pippin, *Hegel on Self-Consciousness*.

be a normative one (between what is taken to be K and what is K) by appealing to what unproblematically turns out to be empirically unsatisfying (a human cannot eat rocks), this simple empirical disconfirmation remains the only clear example we have of how this distinction can get cashed out. The absence of any such unproblematic "claim settler" in any more complex human claim to appropriateness or propriety is why, I am claiming, Hegel's interest turns so quickly to the issue of a *Kampf*, a fight or struggle for recognition, again an issue that Brandom leaves out.[69] It is also why, in Brandom's account, the problem with the Master's assertion of mastery is simply a matter of the Master "overgeneralizing" the human capacity for self-constitution by being insufficiently sensitive to the importance of the distinction between how I take things and how they are.[70] But the Master in Hegel's drama has not simply *made an error*. He represents an immediate option in the unavoidable struggle to determine how we shall make that distinction, once we move beyond the edible and the inedible and the like.

This Hegelian contestation also does not seem to me captured by the notion of ongoing negotiations between individuals and scorekeepers. For one thing, there is no reason to expect that a "neutral" notion of what counts as proper negotiation is available to both parties. The relevant distinction, therefore, to use Kantian and Sellarsian phrasing, is not so much between the space of causes and the space of reasons, between subsumption under law and acknowledgment of the concept of a law, but between the illusory appeal to legitimacy and authority, and a justifiable appeal—between, as it were, the fact of power and the fact of reason. The absence of such a common measure in what counts as negotiating is one of the reasons why the question of the *proper* distinction between the fact of power and the fact of reason constantly arises and why it forms the narrative core of Hegel's *Phenomenology*. (I should also note that Brandom is certainly aware of this issue and raises such a "Foucault" problem in his response to Habermas. But here again he just notes that playing the game of giving and asking for reasons *is*

69. He does, in "The Structure of Desire and Recognition," note that a commitment, especially a basic, or identity-constituting commitment, is the sort of thing one will have to make sacrifices for, but he treats the story of a risk of life as a "metonymy" for this sacrifice.

70. It is not clear to me why, on Brandom's premises, he feels entitled to this flat-out claim about "overgeneralization." Suppose as a matter of empirical fact that all the other scorekeepers *agree* that the Master is fully entitled to constitute himself as he will. What justifies Brandom's claim to "overgeneralization"?

categorically different from doing things with words like exercising power, without telling us *how* to make that distinction, and as if the latter could not go on well disguised as the former, which, according to the early Foucault, it always does.)[71]

## IV

Brandom's view on what he needs to say about human sociality to satisfy the requirements of his theory of conceptual content is certainly not one that leaves no room for the "challenges" that initiate "negotiation."[72] And he has provided a way to think about the developmental process that results from such challenges and responses. I have already expressed skepticism that the "negotiation" model will get us very far along on Hegelian tracks, but this image requires an independent hearing. There are two premises we need to examine first.

Brandom interprets Hegel's striking remark that the "I," the self-conscious subject of experience, *is* the concept, *der Begriff*, as that concept "has come into existence,"[73] as affirming that, just as one becomes a contentful self only in recognitive relations with others, so concepts are contentful only in the social game of giving and asking for reasons, in the double bookkeeping game of undertaking and attributing/assessing. Spirit as a whole is modeled on being a self, and that means that it is "the recognitive community of all those who have such normative statuses, and all their normatively significant activities."[74] This interpretation is then linked to a fundamental Brandomian theme.

> All there is to institute conceptual norms, to determine what we have committed ourselves to by applying a concept, is other applications of the concept in question. . . . Thus the applications of the concept . . . that have already been made already have a certain sort of authority over candidate future applications of the concept.[75]

71. Brandom, "Facts, Norms, and Normative Facts," 360.

72. Cf. *MIE*, 178.

73. Brandom, *TMD*, 226.

74. Ibid., 227.

75. Ibid., 229.

But also:

> The authority of the past applications, which instituted the conceptual norm, is administered on its behalf by future applications, which include assessments of past ones.

The model is common-law applications of case law, where each judge inherits a tradition of past decisions about cases and must rely on, can *only* rely on, those past cases to decide about new, sometimes radically new, cases. The authority of the tradition "consists in the fact that the *only reasons* the judge can appeal to in justifying his decisions are procedural."[76] Brandom takes this to be a good model for the Hegelian dialectical claims for both continuity and change in a normative tradition, for the fact that normative developments are in some sense "found," in another "made." The model also fits Brandom's theory well, and aspects of Hegel's, because it is crucial to both that the normative significance of some move or commitment I make almost always "outruns" what I may consciously be taking myself to be committed to, and "catching up," being able to make those further aspects more explicit, can look very much like Hegelian development or *Bildung*.[77]

This model is also said to have the additional benefit of explaining what Brandom thinks would otherwise be inexplicable: how Hegel can talk of the human community, Spirit as a whole, as a "self," but yet insist on the irreducibly social character of that self. Who, in this sense, could be said to hold *Spirit as a whole* responsible to itself, since there is no other social subject outside of Spirit, in recognitive relations with it? These different *time slices* are said to answer that problem. "The present acknowledges the authority of the past, and exercises an authority over it in turn, with the negotiation of their conflicts administered by the future."[78]

However, Brandom is out to solve a problem that Hegel does not have (any more than Brandom does), and the solution, the common-law analogy, while revealing in many respects, does not go far enough in capturing what Hegel means by tying "normative life" to historical time. The problem again

76. Ibid., 231.

77. Brandom calls this aspect of his project "semantic externalism." See Brandom, "From a Critique of Cognitive Internalism to a Conception of Objective Spirit," 250, for an interesting application of the notion.

78. Brandom, *TMD*, 234.

is that Hegel's position is far more substantive, far less formal, than that attributed to him by Brandom. This is because one of the aspects of what has been made explicit across historical time is not just a set of particular normative commitments (which are administered, altered, and perhaps substantially revised by a successor ethical community) *but the nature of normative authority itself*, the "truth" that such authority is socially instituted, tied to claims of reason that are cashed out in terms of social roles embodied in institutions, institutions the basic structure of which have begun to develop in ways finally consistent with, rather than in underlying tension with, the true nature of normative authority. Mutuality of recognitive status (the true source of normative authority), is, Hegel argues, embodied in several modern institutions (the rights-protecting, representative modern state, the modern nuclear family founded on both romantic and parental love, and the modern property-owning market economy and civil society, as well as late Protestant religion and theology and lyric romanticism, the final culmination of art). These are not counted by Hegel as *just* proposals for future administration and alteration. Brandom's common-law model works well when we consider how one might "update" Hegel's substantive institutional story and extend the application of such a civil and ethical status to women and propertyless citizens, but not for the claims Hegel wants to make about the authority of these basic roles and functions themselves.[79] Their authority stems from the developmental justification Hegel has provided for his distinct account of the nature and authority of freedom ("the worthiest and most sacred possession of man").[80] This is all parallel to the way in which Brandom's own account of conceptual content is itself a normative claim, a claim that the matter ought to be rendered explicit in this way, as a matter of inferential articulation, instituted social statuses, and so forth, and is not itself the carrying-forward of a tradition (one among many other philosophical traditions), itself subject later to the "authority of the future." Brandom's account presumably has its own authority, assuming that

79. Moreover, the common-law practice is underdescribed here. By some accounts, what a contemporary judge is trying to do in applying precedent to a new sort of case is to keep faith with an underlying moral principle, the same one animating the earlier decisions, presumably. By other accounts, when the question is what a decider of the earlier case "would now find rational," the model of rationality is something like "insuring that everyone will be better off, in an economic sense." In other cases, one tries very hard simply to imagine what a constitution framer or earlier judge would himself (that real person) actually decide now.

80. Hegel, *Science of Logic*, trans. Miller, 215.

it is meant as itself a philosophical claim, not just the interpretation and application of other claims.[81]

For the same reason, the common-law analogy is too weak to capture Hegel's account of conceptual change. As noted before, Hegel is trying to introduce into a distinct kind of historical explanation an account of the way normative notions can begin to lose their grip, thus are experienced with weakening authority, and that explanation counts crises like incompatible commitments or tragic dilemmas as arising from *within* the community's own experiences, and not because a new case has contingently arisen. It is possible that some of these crises arise from trying to apply a familiar norm to a new, problematic case, but in almost all the significant cases in his *Phenomenology*, that is not so, and the account of the underlying crisis points to the developmental account of the relation between freedom and authority that makes up the basic "plot" of that book. Contemporary concept-appliers are not, in other words, guided only by past cases, constrained too by being subject to future judges. For the most part the nature of normative authority itself is up for grabs, and the Burkean, Whiggish claim at any point that such authority is best understood as transmitted by history, exercising authority over the present, would have to count as an *episode* in that contestation, and could not count as the general *form* of any such contestation.

81. I assume it is obvious that Brandom's antirealist, rationalist, constructivist account of norms in general will, if believed or "actualized" (*verwirklicht*), have all sorts of implications in the real world, from daily social practices to the law (where his position again sounds like legal positivism).

# 3

# John McDowell's Germans

## I. The General Problem

McDowell has made clear in various writings, including "On Pippin's Postscript" and many other works, that the interpretive question at issue in much of what he has written about modern German philosophy—how to understand the relation between Kant and Hegel, especially as that concerns Kant's central "deduction" argument in the *Critique of Pure Reason*[1]—brings into the foreground an even larger problem on which all the others depend: the right way to understand at the highest level of generality the relation between active or spontaneous thought and our receptive and corporeal sensibility and embodiment. From *Mind and World* on, McDowell has indicated that this is in fact a problem so inclusive as to be common to theoretical and practical philosophy; that the issue of how thought informs

1. I argued (*Hegel's Idealism*) that such a focus was the best way to appreciate Hegel's achievement. As I understand him, McDowell agrees with the choice of such a focal point but disagrees about what comes into focus. I understand that disagreement to turn on the nature of the *quid iuris* claim (if any) that arises for distinctly philosophical reflection about the normative dimension of experience (empirical knowledge). And *that* is the problematic most at issue in any interpretation of Hegel's *Phenomenology of Spirit* and therewith how Hegel understands the problem of "skepticism" in that work as a whole. The question is what he means when he calls the work a "thoroughgoing skepticism" and even the "pathway of doubt or even more precisely despair" and what he means in such claims as "This path is the conscious insight into the untruth of phenomenal knowledge, for which the supreme reality is what is in truth only the unrealized Concept" (*Phenomenology of Spirit*, trans. Miller, 49–50).

our sensibility is at bottom the same (raises the same logical or conceptual issue) as the issue of how thought could be said to inform, to be active "in," bodily action; that we can be in the grip of the same bad, misleading picture in accounting for *executing an intention* as in accounting for *acquiring perceptual knowledge*.[2] I agree with, and follow his lead in, setting the basic framework for the particular issues in just this way. With matters so set out, there are two main areas of disagreement: (i) how to state the role of concepts and especially conceptual activity in the sensible uptake of the world and (ii) what to make of Hegel's claim for a speculative "identity" between inner and outer in action, or how to state the role of intentions "in" bodily activity. In both cases, McDowell thinks I go too far: too far in terms of what is philosophically correct, and too far in attributing those positions to Hegel. It is the former topic that is in play in this exchange, although elements of the latter arise as well. There is first an issue lingering from the initial exchange in the collection *Reading McDowell*.

## II. Nature

I had claimed there that McDowell's invocation of "second nature" seems to have real work to do only when addressed to quite a crude naturalist, one who believes that we need to account for the possibility of perceptual knowledge only by appeal to biological, neurophysiological, biochemical, etc. properties *as such*, as any perceiver is presently endowed. McDowell disputes this and claims that his invocation of second nature to explain phenomena like responsiveness to reasons is of a sort that *already* makes it impossible for bald naturalists to appropriate or co-opt it with talk of social conditioning or trained-up neural nets, etc. Such an attempt would be, he says, "too late."

My sense of this problem is the following: if second nature is *not* deeply continuous with first nature ("nature *again*"), his "reminder" cannot do the "exorcising" that McDowell wants. Any discontinuity would introduce dualism or ontological worries. If, however, it *is* continuous enough to ward off

2. Cf. "In order to introduce the attractions of a relaxed naturalism, I have exploited philosophical difficulties about perceptual experience. But this focus was not essential. The difficulties exemplify a type" (McDowell, *Mind and World*, 89; see also 90). One obvious way to sum up the problem type at issue is: how to avoid the Myth of the Given in both contexts, or how to avoid the temptation to appeal to something extraconceptual or preconceptual as explicans for, respectively, perception or action.

suspicions of the un- or supernatural, it is hard to see why our naturalist may not simply help himself to it and do with it as we might expect, develop a theory of psycho-socio-biological development ("bio-*Bildung*," let us say), conditioning, and training as current scientific orthodoxy requires. What exactly *distinguishes* second nature from first nature in a way (of the "sort") that avoids worries about "absolute" naturalism?

The ambiguity that I think is created by McDowell's formulations is that his responses to two different sets of critics are given in different registers. It is certainly true that placing something ("responsiveness to reasons") outside the scope of natural-scientific *intelligibility* need not at all commit one to placing that phenomenon *outside of nature.*[3] Second nature is always *nature* again. So much for any un- or supernaturalists (or "re-enchantment" specialists), eager to sign on to McDowell's program. But to those who concede this as only a temporary result of the current limitations of scientific understanding, he notes that there is something about some human capacities that, while part of nature, will *never* be explicable scientifically, no matter our eventual knowledge of "feedback loops" and brain reorganization. So much for the crude naturalists. It is *second* nature that is nature, and second nature is not and cannot be understood strictly in first-nature terms. It is this result, *framed in terms of the problem of nature,* that can look like a "have your cake and eat it too" position. It is understandable that the modern naturalist would ask: *Why not,* ultimately, if second nature really *is* "nature again" and if we have conceded *that* territory, first nature, to the scientific naturalists?[4] If the "meat machine" can do this or that or whatever, eventually the study of the meat machine will tell us how.

By different registers, I mean that one response addresses ontological issues (the nature of nature) and another epistemological concerns (the terms of successful explanations). I think the right response is to concentrate on the latter and to insist that the basic problem concerns the general criteria of explanatory adequacy, the appropriate form of the explicans, not the nature of the explicandum. (The two *might* be logically linked, and one *might* insist that any answer about the latter necessarily sets the terms for the former, but our bald naturalist does not get to assume this. It is what is

3. McDowell, "On Pippin's Postscript," 397: "There is nothing obligatory about equating nature with the domain of natural-scientific intelligibility."

4. Of course we might dispute this too; that is, dispute both the first/second distinction and the claim for the complete or absolute explanatory adequacy of modern science for first nature. That would be a different story.

in question. Perhaps this is what McDowell means by not conceding at the start any "default position" to such a naturalist.) What we want is something difficult and elusive: an answer to the question of what counts as explanatory adequacy, even explanatory "satisfaction," and so why the undeniably possible neurological descriptions of cognition or evolutionary-biological descriptions of "ethical dispositions" are not false but incomplete, and so misleading and inadequate. (So the question that worries me is not how the domain of reason can be "efficacious,"[5] but what is the basis of the claim for the autonomy of the "space of reasons"?) This explanatory satisfaction question is, in effect, a question about us, not about nature,[6] so I still don't see that we gain that much by noting that "second nature is nature too," or that "second nature is not, and never will be, explicable as first nature." The important issue has (finally) nothing to do with nature.[7] There are many conceivable ways of picturing the possible exercise of our spontaneous, rational, and so free capacities in any cognitive "take" on the world or in the bodily movements we count as actions. What we want is some picture of the relation we stand in with respect to the "input" of perceptual knowledge and the "output" of action that does the justificatory and explanatory work we demand of it, and while there are certainly physiological necessary conditions for any such mental activity, the question we are posing does not need to address the properties of the meat machine. Reminders about second nature being nature too just invite our bald naturalist back into a discussion that the proper specification of the normative question should have excluded him from.[8]

5. McDowell, "On Pippin's Postscript," 396.

6. To jump the gun a bit, I think this is exactly what the *Phenomenology* is about.

7. As McDowell's use of terms like "reminder" and "exorcism" suggest, this could all be considered *strictly* a rhetorical or strategic question. If the reminder about second nature *does* pacify the reductive or eliminativist animus of a bald naturalist, no one should object. But it seems very likely that there will come a point when the claim that organic beings can create practices, build institutions, and hold each other to account at a level of complexity and *of a kind* not sufficiently explained by reference to the natural properties of the organism will be challenged in principle.

8. Kant famously worried about a moral skepticism that would hold that morality was only a "figment of the brain," and thought such a skeptic had to be answered. But he never did worry in the first *Critique* that cognition might be a "figment of the brain," that, since human sensibility, and indeed human knowers, were corporeal, our experiential interchange with the world should be accounted for as an element of the natural world, in the space of causes, not reasons, we might now say in Sellarsese. And he makes clear in his famous remarks about Locke that he disagrees with Locke not because the latter had his facts wrong but because he was asking the wrong question. Moreover—and this is the most interesting fact—he also does not treat

## III. The Location of Spontaneity

An important issue is how to state properly the project of representing the sensibility-related conditions of experience as not independent of the understanding-related conditions, or how to state (with both Sellars and Hegel) that the active/passive distinction is not congruent with the spontaneity/receptivity distinction, and so how to explain genuine "receptivity" that is nevertheless not *mere* passivity (as in nonconceptual content "triggering" conceptual activation). One way or another this issue comes up in everything that follows. In this regard, McDowell objects to my characterizing his position on Kant as not going so far as to make apperceptive spontaneity "at work" in sensible intuition. (I had thought that by denying activity *by the subject* in sensibility, McDowell must have meant only to refer to a relatively weak argument: that we can be shown to be entitled to assume that the manifold of sensibility must exhibit the discriminability required by the understanding in order for there to be experience.)[9] But in his response, he says that he *does* mean apperceptive spontaneity to be at work in intuiting,[10] so much so that my version of the deduction (which depends on some sort of notional separability between intuitional and conceptual elements in experience—albeit one entertained in order to be denied)[11]

---

the possibility of a "spontaneous faculty of judgment" as an unknowable "noumenal" capacity. Whatever this "third way" is (neither naturalistically explicable, nor a manifestation of noumenal ignorance that requires a postulated capacity)—a way, I have argued, adopted by Hegel—it explains why Kant needs no second-nature reminder. See Pippin, "Kant on the Spontaneity of Mind."

9. It is weak because there are all sorts of ways in which such a manifold could be said to exhibit the discriminations we "require," as when a manifold might be metaphorically said to "allow" us to do with it whatever we will. And I offered this possibility while realizing that McDowell says such things in *Mind and World* as "If we try to keep spontaneity out of the picture but nevertheless talk of conceptual capacities operating in experience, the talk of conceptual capacities is mere word play" (13). See also the contrast between what he calls "actualization" of conceptual capacities and their "exercise" in McDowell, "Having the World in View," 439–40.

10. The precise formulation here is obviously both important and tricky. In "On Pippin's Postscript," McDowell writes both "I do not object to Kant's understanding intuitions as manifestations of apperceptive spontaneity" and "in intuiting we are not actively judging or spontaneously at work." McDowell believes both claims are consistent because the proper formulation is "capacities that belong to our spontaneity, are actualized in intuitions" (430).

11. And which Kant never does figure out how to *entertain* while ultimately *denying*. Ultimately, I claim that the success of the standard version of the Deduction, proving the objective validity of the pure concepts of the understanding, depends on posing the problem in terms of

is for McDowell already a nonstarter. So McDowell does not mean by his own denial of strict separability that the sensible uptake of the world is a *judgmental* ordering. (And he now says that he does not want to be taken to claim that intuited content is propositional or even "fragmentary" discursive content, as in Sellars's "this cube" locution.)[12] But he thinks there is another (nonjudgmental) form of apperceptive spontaneity at work that is not judgmental or even protodiscursive but still conceptual and active. I am not sure what this amounts to. It led McDowell in *Mind and World* to such phrases as "experiences are actualizations of our sentient nature in which conceptual capacities are inextricably implicated."[13] In a more recent piece, he says, "But intuitions immediately reveal things to be as they would be claimed to be in claims that would be no more than a discursive exploitation of some of the content of the intuitions," and:

> If intuitional content is not discursive, why go on insisting it is conceptual? Because every aspect of the content of an intuition is present in a form in which it is already suitable to be the content associated with a discursive capacity, if it is not—at least not yet—actually so associated.[14]

One apparent difference in "conceptually shaped" sensible engagements with the world that distinguishes them from judgings is that the former are sometimes said to be "wrung out of us," or "involuntary,"[15] a presence of the sensible world to the mind that an experiencer might subsequently (judgmentally) affirm or not, or go beyond, given more refined recognitional capacities.[16] But in general, unless McDowell means something like what

---

a separability between the pure forms of intuition and pure concepts that the attempted proof itself undermines, thus rendering the standard formulation of the goal quite misleading. Since McDowell is not that interested in the problem of synthetic a priori judgments or standard transcendental idealism, and since he criticizes Kant's "setup," his assuming such separable pure forms of intuition as "idealizing" (in the bad sense), as a mistake, I assume there is *some* version of this general claim he accepts. Which version is what is at issue.

12. McDowell, "Avoiding the Myth of the Given," 256–72.

13. McDowell, *Mind and World*, 89–90.

14. This and the previous quotation are also from McDowell, "Avoiding the Myth of the Given," 256–72. I note that in these two passages the weaker claim, that intuitions must merely exhibit the discriminability required by the understanding, seems to predominate. I am not sure where this leaves us.

15. McDowell does not put things this way any more.

16. Nothing in McDowell's position has ever committed him to the jejune view that we are

Sellars called "relative spontaneity"[17] in describing this conceptual engagement (and I don't think he does), I am still not sure that I understand what he means by "capacities being at work" when "we are not."[18] The former seems to give with one hand what the latter takes back. But the issue will emerge again very often in many guises and might be better approached more indirectly.

## IV. How to Read Kant's Deduction

McDowell sees my reading as having as its point to reassure us that our ways of categorizing things are a good fit with objects as they make themselves present to our senses, whereas McDowell thinks the project of the deduction is more radical. It is to explore the very possibility of objective purport at all, the very possibility that thought, representational activity, *could* have determinate content (and in particular to show that spontaneous thought and its pure concepts, contrary to all our commonsense intuitions, are required for such a result).

---

somehow "locked up inside" a point of view that is fixed, even for perception, by the concepts we happen to have. And the fact that experience should not be understood as a conceiving that renders intelligible some nonconceptual content does not mean that it cannot be the case that perceivers with a more adequate recognitional arsenal can "make more" out of what they see. The point is only that conceding this does not concede a mode of givenness in which nothing plays any role qua nonconceptual (for epistemic perceivers like us, anyway).

17. Sellars, ". . . this I or he or it (the thing) which thinks . . . ," 20.

18. The basic idea is clear enough. It seems quite wrong to deny that a fairly rich, determinate "having the world in view" (McDowell) can come into focus directly in a sensible exchange with the world, without my yet being able to resolve just what it is I am seeing, without my affirmative judgment. But these initial presentations of such a view are wrongly described, I think, as *simply* "wrung out of us." I think that we can call such views "a way the world is taken to be" without fearing that this will look like takes *on* an independently given sensible "material." We *are* active in such sensible uptake and therefore, admittedly, much farther away from even a reformed empiricism than McDowell's version, but I do not at all mean that such activity should be construed on the model of judging (what would be, I suppose, extremely rapid judging), any more than I think that the intentional nature of ascribable actions requires explicit deliberation, self-conscious commitment, and acts of will. Such a claim for "conceptual activity but not judging" *in* intuiting versus "conceptual capacities being at work even though we are not" *in* intuition (the sort of alternative that provokes a "pox on both your houses" response by those worried about overintellectualizing perception) would require a much longer discussion. I think we can get very far by noting that we are able to *distinguish* a number of elements in experience that are not, to use McDowell's words, "even notionally *separable*" in experience. See Pippin, "Concept and Intuition: Distinguishability and Separability."

> Kant's question is this: given that our intellectual engagement with reality requires the availability of objects to the senses, how can we know a priori, concerning forms required by the pure understanding, that they provide for objective purport in instantiations of them?[19]

The "threat" at issue in the deduction is the threat that "a possibility of objects being present to our senses is completely provided for by conformity to the requirements of our sensibility, independently of any condition involving thinkability."[20] And whereas, for McDowell, I take off from the "reassurance" misreading just mentioned and also saddle *Hegel* with a dead-end skeptical program—a worry about whether our form of mindedness is merely *our* form of mindedness, and not the form of things—McDowell wants to keep Hegel inside the Kantian project as described by McDowell, showing "how forms required by a pure understanding can be a priori guaranteed to be forms of mindedness—of thought about reality, right or wrong—at all."[21] (This will eventually lead McDowell to say that by these Hegelian lights, the difference between a transcendental logic and, simply, logic, becomes unnecessary.)[22]

I am not sure here where the line between the historical Kant and the improved, very radical Kant, of relevance to us, is being drawn. The stated aim of the deduction is to prove the objective validity of the pure concepts of the understanding, where that means proving that the objects of experience do necessarily and universally conform to these categorical requirements. This would make little sense except under the threat that they (such objects) might not so conform. That is, we are out to answer the question: By what right do we claim that (experienced) reality embodies categorical distinctions that were not themselves derived from experience of that reality? The point is to prove that there is synthetic a priori knowledge: to answer Hume and so forth. Consider: "Appearances might very well be so

19. McDowell, "On Pippin's Postscript," 399.

20. Ibid., 400.

21. Ibid., 404.

22. "Hegel does not need to work at making a place for transcendental logic. In the new environment, an investigation of the pure forms of thought already belongs, just as such, to a logic that is transcendental in something like Kant's sense" (ibid., 406). (I should note here that I now think I finally understand what McDowell means by this and agree with it. Or at least I agree with what I think he means. See Pippin, "What is Conceptual Activity?" and "The Significance of Self-Consciousness in Idealist Theories of Logic.")

constituted that the understanding should not find them to be in accordance with the conditions of its unity."[23] We must show otherwise. Even if this means that we must show that this (this strict *putative* separability between the sensory deliverance of a manifold of appearances and the conceptual conditions of unity) really is *not* a possibility (which is what I think the goal of the deduction is), it still must be shown. (Kant must *entitle* himself to the famous claim at A79: "The same function which gives unity to the various representations in a judgment also gives unity to the mere synthesis of various representations in an intuition.") And there is the oft-quoted (at least by me) passage in B, "The synthetic unity of consciousness is, therefore, an objective condition of all knowledge. It is not merely a requirement that I myself require in knowing an object, but a condition under which every intuition must stand in order to become an object for me."[24]

But, as I understand it, this is not an account that competes with McDowell's more radical one. It (this version) depends essentially on a resolution of just the question McDowell has Kant pose: Exactly *how* is objective purport, thought's being about things, at all possible in the first place? The key to the connection between the two issues is the last phrase in the B138 passage: "in order to become an object for me." There is no possibility that the categories are mere subjective requirements of thought imposed on the "matter" of sensible intuition because the very possibility of determinate conceptual content at all, even in the intuitional presence of the world to consciousness, requires both categorical and intuitional conditions. And this (ultimately) means a distinction between objective and subjective time ordering that, Kant argues, cannot be supplied by experience. There could be "nothing" contrary to these conditions because such a putative exception could not even be a content of thought; it would be "less than a dream."[25] The object just *is* "that in the concept of which the manifold is united"; representation of an object just *is* rule-governed unity of

23. Kant, *Critique of Pure Reason*, trans. Guyer and Wood, A90/B123.

24. Ibid., B138. So all I want to claim is that (a) Kant sees that his transcendental approach creates the impression that *this* is how he will prove objective validity, (b) he must demonstrate that this is *not* so, and (c) the goal after "under which every intuition . . ." explains the second half of the two-part B deduction.

25. This is all obviously a terribly compressed summary. Such a putative exception could *not* be, ultimately, a content of thought because it could not be self-ascribable by an apperceptive subject continuous in all its experiences. Demonstrating the role of that sort of claim is at the heart of a lot of deduction-work, and would clearly require at least a book to spell out and defend.

consciousness. This is supposed to turn out to be true whether we consider a sensory manifold already delivered up in its intuited form, or whether we consider it in its very being-delivered. (Hence the two parts of the B deduction; another long story.)

Indeed, as far as I understand him, McDowell accepts something like just this linkage. That is, the possibility that categories are "external" to sensible conditions just *is the worry that they are mere subjective impositions on exogenous material,* and so the worry that objects need not manifest categorical unity in order to be present to the mind as objects of experience. When he writes,

> Kant's question is this: how can we know a priori that the forms required by the pure understanding enter into providing for the possibility of objective purport? The question is urgent because Kant thinks our intellectual engagement with reality requires objects to be given to our senses,[26]

he is, in my reading, entertaining the possibility of a gap only to deny it exists. That is the ultimate task of the deduction, although it competes in Kant's reflections with a more standard version. The latter, more standard account is a "gap-crossing" version; this "more radical" version is a "gap-denying one," but the latter does nonetheless serve to provide a warrant of sorts for categorical objectivity.

If it turns out, as it begins to seem in the second-edition deduction, to be impossible to consider the intuited manifold "purely" and as a separable component of any knowledge claim, if "what presents themselves to the senses" must be considered always already conceptually articulated and that conceptual articulation cannot be considered an immediately *given* aspect of the manifold as such, then any a priori claim about the fixed, necessary conditions of receptivity and thereby strong objectivity in experience (the language of "fit" and not possibly being "other-minded') cannot be made in the terms originally proposed by Kant. In Hegelian terms, this means that there cannot be a fixed, a priori determinable separation between the subject of experience on one side and some formal consideration of all possible deliverances of sensibility on the other; or, more familiarly, the subject and

26. McDowell, "On Pippin's Postscript," 403.

the object side of this equation are far too intertwined to allow one to say that what the subject side requires from the object side can never be contravened by any deliverances from the object side. The interesting question is what follows if, as McDowell says, the deeper point is to show that "receptivity does not make an even notionally separable contribution to the co-operation" (of the conceptual and sensible).[27] This is an especially interesting question because it was Hegel (together with Fichte) who saw just how much was at stake in the version of the deduction that begins to emerge in the B160 note.[28] I don't yet see, apart from ambiguities in formulations, why McDowell keeps insisting there is such profound disagreement here.

Said another way (and it too is a formulation important for Hegel), the Humean worry that motivates the *Critique* is not that there might be some better or more accurate way to characterize thought's grip on the world, that we might be "better-minded" than we are, but that there could be *no* empirically independent but epistemically warranted determination of such conceptual shaping at all; a denial that a conceptual determination formulated without a basis in experience could nevertheless apply to all possible objects of experience.[29] I agree that "guaranteeing a fit" with the manifold is the wrong phrase here, precisely because it turns out, as the logic of Kant's own argument leads him to claim, that the "separability" assumption on which such a strategy rests is impossible, but again, Kant's procedure entertains the possibility of such a separability (as at A90/B123 and B138) in order to rule it out eventually, and *the way it is ruled out* then causes problems for what I have been calling the standard version of the deduction. He rules it out in a way that links what McDowell calls the more radical "possibility of objective purport" dimension with the more conventional view of the problem of the objective validity of pure concepts, and whatever the successor notion of that problem amounts to once we take fully on board the intertwined nature of concept and intuition.[30] It is true that Kant wants to

27. McDowell, *Mind and World*, 9. Note that he says "separable." The claim is not that the deliverances of sensibility make no contribution.

28. See chapters 2 and 3 in Pippin, *Hegel's Idealism*, for a defense of this claim, and also Pippin, "Fichte's Alleged Subjective, Psychological, One-Sided Idealism," on Fichte.

29. Again, *by* being constitutive of the thought of an object at all.

30. A successor notion suitably transformed into the issue of what can be said to be true of the shape of our experience (of the mind-world relation), which we can claim to know independently of what we learn from experience, what must necessarily be so of such a "shape." This

respond to skeptical doubts about the possibility of a priori synthetic knowledge by insisting we have first to establish that thought could have content at all (*the conditions of the possibility of experience*), but the latter is still a strategy in the service of *some* version of the former issue (*the conditions of the possibility of objects of experience*). So I am not ignoring the more radical question in favor of a misleading skeptical worry. I am trying to understand the role of Kant's radical question in the overall strategy of a proof for the legitimacy of empirically nonderived conceptual determinations, trying to understand, as Hegel did, the "identity claim" at the heart of Kant's enterprise, "The Highest Principle of Synthetic Judgment": "The conditions of the possibility of experience are at the same time the conditions of the possibility of objects of experience." It is true that once Kant starts to waver on the strict separability of concept and intuition, *his* conventional strategy for establishing objective validity is no longer available. However, the issue of a nonempirical warrant for nonderived claims about concepts does not go away, and will resurface in a different form in Hegel. It is not enough, in other words, just to construe the deduction as an argument to show that "the understanding's" activity is necessarily involved in the possibility of objective purport. (It is *a lot* to show this. Given the reasonable insistence that objects are available to us only through the senses, to show that sensory states just as such, without the involvement of conceptual activity, could not be said to be directed to, to be about anything, to have content, is a major achievement and has a number of implications.) However, in order to get Hegel into this picture (and a good deal of the historical, if reformed, Kant), we have to note that such a claim is opening the door to a nonempirical determination "by thought of itself," as Hegel would put it.

And when we do face the question of the different status between concepts whose content and authority are established by experience and a conceptual form of experience whose content and authority are not and cannot be, when we get to that level, we reach the issue that links Kant and Hegel. The fact that there is room for doubt and uncertainty about just what are "the" forms of any discursive engagement with reality is what generates the

---

is an issue that has both a formal-logical level (where we argue, say, for the unacceptability of any form of subject-object "gap," the existence of which poses the problem of "crossing" it) and a determinate "phenomenological" level, where the form of experience presupposed by a "shape of *Geist*" like *Verstand* or "observing Reason" can be phenomenologically tested, imagined as "lived out."

different "shapes of consciousness" (*Gestalten des Geistes*) entertained as possibilities in Hegel's *Phenomenology*.

## V. Implications of the Deduction Issue

At this point, one can simply plead that one is focusing on "the Kant that can speak to us" and point out that the main value of this picture of a conceptually articulated sensory uptake (where the engagement of concepts in sensation does not mean full-fledged judging) is to make clear how we are doomed neither to a causal theory of perceptual knowledge and a picture of nonconceptual content inconsistent with the normative nature of inference and judgment, nor, on the other extreme, a "frictionless spinning in the void," a coherentism like Davidson's. Kant, understood in this sort of "Hegel-leaning" direction, simply gives a better overall picture here of how *empirical knowledge* works than a picture based on the non-Kantian and non-Hegelian assumption that this is finally the only sort there is. Perceptual knowledge is also a corporeal process, of course, but that too need not lead us down the path toward neuroepistemology and hard naturalism as long as we remember that human nature is a second nature too, that visual acuity and discernment can be educated to discern what needs discerning.

But if we want to retrace the Hegelian path from these reflections, we need another component not prominent in McDowell. For even though Hegel has in effect given up the Kantian strategy for demonstrating the objective validity of a fixed set of categories, he still maintains, I argued in the "Postscript," that understanding the very possibility of objective purport requires that we consider determinate conceptual projections of possible experience (ways of framing the concept-sensibility relation as a whole, let us say), *one sort rather than another*, the normative authority of which cannot be tied to an empirical derivation. Hegel also thinks that principles or norms for *action* are not in some way rationalized strategies for the satisfaction of "given" desires and interests, nor are they formal legislations by pure practical reason to the "material" of motivating inclinations, and this too means we need to consider possible "models" of the relation between intention and bodily action in order to arrive—in the usual "dialectical," determinate negation way—at a satisfying (nondualistic) model. So the issue of the authority or legitimacy of nonderived (and noninstrumental) norms, once this mind-world model changes from Kant's (or once the genuine "spirit" of Kant is emphasized), extends very far in Hegel. The *quid iuris* question survives in Hegel, even if it is not pointing toward a "deduction strategy" based on separable pure forms of intuition. Does that mean we are left with some (for Hegel quasi-psychological or even quasi-social) claim about subjective indispensability, an enterprise of frictionless spinning? Or a metaphysical claim about the "conceptual structure" of reality in itself? It should not lead in these directions since the outcome of Hegel's take on the deduction is supposed to involve an altered way of seeing the "subject and object" relation, such that interpretations like these will seem to have made several distorted assumptions. The course of his attempt to convince us of this and to illuminate this altered sense of the mind-world relation is, I argued, the task of the *Phenomenology of Spirit*. It is also indicated in summaries like this from the *Encyclopedia*:

> *Philosophy, then, owes its development to the empirical sciences.* In return it gives their contents what is so vital to them, the freedom of thought—gives them in short an a priori character. These contents are now warranted necessary, and no longer depend on the evidence of the facts merely, that they were so found and so experienced. The fact as experienced thus becomes an illustration and a copy of the original and completely self-supporting activity of thought.[31]

While passages like this make clear that Hegel never dreamed he would be taken to say that thought supplies itself with its own *empirical* content, they raise the question of why Hegel is talking about development this way and what "philosophy" adds to what the "evidence of the facts" shows. In my view this requires even a bigger step back from these issues so that we can see the whole.

## VI. Hegel

Someone who is taken to deny that there are unique representations with nonconceptual content that play a cognitively significant role in experience is often taken to deny that such representations could be said to "provide" exogenously the content for thought. (How could they if there aren't such separable elements?) The natural inference is that such a denial must entail

31. Hegel, *Hegel's Logic: Being Part One of the Encyclopaedia of the Philosophical Sciences*, trans. Wallace, 58.

that, therefore, thought must be said to "fill out" such content on its own, to "give itself content." Now this is exactly the way Hegel *does* talk, and it is no surprise to see hands thrown up in frustration at this point. But the frustration is premature.

For example, Hegel speaks frequently of the Concept's self-determination, that the Concept gives itself its own content, even that the logic of the Concept is the logic of freedom (as autonomy). Here is the most poetic, sweeping passage:

> This pure being-on-our-own [*reine Beisichsein*] belongs to free thought, to it in its free sailing on its own, where there is nothing under it, or above it, and where we stand in solitude with ourselves alone.[32]

McDowell's phrase for all this from Lecture 2 of *Mind and World* (or what, at any rate, I choose to interpret as a gloss on these sorts of claims) is a very good one: the "unboundedness of the conceptual." It has suggested to several readers (such as Michael Friedman)[33] that he has slipped back, despite his avowals, into a "frictionless spinning" model. The same is said of Hegel (again by Friedman, and others). In both cases such charges are quite hasty, as if again inseparability is being confused with an indistinguishability claim. (As if the fact that the deliverances of sensibility cannot be neatly separated as having distinct cognitive work to do must mean that there is no difference between receptivity and spontaneity.) If one is careful about that distinction, then such Hegelian claims only first mean to insist that a relation to objects is not, as it were, "secured" by receptivity, by the deliverances of sensibility, *alone*. The unboundedness claim just states that it is only because our uptake of the sensory world is already conceptually articulated that these deliverances can assume a *justificatory* role. Indeed, since the sensory world is an immediate sensory take *on the world*, the claim could just as easily be taken to be realist; reality itself is conceptual in this sense: offers up "what could be taken to be the case." In the *Tractarian* language McDowell sometimes invokes, thought does not "stop short" of the world; a way of thinking about an object (a *Sinn*) is not an intermediary entity between us and the referents of thought; it is a way of seeing the world. There is still plenty of substantive content and empirical guidedness in experience on such a pic-

32. Ibid., 18.
33. Friedman, "Exorcising the Philosophical Tradition."

ture. The broadest way to restate the point is simply the familiar point that the domain of the normative is autonomous. Principles constraining what we ought to believe, what could count as a possible object of experience or as a satisfying explanation of what one ought to do, are wholly independent of claims about how the mind works or what people generally do. Fichte appreciated this point in the deepest way and built his whole philosophy around it. On all these matters I take myself to be in agreement with and guided by McDowell's view.

With all that said, though, if the conceptual is unbounded (by anything nonconceptual), the normative domain autonomous, what *does* help account for the determinate principles constraining and guiding (normatively constraining and guiding) thought and action? What is the nonmetaphorical meaning of the notion of the Concept's "self-determination" (in Kant's *Groundwork* terms: our self-authorship of the law)?[34] But that question depends on another. When everything is formulated this way, is this sort of version of Hegel even an idealism? And if so, in what sense?

The most expansive summary of such claims sometimes used by McDowell is that *the forms of judgment, the forms of thought, are the forms of things, of objects and events.* At this extreme altitude one is reminded of similar controversial claims by Wittgenstein in the *Tractatus,* as at 5.6, "the limits of my language mean the limits of the world," something Wittgenstein provocatively calls "the truth in solipsism" and expands in 5.61 as "We cannot think what we cannot think; so we cannot think what we cannot say either." Again at altitude like this, there are parallels in the discussions such similar claims have prompted. There are parallels in the distinct uses by Wittgenstein of "my" and "we" and Kant's "subject of experience" and "subjective" (and the "I" in the "I think that must be able to accompany all my representations"). For both, these terms refer to nothing in the world but express the limits of the world, set the limits of what could be a world. Any encounter with anything in the world would presuppose, could not "discover," such a subject.

Now, in this way of looking at things, there *is* a benign sense in which the notion of a "world" can be said to be "limited," to have a boundary. The boundary in question is just the difference between what could count as a world and what not. The latter (what could not so count) is not a kind of world "beyond" what could be conceived by us. It is just not a world. (We

34. Pippin, *Hegel's Practical Philosophy,* chap. 3.

are not "limited" in being unable to understand as a world what could not be a possible world.)

For both as well, since this last point means that the basic statement of idealism involves no reference to an empirical psychological or actual social subject (is no species, as Williams notes, of any sort of "Whorfian" claim about language and worldviews),[35] or idealism is not invoked here as an explanation, the form of thought or the form of language does not *explain* "why we experience the world as we do"; the claim threatens to seem either a tautology or as McDowell puts it, a platitude. The natural temptation is to see all this talk of nonempirically warranted "shapings" of our experience, and all these presuppositions about normative authority, explanation, projections of the mind-world, and agent-action relation, so deeply assumed that the language of "presupposition" is inappropriate, as a preliminary to a claim about relativism and incommensurability. This point about "shapes of *Geist*" not being objects in any sense "in" the world, and so not fixed "limits" with an "outside," is supposed to prevent drawing such an inference, and it is a point loudly reverberating in Kant, Fichte, Hegel, and then again in Wittgenstein and McDowell. But it is an elusive and difficult point to state, and one is driven to pointing out that it is not a "claim" at all.

The former "tautology" or triviality danger in the formulations is clear enough. The basic statement appears to say: that which we can understand and state, we can understand and state; that which we cannot, we cannot. (This triviality danger is also evident in interpretations of Kant as "restricting" knowledge to our "epistemic conditions." Any view like this that is *not* a tautology threatens to introduce a substantive or empirical subject and thus a substantive or material notion of "limit.")

The latter possibility, that the basic statement is not a claim at all but still shows us something, appears to be the way Wittgenstein understands it, but it opens a potential disanalogy between Kant and Wittgenstein. How wide a disanalogy and what the relevance is for Hegel are challenging questions. For Wittgenstein, coming to understand what, say, "comprehending the meaning of a term" amounts to *for us* is not an empirical report on how we go on. It is coming to understand what comprehending the meaning of a term or a rule *could be*. (The Kantian parallel would be: *all* that being an object of our experience could be. The point is the same as the one made about a possible world.) Even though Wittgenstein later seems to entertain

35. Williams, "Wittgenstein and Idealism."

the possibility of beings minded other than we are (in the Hegelian mode, our being minded other than we now are), his point seems to be to show ultimately that there couldn't (intelligibly) be beings minded other than us. If we insist, "But the impossibility of entertaining such other-mindedness holds only by *our* lights, for us," then we have not understood what was just explained: that there is no we or I *in* the world "for" which things are; that the point of introducing the notion of "our" forms of thought is to help us see that there could be nothing else but "ours," if *forms of thought*. The truth in solipsism, in a famous Wittgensteinean twist reminiscent of Hegel's style, is the truth of realism; the "we" in Jonathan Lear's phrase is, if properly understood, a "disappearing we."[36] Kant's idealism is a robust empirical realism; imagining an intuitive, not a discursive, intelligence does not render our forms of thought "limits" beyond which there is something in principle knowable, but not knowable by us.

But here the disanalogy (with Kant and ultimately with Hegel) begins. Wittgenstein clearly does not want the limits of language to be the sort of limit that has an other side, a limit like a fence or a barrier. Yet a phrase like "the limits of my language" does imply a restriction *of some sort*. That is why the Wittgenstein version of the basic claim is not a tautology, even if not a claim in the normal sense. (Not, perhaps it would be clearer to say, an *explanation* of the forms of things by appeal to the forms of thought. This is the same sense in which the claim that mindedness requires a "spontaneity" is not pointing to a noncausal power in order to offer *explanations of mental activities*.)[37] There *is* a point at which nonsense *begins*, something we could not make sense of but can recognize as nonsensical. This restriction, however, is only available "from the inside," as Bernard Williams puts it, by "finding our way around inside our own view, feeling our way out to the points at which we begin to lose our hold on it (or it, its hold on us) and things begin to be hopelessly strange to us."[38]

Kant does not seem to think of things this way and *does* seem to use the notion of a limit as a barrier with another side, for which he was famously taken to task by Hegel. (One has to straddle the limit, stand on both sides, to understand it as a limit in this sense. In which case it is not a limit in that sense.) This did not appear to be solely because we arrive on the scene just

36. Lear, "The Disappearing 'We.' "
37. Pippin, "Kant on the Spontaneity of Mind."
38. Williams, "Wittgenstein and Idealism," 160.

stuck with distinct forms of intuition, but because it does not unproblematically just follow from the fact that we judge in subject-predicate or hypothetical forms of judgment that the contents of experience must include substances and properties and causes and effects. It is in establishing this claim that the objective validity of the claim comes to be seen as restricted or limited just by the unique way in which the claim can be established. It cannot be established "in itself." So the question is: Given all of this sympathy by Hegel with these sorts of critiques of limit notions, does this mean that we should understand Hegel's "idealism" not to be like Kant's but to be as little a substantive claim as Wittgenstein's, a way of showing the *disappearance* of the relevance of any "we"?[39]

The right response here is "In the long run, yes," but where we end up in the long run is not clear and defensible without the run itself. (This is at least how I understand McDowell's correct claim that "it takes work to enable it to present itself [the identity-in-difference of thought and reality] as the platitude it is.")[40] It is when we face the issue of the determinateness of what are claimed to be candidates for the "forms of thought of any world," and the unavailability of the Kantian separable forms of intuition, that a new form of skepticism emerges, the skepticism that forms the heart and soul of the *Phenomenology* (that "pathway of doubt and despair"). That is, to take the quickest route to the issue in Hegel, if a condition for possible objective purport is some sort of prior-to-experience projection of possibility, conditions that cannot be accounted for empirically or deduced by pure reason from the possibility of thought at all, normative constraints on what could be conceptual content and self-conscious engagement with reality at all, then we must also have some way of taking into account that the normative authority of such principles not only cannot be established once and for all by a deduction, but that this authority also can break down ("internally") and has broken down historically. The reassurance we can be said to require given this possibility and this fact cannot at all be the reassurance that objects, considered independently of such conditions, can be said to fit or match what we require. Agreed. But this does not mean that there is no "skeptical" problem to resolve, not at least according to many passages in the *Phenomenology*'s Introduction. In what we might call "normal" experi-

39. I discuss this issue in much more detail in "Finite and Absolute Idealism," in Gardner and Grist, *The Transcendental Turn*.

40. McDowell, "On Pippin's Postscript," 405.

ence, within what Hegel names a "shape of spirit" (a "form of life" perhaps), there are norms that cannot be questioned because they are the basis for the possibility of any questioning, norms that both Hegel and Wittgenstein say we are "certain" of. That consciousness is direct and immediately presented with determinate objects it can pick out and refer to indexically is not a theory or claim about objects in the world. It is more like a picture of what experience might be, what the mind-world/agent-action relation is; and, as in the comments about the subject of experience, this is not an object in the world. That such a form of thought is the form of objects (constitutes objecthood) in *such* a context must function as a platitude. (But only, as he says, "for consciousness" at such a stage or time.) And Hegel "examines" its sufficiency, he says, by "watching," looking on, as an experience so shaped could try to say what it knows, according to its own "conditions for possibility." It cannot, and another picture is introduced.

I don't think the right way to describe what is going on here is that such "models" are introduced as a series of hypothetical possibilities concerning the concept-sensibility relation, and that we are shown how the temptation to rest everything on some form of immediacy or the Given keeps intruding, as if the temptation were constantly irresistible and as if we kept forgetting what just got us into trouble. The process is more systematic, and the education of consciousness is progressive. To be sure, in the Consciousness–Self-Consciousness–Reason chapters, Hegel is presenting an idealized picture of the education of consciousness about its own possibility, and so he is entertaining highly idealized and partial dimensions of *Geist*'s experience, all meant to show such partiality and incompleteness. But the point toward which such education leads is a final corollary of sorts to the inseparability of mind and world that was the key point in Hegel's appropriation of Kant's deduction. This inseparability does not mean that transcendental logic simply is logic, constitutes what the form of objects could be. The Hegelian direction actually goes the other way. A logic is interwoven in a form of life, a form of actual, historical life, that cannot be rightly understood in abstraction from, separate from, the "life" it regulates, and these forms or norms fail or break down in time. It is such a breakdown in authority, such a loss of grip on the actual world, that raises the suspicion of merely subjective forms of mindedness and so is the source of that thoroughgoing skepticism and even "despair" spoken of in the *Phenomenology*'s Introduction. This loss of authority and suspicion about "just our way of going on" is the logic, we might say, of the perpetually reappearing "We."

## VII. The Social Bases of All Normative Authority

Hegel has a narrative story to tell about such breakdowns, and it has to do essentially with the various ways we hold each other to account in normative discourses and practices. This issue of the social basis of normative authority is relevant even to issues like what counts as credible empirical knowledge. Here is a rather high-altitude view of the task of Hegel's revolutionary book.

Officially, the *Phenomenology* is the "science of the experience of consciousness," as in its alternate title. Experience, however, cannot be described from a sideways-on or third-person point of view. If it is to be made present to us it must in a sense be reenacted, as if from the point of view of the experiencing subject. It must be presented in a "phenomenology." (This sort of a reenactment must be a kind of dramatic exercise, so it is not for nothing that the *Phenomenology* is often called a *Bildungsroman*.[41]) We must be told "what it is like" to be *Geist*, as in one well-known formulation of the subjective viewpoint. But this experience is also said to be developmental. There is no such thing as "what it is like to be *Geist*" *simpliciter*. Besides the various dimensions covered by such a loose expression (what it is like to be perceiving, desiring, goal-pursuing, art-making, and religious *Geist*, for instance), the question (ultimately, once the ineliminable dimensions of *Geist* as such are understood in their unity)[42] can always only be posed as: what it is like to be *Geist* at a time, in relation to a certain past, projected into a possible future. Hegel claims to achieve a general purchase on all such issues by considering all of them as experiences of attempts at the realization of norms. What it is like to be *Geist* in all these dimensions is to be "fraught with ought," to be a claim-making and action-guiding being, always subject to challenge about such normative constraints and direc-

41. By Josiah Royce, for example, in *Lectures on Modern Idealism*, 147–56.

42. I refer here to the controversial relation between the first five chapters of the *Phenomenology*, which cover the dimensions of Consciousness, Self-consciousness, and Reason, and the historical chapters on *Geist* and Religion. I take the former chapters to be preparing us for the thesis about the necessarily historical character of human subjectivity when finally in view as such in all its relevant dimensions, and the latter as realizing such a requirement by providing us with an actual phenomenology of *Geist*'s experience of itself. I think Hegel says as much several times. (See the following footnote.) But there is certainly room for controversy here, and this is an area of very large disagreement with McDowell. For a defense of this reading see Pippin, " 'You Can't Get There from Here': Transition Problems in Hegel's *Phenomenology of Spirit*" and *Idealism as Modernism: Hegelian Variations*.

tives. The experience of *Geist* itself counts as the education of a "natural consciousness" burdened with many dualisms that disrupt the experience of what it would be to "live," experience in a way so constrained and guided (subject and object, self and other, individual and community, inner and outer, human and Divine) up to the standpoint of "absolute knowledge" (*das absolute Wissen*), which is absolute precisely by having reached a way of understanding human experience (and therewith a way of experiencing) that has overcome without collapsing such dualisms. The "engine" driving forward this development is abstractly described as *das Negative,* and more poetically is said to be a kind of "violence" that consciousness suffers at its own hands, as it struggles with its most basic issue—its attempt at self-knowledge.[43]

This is all rather breathless, but the general point is this: once Hegel has shown us the internal insufficiency of the basic model of "consciousness" (as if the mind-world or subject-object model of experience could be sufficient as a model, as if individual experiencers processing information and theorizing as monadic units could be a "world"), then the very possibility of mindedness (or objective purport) is shown to depend on forms of social self-regulation about all matters normative, forms that can be theoretically distinguished from, but never rightly understood as separable contributions to, the world's direct coming into view in perceiving, and forms that can "fail" in a distinctive way. This will look different when the questions about normative proprieties are questions about distinct sorts of normative thinking (understood as conditions of intelligibility, and not as particular beliefs) and so about the exercise of power in politics, religious condemnation, appraisals of art, certification of experts, and authoritative models of cognition, but Hegel is a social holist and believes that such claims of authority have something essential to do with one another at a time. I realize how many trainloads of baggage such a claim carries with it, but I am just trying by this circuitous route to admit that the answer to McDowell's incredulous question "Are we to suppose that members of downtrodden minorities, say, or those who oppress them, cannot have their empirical thinking rationally controlled by objects they perceive?"[44] and this because they do not belong to a community shaped by mutuality of recognition among free,

43. For Hegel's view on the relation of the *Phenomenology* to history, see *Phenomenology of Spirit,* trans. Miller, 412–18.

44. McDowell, "On Pippin's Postscript," 406–7.

rational beings, is simply: Yes, of course. McDowell himself has emphasized how differently we must understand the bearing on and role in experience played by the deliverances of sensibility when the subject is a rational, self-conscious (and I would add essentially historical) being. *Whatever* might be the right way to state the inseparability of conceptual and sensory elements in the world's "coming into view," whenever we introduce the question of the determinate conceptual arsenal that is "at work" in such a sensory uptake, it will be very hard to continue to maintain the commonsense view that Greek slaves and modern data programmers must at some level have a common perceptual world in gazing out at the Aegean, that they are "controlled by objects" seen in the same way.[45] Living in a world everywhere animated by intentional natural forces, one "*sees*" their effects; socialized into a community of feudal order, there are visible inheritable properties in blood that entitle a family to rule over many generations; when there is a Great Chain of Being, its orders of reality are directly manifest to all "with eyes to see"; when souls reincarnate, the effects can be everywhere perceived; one "sees" the soul in bumps on the head; and so on and so on. These are all not simply empirical mistakes or bad science for Hegel, and are not beliefs that go beyond the right sort of (directly wrung out of us) "givens," or theoretical impositions on an empirical experience everywhere and at all times available to any properly equipped receptor.[46] This is the price of "blurring

45. See MacIntyre's useful formulation in *After Virtue*, quoted below in chapter 11: "The twentieth-century observer looks into the night sky and sees stars and planets; some earlier observers saw instead chinks in a sphere through which the light beyond could be observed" (79).

46. One has to be careful about this point. First, a good deal of work would have to be done to distinguish a variety of beliefs one might have "*about* what one sees," or inferences one might draw from what one sees, and the differing modalities of perception itself. Second, the nature of the link between the possibility of agency or knowing and historical actuality is not meant, in my version of Hegel, to entail that, say, a Greek slave is somehow a *materially* deficient perceiver or knower, compared to us, or whose agency, whose capacity to act intentionally, is but a dim shadow of ours, *as if a lower species*. Whatever it is to perceive or whatever it is to act, for one's brain to be functioning properly, Greek slaves in that sense perceive and act as we perceive and act. Hegel, however, wants to make great hay out of the possibility that at the deeply implicit reflective level (and this means for him at some commonly minded level), given the historically located "form of Spirit" in which they participate, they (again implicitly and unthematically) misunderstand what it is to perceive and act, or take themselves to be following norms in ways not consistent with what it actually is to follow norms, etc., and that this form of incomplete self-understanding is reflected in their perceptual lives and so is as relevant to "what they experience" as the health of their optic nerves. This sets up a conflict between what he calls the "in-itself" and the "for-itself" that he wants to argue leads to a particular sort of breakdown. Ulti-

the boundaries" between concept and sensibility, from Hegel to Heidegger (and so of course for the empirically bloody-minded it counts as a *reductio* of such a blurring). What *counts* as having one's thought "rationally controlled by the objects" is not simply itself another event in the world, but an aspect of a complex norm inseparable from the practice of giving and asking for reasons in a community over a time.[47] There are obviously bookloads of work to do to get from questions about perceived cubes and color predicates to such heady talk, and so baldly stated one seems to be proposing a renewal of a stale cultural anthropology debate, but such a move (or slide) is, I think, unavoidable.

We can put this result in terms of the earlier discussion of the inseparability issue. The claims are:

(i) The possibility of conscious intentionality requires a kind of relatively unreflective (but still potentially apperceptive) conceptual unification in even taking up a minimal view of the world, one that is not a judgment I "stand behind" but a provisional view. In any account of such a view, while the conceptual and sensory-material elements can be distinguished, they cannot be understood to play their roles even "notionally" separably, to recall McDowell's claim.

(ii) The question, then, is the right way to state the unique way such intuitional, minimally conceptual views (which have to count as unifications, orderings of a sort) can be said to be embodied in a sensible perceiver, rather than understood as concepts imposed on something separable, or as terribly rapid judgments, but while conceptual still nonjudgmental, even, as McDowell stresses, not even partially discursive.

(iii) To make these two points clearer and to emphasize the "price that must be paid" claim, consider a practical example of such an "embodied shaping" of experience. Imagine a contemporary person-

---

mately the claim is that whatever reflective account of perceiving and acting is the right one, we will now be able to know it as right without understanding the "pathway of doubt and despair" leading from that early take on things to a later "more self-conscious" one.

47. This bit of Brandomese should not be taken to signal agreement with Brandom's own "two-stage" theory of his relation between sensory interchange and social normativity, as noted in the previous chapter. Cf. also McDowell's discussion (especially of chicken sexers) in McDowell, "Brandom on Observation."

> nel office of a large corporation. A candidate is being interviewed for a managerial job. In the course of the interview, as the company representative interrogates the candidate's credentials, asks a variety of hypothetical questions, probes experiences at past businesses, it never once occurs to the interviewer, and so is never expressed, that the candidate is an African American woman. Such an issue (in our imaginary world) has become as little salient as eye color or shoe size. Our interviewer has never reflected on the meaning of equal opportunity, has never had occasion to formulate any principle of equality and so forth. She has simply come to maturity in our (imaginary) world where racial and gender issues have no bearing on deliberations about qualifications. She doesn't see them in the world as relevant, let us say (as opposed to seeing such features as possibly relevant and discounting them). While in one sense she is "following a rule blindly," I think we still ought to say that she is observing a normative propriety and can be credited with acting justly.[48] (If someone were to raise the issue as relevant, for example, she would immediately protest.) Her world is shaped by conceptual norms she shares with others, and, quite contrary to many criticisms of McDowell's, our picture does not suggest an "overintellectualizing" of her view of the practical world of work. Quite the contrary.[49]

I hope the relevance to our Greek slave is clear. Once we stress the "inseparability" claim, make clear that it is not an "indistinguishability" claim, and once we add *any* flesh and bones to *any* notion of a conceptual shaping of intuitive access beyond "thinkability understood as general logic," we are at a point common to the slave and the above case. Once one starts talk-

48. Another and very famous and contested example would be the way one can be said, according to Kant's third *Critique,* to be "reflectively engaged" in aesthetic perception, subject to the norm of beauty and entitled to require it of others, without this being a matter of the application of a concept, or a matter of being merely sensuously absorbed. The role there of the *sensus communis* would be an important analogue to the example presented here.

49. This is a point made very well in McDowell, "Avoiding the Myth of the Given." It is also relevant to his "What Myth?" and exchange with Hubert Dreyfus. McDowell wants to say that what Dreyfus calls embodied coping is just as conceptually permeated with rationality as perception, but that this does not involve applying a general rule to a particular situation, a rule that can be specified apart from the situation one is in, and neither does it involve some always available self-conscious rendering explicit and assessing one's rational commitments.

ing about the conceptual "shaping" of the intuitional uptake of the world, I don't see how to prevent such an extension.[50]

This issue flows naturally into McDowell's doubts about the self-legislative as well as the social side of this theory of normativity.

## VIII. Self-Legislation

A couple of points on which we agree. Any model of the self-legislative source of value or obligation must have an "element of receptivity" to it. That is just another way of saying that any picture of such a self-legislative source cannot have it be arbitrary, either in its initiation or in its sustenance. So no "I am only bound because I bound myself, so I hereby unbind myself." That would be like someone playing chess who moved his rook diagonally and tried to justify his authority to do so that way. The point is not that he is violating what everyone can see is this ideal object, "Chess," but that he is contradicting *himself*, his own agreement to play chess and all that that commits him to. The only point in making the *strong* self-legislation claim is to caution that this concession (no arbitrariness and so "an element of receptivity") does not open the door to objective value, natural law, or any other naturalistic or realist theory, as if all self-legislation meant was that I am determining for myself, upon rational reflection and relying on that alone, the truth about such moral facts. Of course, once practices *are* instituted, people "see" what to do and do not have to go through any process of value creation and self-obligating. Once there is a practice, there are reasons to do things that exist independently of any individual or group constantly and explicitly acknowledging that reason, reasons that participants are genuinely responsive to.

Likewise I agree with what McDowell calls the plausible version of the

50. I think that this is relevant to an interesting point McDowell makes in "Avoiding the Myth of the Given" in citing Michael Thompson's claim ("The Representation of Life") that our discrimination of nonliving from living beings is not a matter of noting empirically distinct markers as *contents* in our experience, that "life thoughts" are distinct *forms* of thought, that they have their own "logic." In discussing the perceptual awareness of a bird, McDowell notes: "But perhaps we can say it is given to me in such an experience, not something I know by bringing a conceptual capacity to bear on what I anyway see, that what I see is an animal—not because 'animal' expresses part of the content unified in the experience in accordance with a certain form of intuitional unity, but because 'animal' captures the intuition's categorical form" (261). I want to say: if "animal" can be an intuition's categorical form, so could, however partial and unable to sustain an experience so viewed, gods, evil spirit, higher and lower orders of being, and so forth.

claim that values and reasons to do or refrain from doing depend on historically instituted and sustained social practices, and certainly that shifts in practices need not themselves have been the object of anyone's intentions. (The "need not" is important; sometimes the attempt at a shift is all too deliberate, as with the Jacobins or Leninists.[51] Sometimes bestowing authority is explicit and intentional, like establishing a fiduciary relation or agreeing to arbitration; sometimes quasi-explicit, as when one plays a game with an umpire, and so forth.) I certainly did not intend that according to my Hegel there must be something like periodic explicit, intentional, conscious, authorizing, self-obligating ceremonies of some sort to explain the authority of any norm. The gradual invention of opera, say, cannot be said to be something someone or some group intentionally invented like this, but it was *invented*, and "by" human beings.[52] And subscribing to the values of opera need involve no "I hereby do subscribe," etc. But the values of opera only bind those who *do* subscribe, those who bestow it with authority, by trying to sing in one, for example.

Sometimes McDowell seems to want only to concede that authority must be rationally acknowledgeable, open to rational criticism, etc., for it to count as genuinely normative authority. This would leave open the question of whether such an exercise of reason could discover, for example, "the" normative structure of the world. Although it is a matter of great controversy in Hegel scholarship, I think Hegel closes down that option, and statements by McDowell seem to go further than such an option by conceding that such authority is also, must be, *instituted*, and this in a way that means such authority can *fail*. (Again, none of this means instituted out of whole cloth, out of the nonnormative ooze, by an act of mere will, or intentionally and explicitly.) For me, and I think for Hegel, that is the most interesting and telling aspect of normative authority. It can fail. (Indeed such failure is an important subtheme in all these remarks. It is why it is necessary to talk about a "*Re*appearing We," an anxiety about "mere" self-legislation.) In the simplest sense all that it means for it to fail is that it is no longer acknowledged as authoritative by a wide enough spectrum of a community so as to make its continual enforcement and sanction, after such a breakdown, the mere

51. Or explicit in the way Descartes and Hobbes explicitly called for scientists simply to stop doing scholastic science.

52. For more on this issue (formulated often in terms of this example), see my response (in "The Conditions of Value") to Joseph Raz's Tanner Lectures.

exercise of power. But that is just the simplest sense. Obviously, we would want to make distinctions like that between contingent "failure" (world-historically insignificant, perhaps a matter of famine or decadence or collective irrationality) and the sort of breakdowns Hegel spends so much time on in the *Phenomenology,* like the breakdown he thought he saw coming in the individualist moralism that he took to be at the heart of the central institutions in the West. But that would launch us into a much longer and independent topic.

# 4

# Slavoj Žižek's Hegel

## I

It takes some courage to give a book this size the title *Less than Nothing*. Žižek must know that the first, powerfully tempting phrase that will occur to any reviewer, even before reading the book, will be "Aptly titled." The book has already inspired dismissive reviews in widely read publications, reviews that seem to be reviews (and dismissals) of Žižek himself (or of the Žižek phenomenon, the Symbolic Žižek) and mostly ignore his massive tome. But he has written a serious attempt to reanimate or reactualize Hegel (in the light of Lacanian metapsychology and so in a form he wants to call "materialist"), and in the limited space available to me I want to try to summarize what he has proposed and to express some disagreements.

The question of the possible relevance of Hegel to contemporary concerns divides into two questions and immediately confronts two objections that have long proven deeply compelling for many. There is first the question of what can be said about Hegel's "system." He is taken to be a hyper-rationalist holist whose central claim is that the Absolute (something like what Kant called the unconditioned) is the Idea, and that everything there is can be understood as the actualization, in nature and across historical time, of the Idea. (And, of course, contra Kant, he is thereby claiming to know what Kant had denied we could possibly know.) Second, there is the question of Hegel the *Versöhnungsphilosoph*, the philosopher of reconciliation. On some accounts of this side of Hegel's project, Hegel believed that we had reached the "end of history," both in philosophy (his own position had successfully accounted for all possible philosophical options, in their interconnection with each other) and in politics, art, and religion. Human freedom had been realized in the modern state as described in his *Philosophy of Right,* in the rather doctrinally thin Protestant humanism Hegel championed, and in romantic art, an art form in the process of transcending itself as art, actualizing art in a way that signaled its end as a significant vehicle of human self-knowledge. (The link between the two aspects of Hegel's position is taken to be his theodicy, the role of the Absolute's [or God's] self-actualization in time in accounting for the rationality and culmination of political and intellectual history.)

The objections to both versions of Hegel and Hegelianism are well known. There are a host of objections to Hegelian rationalist holism from the empiricist, scientific naturalist, and analytic approaches to philosophy. (The Anglophone version of that school famously began with the rejection of Hegel.) But in Europe the objections were more often directed at Hegel's uncompromising and supposedly "totalizing" rationalism: his inability, it was charged, to do sufficient justice to the concrete particularity of human existence, the unconceptualizable human individual, the role of unreason in human motivation, the contingency of historical change, and the phenomena of interest to psychoanalysis, like repetition and the death drive. Objections to the second dimension are more varied and more interesting, because Hegel succeeded in convincing even many of his critics (like the "young Hegelians") that philosophy must have a historically diagnostic task (it must be "its own time comprehended in thought"), even while many also rejected Hegel's "idealist" version of that project and his conclusions about "where we are" in any such process. Others simply point to the fact that no one has succeeded in writing *The Phenomenology of Spirit, Part Two*. The historical world that developed after 1831 and after the twentieth century cannot, it is assumed, be properly understood in Hegelian terms, the world of mass consumer societies, postcolonial states, globalized capitalism and therewith greatly weakened nation-states, the culture industry, pervasive reliance on technology in all facets of life, and so forth. Moreover, it is argued, it is not possible to "extend" even a roughly Hegelian analysis to such phenomena, especially to reason-defeating, irreconcilable-with phenomena like Nazism, the Holocaust, Stalin's crimes, or a communist China full of billionaires.[1]

1. See Žižek's remarks on Hegel and contemporary finance capitalism (*Less than Nothing,*

Simply put, Žižek's ambitious goal is to argue that the former characterization of Hegel attacks a straw man, and when this is realized in sufficient detail, both the putative European break with Hegel in the criticisms of the likes of Schelling, Kierkegaard, Nietzsche, Deleuze, and the Freudians will look very different, with significantly more overlap than gaps, and this will make available a historical diagnosis very different from the triumphalist one usually attributed to Hegel. (One of the surprising things about the book is that despite its size, what interests Žižek, by a very wide margin, is the theoretical presuppositions for such a diagnosis rather than much detail about the diagnosis itself.)[2]

The structure of the book is unusual. It is based on the adage that the second and third most pleasurable things in the world are the drink before and the cigarette after. Hence we get "*the drink before*," the pre-Hegelian context needed to understand Hegel's option (a lot of attention is devoted to Plato's *Parmenides*, Christianity, the death of God, and Fichte); "*The Thing Itself*" (twice! once with Hegel, once with Lacan); and "*the cigarette after*" (Badiou, Heidegger, Levinas, and a concluding chapter on "the ontology of quantum physics"). A lot of this, especially the occasional digressions about Buddhism and the quantum physics discussion, not to mention the intricacies of Lacan, is well above my pay grade, so I will concentrate in the following on the interpretation of Hegel and the implications Žižek draws from that interpretation.

## II

Let us designate the basic problem that the book addresses as the ontological problem of "subjectivity"; *what is it* to be a thinking, knowing, and also acting and interacting subject in a material world? Žižek begins by claiming that there are four main kinds of answers to such a question possible in

---

244). Perhaps Zadie Smith's trenchant summary is the best: states now "de-regulate to privatize gain and re-regulate to nationalize loss." Smith, "The North West London Blues."

2. There is a sober, clear statement of what, from a Hegelian point of view, we now need: "breaking out of the capitalist horizon without falling into the trap of returning to the eminently pre-modern notion of a balanced, (self-) restrained society" (Žižek, *Less than Nothing*, 257). But as he goes on to explain this position, the core turns out to be that "the subject has to recognize in its alienation from substance the separation of substance from itself" (258). I have not been able to understand how that helps us do what the sober statement insists on. This is an issue that will recur frequently below.

the current "ideological-philosophical field": (i) scientific naturalism (brain science, Darwinism); (ii) discursive historicism (Foucault, deconstruction); (iii) New Age Western "Buddhism"; (iv) some sort of transcendental finitude (culminating in Heidegger).[3] Žižek's thesis is that these options miss the correct one, which he calls the idea of a "pre-transcendental gap or rupture (the Freudian name for which is the drive)," and that this framework is what actually "designates the very core of modern subjectivity."[4]

This all means that the discussion must proceed at a very high level of abstraction and will require a difficult summary of the basic positions of the "gang of four" (Kant, Fichte, Schelling, and Hegel) that Žižek thinks he needs on the table in order for him to present the core issue he wants to discuss. In the language developed in this tradition, at that high level of abstraction, the problem is the problem of the ontological status of "negativity," nonbeing, what is not (or is not simply the fullness or presence of positive being). In the simplest sense, we are talking about intentional consciousness, say in perception or empirical judgments, and the ontological status of agency. Consciousness is not a wholly "*positive*" phenomenon in this (Kantian and post-Kantian) way of looking at it. If it were it would be something like a mere complex registering and responding device (of the same ontological status as a thermometer). But an empirical judgment about the world ("there is a red book on the table") is not simply wrung out of one by a perceptual episode. One is *not* simply wholly absorbed in the presence of the world to one, and that "*not*" is the beginning of all the German problems Žižek wants to trace out in order to get to his own interpretation. In making any such judgment I "negate" the mere immediacy or givenness of perceptual content, negate it as immediate and putatively given, and take up a position of sorts about what is there.[5] And in agency I am not simply causally responsive to inclinations and desires; there is no

3. Lots of quibbles and qualifications are possible here. I can't see why anyone would take (iii) seriously. I would include "deconstruction" under (iv), not (ii), would argue for more categories (pragmatism, of the analytic [Brandomian], Rortyean, or Habermasian variety; anomalous monism; phenomenology, which is still alive and kicking in some quarters; Wittgenstein's approach), and I would defend a Hegelian version of compatibilism. But what is important is what Žižek is for; his own position.

4. Žižek, *Less than Nothing*, 6–7.

5. In a more extensive and so more careful discussion, several caveats would be necessary here. The case of perceptual consciousness, while apperceptive, is not of the same logical type as a judgment, an empirical claim to knowledge, and more care would be needed to account for the

fullness of positive being here either. I interrupt or negate merely positive being (what I feel inclined to do, experience as wanting to do) by deliberating and resolving what to do. Any such inclination cannot count as a reason for an action except as "incorporated" within a maxim, a general policy one has for actions of such a type.[6] So when Hegel reminds us in the Preface to the *Phenomenology of Spirit* that we must think "substance" "also as subject," he does not, it would appear, mean for us to think subject merely as an attribute of substance or an appearance of what remains, basically, substance, or an epiphenomenon of substance.[7] The whole point of speculative idealism is to think substance as not-just-substance, the negation of mere substance as such; and to think subject as substance, what is not-mere-subject. A tall order. The closest first approximation of what he means is Aristotelian: subjectivity (thinking and acting according to norms) is the distinct being-at-work (*energeia*, Hegelian *Wirklichkeit*) of the biological life-form that is the human substance; this in the same sense in which Aristotle says, if the eye were body, *seeing* would be its form, its distinctive being-at-work. This being-at-work is how that substantial life-form appears, and not any

---

role of spontaneity. But perceptual consciousness is not mere differential responsiveness, and that is what we need for the "negativity" problem. See "Brandom's Hegel" herein.

6. The "incorporation thesis," given that name by the Kant scholar Henry Allison in his *Kant's Theory of Freedom*, emerged as an explicit theme relatively late in Kant's work (his *Religion within the Limits of Reason Alone* [1793]) and does not mean "causes only affect me insofar as I allow them to affect me" (Žižek, *Less than Nothing*, 169–70). "Only insofar as I count them as reasonable grounds to do something" would be more accurate, and inclinations causally affect me (I can be powerfully inclined to do something); they just cannot be said to produce on their own the bodily movement, if it is to count as an action. There are not many such errors and slips, but they are irritating when they occur. The *Critique of Pure Reason* appeared in 1781, not 1787 (11); Henrich's famous article referred to "Fichtes ürsprungliche Einsicht," not his "Grundeinsicht." And (for me the most significant) the newspaper editor at the end of *The Man Who Shot Liberty Valance* did not say, "When reality doesn't fit the legend, print the legend" (420). He said something much more relevant to Žižek's concerns: "This is the West, sir. When the legend becomes fact, print the legend."

7. I say "it would appear" in order to acknowledge that for Žižek, we *should* say *something like* "substance" negates *itself*, creates a kind of "gap" and incompleteness, and that "space" *is* the subject. (But in what sense could the subject also be said to "substantialize itself"? Negate itself as subject just by being substance?) At any rate, Žižek doesn't mean that a subject is just a kind of property of material substance. I think I understand what the gap or self-negation view would mean in Freudian terms—that natural, even biological maturation *itself* produces a subject divided against itself, unable to realize or satisfy the primary processes—but I don't think that is the problem the post-Kantians were addressing, and I will try to say why below.

attestation of the self-negating Gap that is substance. (This is in disagreement with Žižek's Lacanian reading, as at p. 380, inter alia.)[8]

The way Žižek poses the question itself, then, reveals a deeply Schellingian orientation at the beginning and throughout the whole book. (This will not be surprising to anyone who has read *Tarrying with the Negative* or *The Parallax View*.) That is, the question this observation is taken to raise is: What could such a subject with such a negating capacity *be*? And even more sweepingly: What must *being* be, such that there are, can be, "positive" beings and such "negating" ones? For the early Schelling, this led to the conclusion that the distinction between such subjects and objects could be neither an objective distinction nor a subjective one, so the "ground" of the possibility of the distinction must be an "indifference point," neither subject nor object (prompting Hegel's famous, friendship-destroying remark, that this is the night in which all cows are black). And in what could be called the Schellingian tradition, the assumption has long been that neither Kant nor Fichte had, could have, an adequate answer to this question because for them, "being" is "secondary," not primary (an "appearance," or a posited "not-I"),[9] and the "Absolute" is such a "groundless" or putatively (but impossibly) self-grounding subject. The interesting question has always been how to locate the mature Hegel in this field of possibilities.[10] As already noted, for Žižek that position involves a commitment to a "gap" or "rupture" in being. "Speech (presup)poses a lack/hole in the positive order of being."[11] "The void of our knowledge corresponds to a void in being itself, to the ontological incompleteness of reality."[12] There are many such formulations.[13]

8. I have no space to discuss Žižek's interesting parallel reading of substance-subject and id-ego except to agree that in neither case does "wo es war, soll ich werden" amount to a rational appropriation of or control over or simple reconciliation with the "*nicht-Ich*." See Žižek, *Less than Nothing*, 389 ff.

9. Not an unreasonable view. See Fichte, *Introductions to the "Wissenschaftslehre" and Other Writings*, trans. Breazeale, 84.

10. According to Žižek (*Less than Nothing*, 144), Hegel's unique position is to deny that we need any "third" to ground both subject and object. "His [Hegel's] point is precisely that there is no need for a Third element, the medium or ground beyond subject and object-substance. We start with objectivity and the subject is nothing but the self-mediation of objectivity." But this simply *is* objective idealism and has not yet differentiated Hegel's view, as I will try to show.

11. Žižek, *Less than Nothing*, 75.

12. Ibid., 149.

13. Cf. Žižek's claim that Marx and Freud can only understand "antagonism" as a feature of social or psychic reality; they are "unable to articulate it as constitutive of reality, as the impossi-

This all has deep connections with the original Eleatic problems of non-being (how I could possibly say "what is not" in uttering falsehoods; a problem because what is not *is not*, is impossible); hence Žižek's sustained attention to the second half of Plato's *Parmenides*. But the German version has a unique, different dimension, and that dimension is the beginning of my deepest disagreement with Žižek. To see the problem (or to see it as I see it), consider what Hegel draws our attention to when he is stating his understanding of his deepest connection to Kant:

> It is one of the profoundest and truest insights to be found in the *Critique of Reason* that the unity which constitutes the essence of the concept is recognized as the original synthetic unity of apperception, the unity of the "I think," or of self-consciousness.—This proposition is all that there is to the so-called transcendental deduction of the categories which, from the beginning, has however been regarded as the most difficult piece of Kantian philosophy.[14]

It is *for this reason*—the apperceptive nature of conceiving, the fact that conceiving *is* apperceiving—that perceptual awareness, judgment, actions, any determinate intentional awareness, cannot be understood as simply *being* in a mental state (in the fullness or positivity of being, in the manner in which we would say that a computer "is calculating"). For in perceiving, I am also conscious of perceiving, conscious of myself perceiving. In believing anything, I am conscious of my believing, of myself committed to a belief. In acting, I would not *be* acting, were I not conscious of myself acting. (An action is not something that goes on whether I am conscious of it or not, like water boiling. It is only action if I am conscious of myself acting.)

There are then two complications in this view that require extensive discussion but can only be noted here. The first: as Sebastian Rödl often notes, the above should not suggest, as the grammar might, that there are two acts of mind involved.[15] There is only one. Action *is* consciousness of

bility around which reality is constructed" (*Less than Nothing*, 250). I am with Marx and Freud (and, I think, Hegel) on this one. This touches on the most difficult issue for me in the book, what is announced by the title: that "reality" is "less than nothing."

14. Hegel, *Science of Logic*, trans. Miller, 515. This quotation alone seems to me to foreclose the gloss given by Žižek on the Kant-Hegel-apperception relation (*Less than Nothing*, 286).

15. Rödl, *Self-Consciousness*, 17–64.

action; there is no action unless I am conscious of myself acting.[16] The second: apperception is not a two-place intentional relation. I am not self-conscious in the way I am conscious of objects (or an obvious regress would threaten). One could say that I am conscious of objects apperceptively or self-consciously; never that I am conscious of objects and also conscious of myself as a second object.[17] (This is also why first-order self-*knowledge* is not observational or inferential [not of an object "already there"] but *constitutive*.[18] In any respect relevant to my practical identity [and not any empirical feature], I am what I take myself to be [professor, citizen, social-democrat-liberal]. Or at least I am provisionally; I must also enact what I take myself to be, or it is a mere confabulation or an untested pledge about what I will do. In Žižekian language, there is no self except as posited and enacted, and the apparent paradox [who is doing the positing?] is no paradox.)[19]

When Žižek takes on the apperception claim in his own terms,[20] he notes how implausible it is to think that every act of consciousness is an act of self-consciousness. It seems clearly empirically false. But that is because the supposition concerns two acts, consciousness of the object and consciousness of the subject aware of the object, and the most important claim in the idealist treatment of the issue is that this is not so. There is only one act. Self-consciousness is not consciousness of an object. We do not need

16. Cf. Rödl on a "non-empirical knowledge of a material reality" (ibid., 122). See also 131, 133–34, 138.

17. Put another way, the self-consciousness that is a necessary condition of any human doing or thinking adverts to *a way of one's doing or thinking*, as if adverbially, and involves no self-inspection. See my *Kant's Theory of Form*. One does what one does, one is aware of what one is aware of, one thinks what one thinks, all *knowingly*. Apropos the discussion below, cf. Fichte's formulations in the *Wissenschaftslehre*: "The self and the self-reverting act are perfectly identical concepts"(37) and "It is the immediate consciousness that I act and what I enact: it is that whereby I know something because I do it" (38). Or: "Without self-consciousness there is no consciousness whatever; but self-consciousness is possible only in the manner indicated: I am simply active" (41).

18. Žižek makes this same point himself, correctly, in my view, in an approving summary of Lukacs (*Less than Nothing*, 220). See also Hegel in the *Science of Logic*: "The most important point for the nature of spirit is not only the relation of what it is in itself to what it is actually, but the relation of what it knows itself to be to what it actually is; because spirit is essentially consciousness, this self-knowing is a fundamental determination of its actuality" (37).

19. It is not because there is no original moment of self-origination. One has always already come to be in some position of self-positing, is always becoming who one is. There is a very great deal more to be said about this problem. For discussions of small subsets of these issues, see my *Hegel's Idealism* (chaps. 3 and 4) and *Hegel's Practical Philosophy* (chap. 3).

20. Žižek, *Less than Nothing*, 347–48.

Deleuzian "virtuality," or an ontology with an "actuality of the possible." And there is no link in the treatment of this issue by Kant, Fichte, and Hegel to Žižek's own negative ontology, his claim that "what, ultimately, 'there is' is only the absolute Difference, the self-repelling Gap."[21] What there is, in the sense of this inquiry, is a possible space of reasons, into which persons may be socialized and within which constant self-correction, *self*-negation, is possible.

This may all already be "too much information" for a reader interested in how Žižek proposes to offer a renewed version of dialectical materialism and so a critical theory of late-modern capitalism. But this path through German Idealism is the path he has chosen, and it is important to know if his version is leading us correctly. With many more pages to demonstrate it, the point of the above formulation would be to suggest a different way of understanding the problem of "negativity" in that tradition, one that will not lead us to gaps or voids or holes in being (or "groundless Acts" in the absence of "the big Other"). I do not fully understand the claims about holes in the fabric of being, and at any rate, we do not need the claim if we go in the direction I am suggesting. For if that formulation of apperception is correct, it means we are able to account for the inappropriateness of psychological or naturalist accounts of such states, all without a gappy ontology (in the sense if not in the same way that Frege and the early Husserl criticized psychologism without an "alternate" ontology). If believing is to be conscious of believing, then it is impossible just to "*be*" believing. For me to be conscious of my believing something is to be conscious of why I believe what I do (however fragmentary, confused, or unknowingly inconsistent such reasons may be). When I want to know what I believe, I am investigating what I ought to believe.[22] Such grounds may be incomplete and may commit one to claims one is unaware of as such, and much belief is habitual and largely unreflective, but never completely so. In such a case, it is just a view I am entertaining, not what I believe. Likewise with action. It is constitutive of action that an agent can be responsive to the "why" question, and that means to be in a position to give a reason for my action. (Again, this is not a

21. Ibid., 378. And yet, in other contexts, when, for example, he is discussing the "self-consciousness" of the state, Žižek seems to me to state the point being made here in just the way it is made here. See 406 ff.

22. One of the best-known statements and defenses of this "transparency" condition is Richard Moran's *Authority and Estrangement: An Essay on Self-Knowledge*. See also Rödl, *Self-Consciousness*, chap. 3.

possible exchange: "Why did you do that?" "I don't know, I just did it." Your body may have moved, but you didn't do anything.)[23] Doxastic, cognitive, and intentional states are thus "in the space of reasons," and to ask for, say, neuropsychological causes for having come to be in that state is to make a category mistake, to have misunderstood the question, to offer something we cannot use. Such causes are irrelevant to *my* having the reasons *I* have, and your understanding the reasons I have, all of which must be enunciated and "backed" first-personally. No gaps in being need apply, any more than the possibility of people playing bridge, following the norms of bridge, and exploring strategies for winning need commit us to any unusual gappy ontology to account for the possibility of norm-responsive bridge following. Anyone playing the game is not just acting out responses to cues but is, at the same time as playing and making moves, always "holding open" the possibility of revising strategy, challenging someone on the rules and so forth. This is *what it is* to be following rules, not to be instantiating laws.[24] This capacity is possible because it is certainly actual, and that means that materially embodied beings are able to engage in complex, rule-following practices, the explanation of which is not furthered by reference to their neurological properties. (In his *Phenomenology*, Hegel's formulation of this sort of logical negativity is that consciousness is "always beyond itself," and he frequently, for this reason, characterizes consciousness as a self-negation.)[25]

23. This issue, like every one in this paragraph, is much more complicated than this summary can do justice to. On this last point, the compelling films of the Dardenne brothers make clear how much more has to be said about the issue. In all of their films, characters certainly *look like* they are acting without being able to say why. What is especially interesting is that they manage to suggest a link between this compelling opacity and the disintegrating fabric of late-capitalist working-class life. They integrate these philosophical-psychological elements with the social seamlessly. See *Le fils* (2002) especially.

24. This is also relevant to how the way animals have representations is different from ours. Theirs are intentional in their way, but they do not have the status of "cognitions," in the way ours do. A dog might see a human figure far away (downwind, let us say) and, seeing an unknown person, begin barking, only later to start wagging her tail as the known person it really is comes into view. *But the dog did not correct herself.* Here we do want to say that a perceptual cue prompted a response (one we can even call a rational response), and then a different perceptual cue (with more detail of visual features in view) prompted a different behavioral response. The fullness of positive being, we might say. (I've never noticed, for example, that my dog ever became embarrassed that she made such a mistake—which she often makes—since she has no way of knowing that she made a mistake that she ought to correct. That is not how she sees; she sees one set of cues, then she sees another. This would be one way of saying she has no unity of apperception.)

25. Here is the formulation from the so-called *Berlin Phenomenology* (trans. Petry, 2, my

Now it is possible for Žižek to say that just *that*, that possibility for norm-responsiveness, since it is a materially embodied capacity not explicable in material terms, *is* the gap or void or self-negation he wants to attribute to Hegel's ontology, the "more than material, without being immaterial."[26] But that seems too anodyne for what he wants to say and for the connection he wants to make with Lacan. For, on this way of looking at the matter, there is no need for a paradoxical negative ontology. Of course, it is possible and important that someday researchers will discover why animals with human brains can do these things and animals without human brains cannot, and some combination of astrophysics and evolutionary theory will be able to explain why humans have ended up with the brains they have. But these are not philosophical problems and they do not generate any philosophical problems.[27] (The problems are: What *is* a compelling reason and why? Under what conditions are the reasons people give for what they do "their own" reasons, reasons and policies they can genuinely "identify with"?)[28]

Put another way, Žižek is quite right to note that the importance of the shift from the early to the mature Hegel involves at its core Hegel's realization that "logic" was not a preparation for metaphysics, but that

---

emphasis): "The I is now this subjectivity, this infinite relation to itself, but therein, namely in this subjectivity, lies its negative relation to itself, diremption, differentiation, judgment. *The I judges, and this constitutes it as consciousness*; it repels itself from itself; this is a logical determination."

26. Adrian Johnson, "Slavoj Žižek's Hegelian Reformation: Giving a Hearing to *The Parallax View*." Something like this position is available to Žižek if we understand the space of the Symbolic (in its Lacanian sense) as the space of the normative and so of reason. See his interpretation of Freud's controversial remark about "anatomy" being "destiny," "in other words a symbolic formation," a destiny we must make (*Less than Nothing*, 216).

27. Not that such discoveries could not be relevant to philosophy. They certainly are for Hegel. In §12 of the *Encyclopedia Logic*, Hegel says that philosophy "owes its development to the empirical sciences"; and in the remark to §246 of the *Philosophy of Nature*, he says that the *Philosophy of Nature* "presupposes and is conditioned by empirical physics." See also the Addition to §381 in the Introduction to the *Philosophy of Spirit*. These passages are all relevant to the question Žižek raises at 460.

28. When Žižek addresses this issue, he adopts a Nietzschean stance that seems to me unargued for and question begging (*Less than Nothing*, 429): "What kind of power (or authority) is it which needs to justify itself with reference to the interests of those over whom it rules, which accepts the need to provide reasons for its exercise? Does not such a notion of power undermine itself?" He goes on to call such a regime "anti-political" and "technocratic." But appeals to self-interest are only one sort of reason, and the constraints introduced by such a requirement, if they undermine anything, undermine the notion of mastery and rule. They are not meant to be in the service of such notions.

logic *was* metaphysics. But this means that a consideration of being-in-its-intelligibility is the only sort of metaphysics that is possible (to be is to be intelligible, something like the motto of Greek philosophy and so the beginning of philosophy).[29] But this also means that the "movement" in Hegel's *Encyclopedia* from a "logic of nature" to a "logic of *Geist*" has nothing to do with any "materialist evolutionism."[30] Hegel's metaphysics is a logic, and the *intelligibility* of nature at some point, speaking very causally, "runs out," is unable in its terms to account for the complex, rule-governed activities materially embodied beings are capable of. This is not a new, nonnatural capacity that emerges in time, but it emerges in a systematic consideration of the resources for rendering intelligible that are available to accounts of nature.

There *is* a phenomenological account in Hegel of the context within which materially embodied organic beings, living beings in a minimal self-relation (a self-sentiment necessary to preserve life) can be imagined interacting in a way that "for them" transcends mere self-sustenance, a "move" that will not be comprehensible as a move in the game of mere animal life. That is the famous account in chapter 4 of the 1807 *Phenomenology of Spirit*. The problematic is to imagine such living beings struggling, perhaps over resources, to the death if necessary, when the possibility is introduced of a participant's indifference to his own life in the service of a demand to be recognized (a "nonnatural" norm), when what one demands is not mere submission but a pledge of service, an acknowledgment of the other's entitlement. "Spirit" emerges in this imagined social contestation, in what we come to demand of each other, not in the interstices of being. This is a phenomenological account (what *it is like* to be and come to be *Geist*), not an encyclopedic logic, but it also introduces the Hegelian account of reason. We see that it is not to be understood as a mere capacity for calculation or merely strategic, but as a sociohistorical practice, what Brandom calls the "game of giving and asking for reasons"[31] to each other, and it introduces

29. The skeptical anxiety that we would thereby be treating being only as it is intelligible "by our finite lights" is illusory anxiety that Hegel takes himself to have methodically destroyed in the *Phenomenology*, the "deduction" of the standpoint of the *Logic*. The extraordinarily influential Heideggerian anxiety that this all represents the "imposition" of human will "onto" the question of Being is a matter for a separate discussion. See Heidegger, *Nietzsche*, vol. 4, and my "Heidegger on Nietzsche on Nihilism," chap. 8 below.

30. Žižek, *Less than Nothing*, 238.

31. Brandom, *Making It Explicit: Reasoning, Representing, and Discursive Commitment*.

the central question of Hegel's historical narrative: Is it plausible to claim that we are getting better at justifying ourselves to each other or not?[32]

One can see this (that the above account is not Žižek's direction) in his very detailed treatment of Fichte.[33] Žižek follows closely the account of Fichte in the recently published undergraduate lectures given by Dieter Henrich at Harvard in the seventies (*Between Kant and Hegel*), and this creates two problems.[34] In the first place, Henrich confuses the problem of apperceptive consciousness in experience and action with the problem of reflective self-identification, how to find and identify my unique self. Those are two different problems, and there is no indication that Fichte confused them and plenty of evidence that he was aware of the difference.[35] Secondly, Žižek accepts Henrich's charge that Fichte confused "logical" with "real" opposition, switching from one to the other, and so could provide no satisfying account of the relation of the I to the not-I. But Fichte was quite clear on the difference, and his remarks track closely the remarks made above about the status of the normative in Kant and the early idealists. A few examples will have to suffice. Here is Fichte in a typical statement of general principles:

> The basic contention of the philosopher, as such, is as follows: Though the self may exist only for itself, there necessarily arises for it at once an

32. In Kantian terms, the role of reason can be said to emerge in any attempt to lead a "justified" life (and so a free one), to seek always the "condition" for anything "conditioned." See my discussion in *Hegel on Self-Consciousness: Desire and Death in the "Phenomenology of Spirit,"* 55–58.

33. It is also the case that this sort of interpretation would mean a disagreement with Žižek's characterization of the beginning of all this in Kant. It is not the case that Kant and the Idealists (certainly not Hegel; see *Belief and Knowledge*, 62–70) conceived the subject as a "spontaneous . . . synthetic activity, the force of unification, of bringing together the manifold of sensuous data we are bombarded with into a unified representation of objects" (*Less than Nothing*, 106; see also 149). It is not the case that "apperception . . . changes the confused flow of sensations into 'reality,' which obeys necessary laws." In the first place, Kant often says this impositionism is exactly the position he rejects, because it would give the "skeptic exactly what he wants" (B168). See also B138, B160n, and the "same function" passage at B105/A79. Nor is it the case that this synthetic activity "introduces a gap/difference into substantial reality" (*Less than Nothing*, 106). The negativity ("not mere being") in question is a matter of the normative dimension of apperceptive experience and action. One could, I suppose, call this a "gap in being," but that seems to me to mystify everything needlessly.

34. Henrich, *Between Kant and Hegel*. An unusual feature of Žižek's book is his heavy reliance on selected secondary sources. Henrich, Malabou, Miller, and Lebrun are the most heavily relied on, even in disagreements (as with Lebrun).

35. I present this evidence in *Hegel's Idealism*, chap. 3, pp. 42–59.

> existence external to it; the ground of the latter lies in the former, and is conditioned thereby; self-consciousness and consciousness of something that is to be—not ourselves,—are necessarily connected; but the first is to be regarded as the "conditioning" factor, and the second as the conditioned.[36]

But we don't know just from this what "condition" means and especially how it relates to the key term, "positing" (*setzen*), the positing of the *nicht-Ich.*

When he tries to explain what he means, though, he reverts to the "autonomy of the normative" language invoked above. From the 1797 Introductions to the *Wissenschaftslehre*:

> So what then is the overall gist of the *Wissenschaftslehre,* summarized in a few words? It is this: reason is absolutely self-sufficient; it exists only for itself. But nothing exists for reason except reason itself. It follows that everything reason is must have its foundation in reason itself and must be explicable solely on the basis of reason itself and not on the basis of anything outside of reason, for reason could not get outside of itself without renouncing itself. In short the *Wissenschaftslehre* is transcendental idealism.[37]

From the Second Introduction to the 1796/1799 *Wissenschaftslehre (nova methodo),* translated as *Foundations of Transcendental Philosophy*:

> The idealist observes that experience in its entirety is nothing but an acting on the part of a rational being.

The most revealing passage follows this claim about the activity of a rational being, and makes clear what Fichte means by referring to such an "activity." The passage is a gloss on "the viewpoint of idealism."

> The idealist observes how there must come to be things for the individual. Thus the situation is different for the [observed] individual than it is for the philosopher. The individual is confronted with things, men, etc., that

36. G. Fichte, "Second Introduction to the *Wissenschaftslehre,*" trans. Heath and Lachs, 33.
37. G. Fichte, *Introductions to the "Wissenschaftslehre" and Other Writings,* trans. Breazeale, 59.

> are independent of him. But the idealist says, "There are no things outside me and present independently of me." Though the two say opposite things, they do not contradict each other. For the idealist, from his own viewpoint, displays the necessity of the individual's view. When the idealist says, "outside of me," he means "outside of reason"; when the individual says the same thing, he means "outside of my person."[38]

Or, in an even more summary claim from Fichte's notes: "The I is reason."[39]

Now this rational self-satisfaction is only something we can "strive" for infinitely according to Fichte, but the larger point is the one of relevance for Žižek's reading. That point concerns the necessary link between the self-conscious character of experience and action, understood this way, and *reason,* a norm that does not play a prominent role in Žižek's Schellingian account. (The other Hegelian issue that does not play a major role for Žižek is sociality, *Geist,* and the issues are related, as I will try to show in the next section.) The condition of modern atheism means for Žižek, in Lacanian terms, that there is and can be no longer any "big Other," any guarantor of at least the possibility of any resolution of normative skepticism and conflicts. But no transcendent guarantor is not the same thing as no possible reliance on reason in our own deliberations and in our claims on others. Even a position (like Nietzsche's, say) that held that most conscious appeals to reasons are symptoms, that true reasons lie elsewhere (not the slave's virtuousness but his ressentiment motivated his submission), is committed to the link. (Ressentiment *is* his reason, counted *by* him—in self-deceit—as warranting action, submission and moralistic condemnation of the Master.) To claim something or to do something is to offer to give reasons for the claim or the deed, and if there are reasons either to reject the reasons or to reject the claim of sincerity, we are still in, cannot exit, the space of reasons. (An immediate consequence: the first sentence of Žižek's conclusion—

38. G. Fichte, *Foundations of Transcendental Philosophy,* trans. Breazeale, 105–6.

39. This is from the notes to his famous *Aenesidemus* review, in *Gesamtausgabe der Bayerischen Akademie der Wissenschaften,* ed. Lauth and Joacob, 11, 1, 287. It is important to get this aspect of Fichte right in order to avoid the commitments Žižek makes on p. 283, where we hear again about the *phenomena's* "self-limitation," the "ontological incompleteness of phenomenal reality," and the ground of freedom in "the ontological incompleteness of reality itself." Insofar as I understand these claims, they are regressive and dogmatically metaphysical as the "ineffable particularists," the worshippers of "the Other," that Žižek rightly criticizes. The link between self-consciousness, reason, and freedom is not based on such appeals.

"What the inexistence of the big Other signals is that every ethical and/or moral edifice has to be grounded on an abyssal act which is, in the most radical sense imaginable, political"—makes zero Hegelian sense.[40] Something understood by an agent as an "abyssal" act is a delusion, the pathos of self-inflating and posed heroism, and the gesture belongs in the Hegelian zoo along with the Beautiful Soul, the Knight of Virtue, and especially the Frenzy of Self-Conceit.[41] And if the act is "abyssal," then "politics" simply means "power," power backed by nothing but resolve and will, likely met with nothing but resolve and will.)

To see the relevance of, on the contrary, the connection between self-consciousness and reason to Žižek's project in the book, we need to turn to his long, explicit discussion of Hegel.

## III

> In this sense, the post-Hegelian turn to "concrete reality, irreducible to notional mediation," should rather be read as a desperate posthumous revenge of metaphysics, as an attempt to reinstall metaphysics, although in the inverted form of the primacy of concrete reality.[42]

Truer words were never spoken in Hegel's voice. In explaining such a claim, Žižek makes a number of salient points about Hegel. For example, one of the most curious things about Hegel's basic position is that it can be fairly summarized by saying that it is no positive position. Rather it is the right understanding of the other logically possible positions. Žižek gets this aspect of Hegel exactly right (cf. p. 387 ff.) and has a number of useful things to say about it and its implications. Moreover, Žižek's interest in Lacan leads him to three other aspects of Hegel that are quite important but often neglected in both conventional (what Žižek calls "textbook") interpretations

40. Žižek, *Less than Nothing*, 963.

41. When it is described as it is, apparently approvingly, by Žižek on p. 427, a true Badiouian act, the "Act," is said to be a "radical and violent simplification . . . the magical moment when the infinite pondering crystallizes into a simple 'yes' or 'no.' " "Magical" is the right word, close to mystified and unintelligible. One shudders to think how many such Actors gloried in the "infinite" crystallizing itself in *them*. The idea is supposed to be that the founding of a new ethical order must perforce be "abyssal," ungrounded and contingent (460), that you can't have 1789 without 1793 (319), and so forth. But this is a completely non-Hegelian notion of "new" and so of "contingency." See Henrich on *Zufälligkeit*.

42. Žižek, *Less than Nothing*, 239.

and more "up-to-date" contemporary reconstructions. This is the dimension, first, of "retroactivity," also sometimes known as "belatedness" (*Nachträglichkeit*), or what Žižek rightly described as Hegel's insistence on the logic of a deed or claim or event that can be said to "posit its own presuppositions" retroactively. (A dream's meaning is constituted by the telling, not "recovered." A trauma becomes *the trauma it is* retroactively, in its interrogation.) In Hegel the notion is most important in his account of act-descriptions and intentions. There is no literal backward causation, but what it is we did and why we did it can be said to come to be what they are only after we have acted (after we have seen what we were actually committed to doing; what others acknowledge, or not, as what we did).[43] Second, in a related claim, Žižek takes much more seriously than most other commentators the unusual and initially paradoxical thesis that Spirit must be understood as a "product of itself." Žižek's discussions of all these topics are, in my view, on the mark and valuable.[44] Moreover, because he does such justice to these themes, especially the latter, he can, third, reject the picture of Hegelian historical action so familiar in critical theory criticisms, especially by Adorno and Adornoitans. This is the picture of *Geist* externalizing itself in its products (its "self-negation"), thereby being alienated from them, until it can "return to itself" in its externality, and so be reconciled with itself in a sublated self-identity (the negation of negation). This is also "the great narcissistic devouring maw" picture of Hegel, devouring and negating otherness in a mad project to become everything, the picture so beloved by Adorno in his dismissal of Hegel as the epitome of "identity thinking" (cf. p. 300). But however right he is in rejecting that caricature, Žižek's own picture seems to me too influenced by his picture of Lacan (not to mention middle Schelling) and so does not allow the true Hegelian alternative in these very abstract possibilities to emerge, especially with respect to the problem of reason (Hegel's "big Other") and sociality.

## IV

This brings us, in other words, to the more practical and "critical" question, as Žižek puts it, of "how to be a Hegelian today," whether it is pos-

43. Another vast topic. See my *Hegel's Practical Philosophy: Rational Agency as Ethical Life.*

44. See his rejection of the "organic model" of Hegelian historical change (*Less than Nothing*, 272).

sible, what the implications are of Žižek's interpretation of the notion he places at the center of a Hegelianism—a "self-negating" or "gappy" phenomenal reality. With that ontology as a background, philosophy is supposed to be its own time comprehended in thought. Our time is still the time of bourgeois capitalism and its central institutions: private property, commercial republics, individual-rights-based legal institutions, the privatization of religion and the ideal of religious tolerance, romantic love, love-based marriages, nuclear families, and the (putative) separation of state and civil society. What does "thought's comprehension"—in this case "dialectical" thought—"comprehend"?

One broad-based starting point for such a Hegelianism, shared by Žižek and most "Hegelians": a commitment to the historicity of norms, but without a historical relativism, as if we were trapped inside specific assumptions and cannot think our way out of them. The "universal" for Hegel—the clearest name for which would simply be "freedom"—is always accessible in some way but as the "concrete universal," a universal understood in a way inflected by a time and a place, partial and incomplete, requiring interpretation and reinterpretation and dialectical extension. For example, if we want to understand why gender-based division of labor became so much less credible a norm in the last third of the twentieth century, and exclusively in the technologically advanced commercial republics of the West, one begins to become a "Hegelian" with the simple realization of how implausible it would be to insist that the injustice of such a basis for a division of labor, the reasons for rejecting such a practice, were always in principle available from the beginning of human attempts to justify their practices, and were "discovered" sometime in the early 1970s. And yet our commitment to such a rejection is far stronger than "a new development in how we go on." The practice is irrational and so unjust, however historically indexed the "grip" of such a claim clearly is.

Žižek proposes to defend a Hegel for whom any claim about historical rationality (like this one) is always retrospective, never prospective and predicting, and in this "open-ended" Hegel, he is surely right. (It often goes unnoticed that Hegel's famous claim that the owl of Minerva takes flight only at dusk, that philosophy can begin to paint its gray on gray only when a form of life has grown old, means that he is announcing that the form of life "comprehended by thought" in the *Philosophy of Right has* grown old, is dying, and only because of this can it now be comprehended by Hegel. It is hardly the image one would propose were one trying to claim that we had reached some utopia of realized reason.)[45] Moreover, the retrospective dimension is quite important. It is only after the world-historical influence of Christianity that Greek philosophy could come to seem unable to provide the resources to account for what would eventually come to be understood as Christian inwardness, subjectivity, and so a very different view of agency. There is no World-Spirit puppet master in this picture.

But the alternative to any "shadow of dialectical materialism" must be something like a "dialectical idealism." This of course means simply that there are no "material contradictions."[46] Contradictions result from some self-opposition in an action or practice directed by a subject. This can be in the form of "performative contradictions" in a speech act, or practical contradictions in action. (Hobbes gave us a fine example of the latter: in the state of nature, everyone doing what is maximally rational for the individual's point of view—preemptively striking others—produces what is for everyone the worst possible outcome. Agents contradict themselves by acting rationally.) On the assumption of collective subjectivity (*Geist*) one can imagine how one might try to show that some institutional practice in a form of life "contradicts," in the means it rationally chooses, the overall ends genuinely sought by that society. And all of this depends on what one can show or not; whether a successor social form can be said to be achieving more successfully what a prior social form was attempting or not: hence, determination negation, internal critique, all the Hegelian desiderata. (Gender-based division of labor came to be understood as inconsistent with the already existing ideal of equal protection under the law and meritocratic social mobility, and at a time when changes in the technology of production and the need for many more workers in the greatest period of economic prosperity in history made possible such a realization.)

But we are certainly far enough from the ("dead") particular historical form of bourgeois society that Hegel thought he had comprehended, and our own form of life could plausibly said be said to be growing suffi-

45. Cf. Žižek, *Less than Nothing*, 263.

46. I see nothing in what Žižek has said to counter the traditional insistence that any claim about such a material contradiction could not be claiming anything, would not be a claim. The argument seems to be: so much the worse for logic, there are such contradictions. But that does not answer the challenge. See Charles Taylor, "Dialektik heute, oder: Strukturen der Selbstnegation," 141–53.

ciently "old" (dysfunctional at least) before our eyes, for us to ask: What *is* the Hegelian account of the large-scale collapse of the state–civil society distinction so crucial to him, the disintegration of the *Stände*, or estates, central to his account of political participation, the emergence of mass consumer societies totally unlike anything in Hegel's political philosophy, the changes in the technology of warfare that make the notion of an occasional war to shake us out of our prosaic complacency suicidal (not to mention the end of citizen armies), the creation of a globalized financial system that renders obsolete even the notion of the "owners" of property, and on and on in such a vein?

Žižek's answer is not surprising, and that answer raises the largest question of all, the one I found the most dissatisfyingly addressed. Like many others, he wants to say that bourgeois society is fundamentally self-contradictory, and I take that to mean "unreformable." We need a wholly new ethical order, and that means "the Act." Its pretense to being a rational form is undermined by the existence of a merely contingent particular, a figurehead at the top, the monarch. (A better question, it seems to me, is why Hegel bothers, given how purely symbolic and even pointless such a dotter of i's and crosser of t's turns out to be.)[47] And, following many others, Žižek claims that the admitted *aporia* of "the rabble" (*das Pöbel*) in Hegel, what appears to be a permanent underclass of poor, is another mark of the fundamental irrationality of the Hegelian picture of modern ethical life (*Sittlichkeit*). He agrees with the analysis of a recent author, Frank Ruda, and says that Ruda "is fully justified in reading Hegel's short passages on the rabble in his *Philosophy of Right* as symptomatic of his entire philosophy of right, if not of his entire system."[48] In other context, Žižek claims that modern secular bourgeois culture and late capitalism produce their own opposite, evangelical fundamentalism, for example, for which there is no "*Aufhebung*," no return to an elevated form of bourgeois politics and reformed capitalism. (All this in the Lacanian manner in which what is repressed is created by the act of repression itself.)

Whether these relatively brief interludes demonstrate that bourgeois society and a capitalist system of production are fundamentally contradic-

47. The real problem with Hegel's political philosophy is the absence of any account of political will and the politics of will formation. The legislature just affirms "what's already been decided." See Michael Beresford Foster's invaluable and neglected book *The Political Philosophies of Plato and Hegel*.

48. Žižek, *Less than Nothing*, 431.

tory (even in the idealist sense sketched above), so that calls for reform would be as absurd as calls for remaining in the state of nature but "reforming it" would be in Hobbes, is too large a topic for this sort of discussion. I can only say that if the basic norm of such a society is, according to Hegel, some institutionally secured state of equal recognitive status, where this also means direct political attention to the material (familial, cultural, economic) conditions for such a possibility, or some egalitarian idea of freedom (no one can be free unless all are), I see no reason to think so, from the occasional remarks given here. The fact that there appears to be ever weakening political will in, for example, the United States for any attention to such a common good (even public schools are now slowly but surely emerging as a target for the ever more powerful far right) is very likely a pathology that needs explaining.[49] Perhaps we need the help of Lacanians to do this (although Hegel was content simply to point out the danger and irrationality of romantic nationalists in his own day), but that great dream of social democrats everywhere—"Sweden in the Sixties!"—does not seem to me something that inevitably produces its own irrational and irreconcilable Unreason, or Other. More lawyers for the poor in Texas, affordable day care, universal health care, several fewer aircraft carriers, more worker control over working conditions, regulated and perhaps nationalized banks—all are reasonable extensions of that bourgeois ideal itself, however sick and often even deranged modern bourgeois society has become. (*Citizens United* was not a logically inescapable result of capitalist logic. It was the result of the ravings of several lunatic judges. We are the only advanced capitalist democracy on earth that allows legalized bribery.) But these are topics for another context (and a soapbox). I will close with a reflection in the Žižekian spirit.

Žižek gives us two images, a literary and a cinematic image, to help us understand the dialectical gymnastics involved in his attempt to reactualize Hegel for contemporary purposes. The first concerns the problem of Hegelian "reconciliation," and the example is the mysterious and moving

49. When Žižek gives his list of "what Hegel cannot think" (qualified by a number of "yes, but . . ." suggestions), consisting of such things as repetition, the unconscious, class struggle, sexual difference, and so forth (*Less than Nothing*, 455), I see no reason to think that Hegel would object to such questions and issues, any more than he needs to provide analyses and diagnoses of various individual and social pathologies. They are not his questions. A plague can completely erode the moral life of some community, and it can stay eroded for centuries. So can ever more frenzied and hysterical consumption, what may be the death spiral of global capitalism (see David Harvey, *The Enigma of Capital*), and the beginning of a centuries-long ecological catastrophe.

ending of J. M. Coetzee's novel *Disgrace*. Žižek invokes the basic logical structure for rendering "negativity" intelligible that he uses throughout his book. David Lurie appears to have "negated" the status quo, the "big Other" of prudence, trust in the police, holding individuals responsible for their deeds, and seeking to redress wrongs done to individuals (justice), because he has come to see the inadequacy of such a faith for the current, postapartheid reality of South Africa. That is all "negated" by his simply doing whatever he can do to minimize the indignities done to euthanized dogs, satisfied with the gesture of providing for a respectful disposal. That, of course, is, pitiably, not very much in the way of reconciliation. He seems to have accepted his daughter's guilt-burdened acquiescence to her neighbor's complicity in her own rape, and internalized it in his own way, as the price one must pay to continue living with some "ethical dignity" (Žižek's phrase) in South Africa. In the world of unavoidable complicity in the South African crimes, the loss of *everything* is a "wager" that "this total loss will be converted into some kind of ethical dignity."[50]

But Žižek claims that there is "something missing" in this ending, some gesture of defiance and revolt that could be called the "negation of this negation," some "barely perceptible repetitive gesture of resistance . . . a pure figure of the undead drive," by which he means a *Versagung*, a refusal, of the initial or first negation that would not return us to the status quo ex ante, but that would originate the realization of "the fantasmatic status of the *objet a* (the fantasy frame which sustained the subject's desire), so that the *Versagung*, which equals the act of traversing the fantasy, opens up the space for the emergence of the pure drive beyond fantasy."[51] The natural thing one wants to say to this suggestion is that any such gesture that would satisfy what Žižek is after would presuppose that everything about David's original position *was* a "fantasy frame," that there is no "big Other," and by disabusing ourselves of this delusion we would be in a position to open up that space for the emergence of a "pure" drive beyond fantasy. *But just this latter sounds like David's original romantic fantasy itself*, that he is a Byronic servant of eros, can see through the hypocrisy and phoniness of "big Other" conventional morality, and so forth. That is the fantasy *he has disabused himself of*, and why his gesture of wholly symbolic generosity is at once so affirmative and dignified and so pathetic and so limited. There is no Žižekian

50. Žižek, *Less than Nothing*, 326.

51. Ibid.

gesture of defiance because David has seen through the dangerous self-deceit in presuming one is "he who is supposed to know." His assisting Bev in euthanizing the dogs and caring for their remains is done in a different way than that expected by Žižek, a "negation of his first negation," a refusal of mere acceptance of his and his daughter's fate. In the last gesture of the novel, he "gives up" the dog Bev had expected him to save, even as *he* has "given" *himself* up to his fate, not merely suffered it. Finally, said another way, there is nothing more un-Hegelian than the idea of the "emergence of the pure drive beyond fantasy." David's gesture means he remains the subject of whatever drives he has, not subject to them. The idea of "pure" drives (or "pure" anything) belongs in the Hegelian zoo mentioned before.

The second example is equally interesting. It is Hitchcock's *Vertigo*. Here the idea of a negation, and a negation of negation, is easier to track. Scottie loses Madeleine, or the woman he thought was Madeleine; she dies. But it was all a plot by Elster to murder his wife. Madeleine was not Madeleine but Judy, a working-class woman Elster had enlisted in the plot. When Scottie finds this out, he can be said to *have lost his very loss*, lost the meaning of his first loss. He had not lost Madeleine, because Madeleine was Judy. He discovers the bitterly ironic truth that the woman he was trying to "make up" to look like a fake Madeleine was (is) actually the real Madeleine, because his original Madeleine was a fake. So, as with *Disgrace*, we get an ambiguous ending: Scottie gazing "into the abyss," looking down where Judy has fallen, either a broken man, disabused of all the idealizations and fantasy that sustain love, or a "new" man, freed from his illusions and reconciled with this new realism. Žižek makes use of this structure to suggest a limitation in a Hegelian "negation of negation": that both the suggested readings of Scottie miss something, because they understand the "antagonisms" at issue still too "formally" (what I called before and defended as "dialectical idealism"). Here Žižek insists that we need to do justice to what falls "outside" of either resolution, an "excess," a "contingent remainder," a "little piece of reality."

As Žižek goes on to explain what he means by this, he seems to me to come close to reverting to the kind of positivistic, pseudorealist metaphysics he had rightly rejected. (See the quotation at the beginning of section III above.) And the talk of excess and remainders makes it irrelevant that Žižek does not mean something that "simply eludes dialectical mediation" but is a "product of this mediation."[52] Such an excess or remainder

52. Ibid., 480.

still functions in his criticism as "unmediated," and that notion remains profoundly un-Hegelian, for reasons I have tried to present throughout.

But there is something quite right about the relevance of the *Vertigo* structure to the German tradition as, I want to say, Hegel would see it. For in that tradition there is certainly the notion of *modernity itself* as "loss." Hölderlin and Schiller come to mind, and the mourning for the lost "beauty" of the Greek world can certainly mirror the sorrow of Scottie over the lost Madeleine-version of Judy. Then one can say that Hegel became Hegel when, for him, that loss was lost, that negation negated, with a more prosaic view of Greek accomplishments. I mean when, under the influence of the Scottish Enlightenment thinkers, he came to see that there was no simple loss in the end of the Greek ideal, and losing that notion of loss was a gain, as he appreciated the development of modern civil society and the error of fantasizing the loss of a more natural harmony.[53] The Helen-like "Madeleine" was really "Judy" all along. (This all in its own way confirms Žižek's insistence that Hegelian mediation does not issue in a "third," synthetic position, but in the right understanding of the antagonism between the "negation" and the "negation of the negation.") This can even be put in terms of Hegel's secularized Christianity—Madeleine *was really Judy*, or Judy had successfully, for Scottie, *become* Madeleine, all prompting her plaintive "Why can't you just love me for who I am?" Every "Judy" is also a "Madeleine," every "Madeleine" really a "Judy" in this egalitarian, Christian vision.

This is of course something Scottie cannot appreciate, and for reasons also relevant to Hegel. For the very structure of the appearance of Judy as Madeleine had been manipulated for gain by Elster, in a way parallel to the ideologically distorted and so false pretensions to achieved equality in contemporary bourgeois societies ("fair exchanges between labor and capital in the marketplace"). The truth of the identity was ruined, made an untruth, because it was *staged*. What Hegel thought was the greatest accomplishment of modern civil society—its ability to educate (as *Bildung*) its citizens to their equal status and profound dependence on each other, and so to educate them to the virtues of civility and trustworthiness—has become a lie (if it ever was the truth), and the shipping magnates and tycoons like Elster "steer" this *Bildung* in a way that ends up wholly theatrical, as in the

53. The indispensable account of this is Laurence Dickey, *Hegel: Religion, Economics, and the Politics of Spirit, 1770–1807*.

"theater of Madeleine" put on for Scottie's benefit and to manipulate him. He cannot be educated to the truth of the speculative sentence that "Judy is Madeleine," that essence is its own appearance, because of this distortion. Accordingly, Scottie's attempts to remake Judy into Madeleine, rather than being a way of realizing that Judy already is Madeleine, come off as manipulative and as reifying as Elster's. (Another, more depressing identity: Scottie and Elster, creators of a false Madeleine.)

This forces the question of whether there is much left in contemporary society that provides any sort of material basis for Hegel's aspirations about these potentially transformative and educative potentials of modern civil society. No one can be anything but profoundly pessimistic about this possibility, but the search for such possible "traces of reason"[54] seems to me a more genuinely Hegelian and still possible prospect than anything that could result from "abyssal Acts."

54. Rüdiger Bubner's phrase in "What Is Critical Theory?," in *Essays in Hermeneutics and Critical Theory*.

# 5

# Axel Honneth's Hegelianism

## I. Hegelian Origins

In the following I want to express enthusiastic solidarity with Axel Honneth's inheritance and transformation of several core Hegelian ideas, and to express one major disagreement. The disagreement is not so much with anything he says as it is with what he doesn't say. It concerns his rejection of Hegel's theoretical philosophy, and so his attempt to reconstruct Hegel's practical philosophy without reliance on that theoretical philosophy. This is of course not a novel claim in the "Critical Theory Tradition." Since Marx and in typical claims by figures like Adorno, any such Hegelian appeal to metaphysics is treated as a "mystification." What I am going to stress, though, is (i) that Hegel calls his theoretical philosophy a "Science of Logic," and he tells us that such a logic *is* his metaphysics (or that it "takes the place" of metaphysics), and (ii) that this characterization has not been successfully accounted for in that tradition (or by anyone else for that matter). The claim will not be that the absence of attention to this theoretical dimension in Honneth's project somehow invalidates the whole project. Hardly; there is much that is of great value even if the criticism I will make is sound. But the claim will be that key assumptions of it are incompletely defended.[1] With-

1. Hegel famously says in the Preface to *The Philosophy of Right* that that outline, or *Grundriss*, presupposes "the speculative mode of cognition." This is to be contrasted with what he calls "the old logic" and "the knowledge of the understanding" (*Verstandeserkenntnis*), a term he also

out that defense, Honneth's truncated Hegelianism appears, despite his occasional demurrals about this, to rely on claims in philosophical anthropology and developmental psychology that are difficult to reconcile with his historicism, and that are extremely difficult to defend against numerous competitor accounts. The underlying general issue is a very large one — the relationship between practical philosophy and metaphysics — but I will try to confine the discussion to Hegel's basic understanding of the relation and why I think Honneth cannot successfully ignore it.

Honneth subtitled one of his books *A Reactualization of the Hegelian Philosophy of Right*. This characterization is not only true of this book alone (*Suffering from Indeterminacy*) but could serve as a general characterization of much of his project. Hegel has been the most important historical figure for him for some time, especially because of Hegel's theory of recognition, but for many other reasons as well, and his latest book, *Das Recht der Freiheit*, is openly inspired by Hegel's approach to social and political philosophy. Those "many other reasons" include a commitment to Hegel's view of that supreme social and political value, the value to which all others are subordinate and derivative, the value that must guide any consideration of what constitutes just social and political institutions: freedom, understood as autonomy.[2] It includes as well a view of the importance of differentiated spheres of human action (the realization of freedom).[3] Market freedom, civic freedom, a "culture" of freedom,[4] moral freedom, all require that the ideal of freedom be understood as always "mediated" in and by such institutional contexts. (This already obviously raises a "logical" problem: what makes such a differentiated concept one concept with many such "mo-

---

uses to characterize all of metaphysics prior to his own. He makes explicit that he is referring to his book *The Science of Logic*. In fact, Hegel repeatedly says in many different contexts that the core of his *entire* philosophy, what everything else depends on, is to be found in that two-volume, three-part book that he wrote while teaching classical gymnasium students in Nuremberg between 1812 and 1816. The first volume is called an "Objective Logic," and it contains a "Logic of Being" and a "Logic of Essence." The third part, the second volume, is called the "Subjective Logic," and it consists of a "Logic of the Concept." This logical structure would also explain what would otherwise seem the accidental "affective" structure of human social needs — love, esteem, and respect — in Honneth's *The Struggle for Recognition: The Moral Grammar of Social Conflicts*.

2. Honneth, *Das Recht der Freiheit*, 122.

3. We need, Honneth says, to understand "sphere-specific freedom" (*sphärenspezifische Freiheit*) (ibid., 11).

4. Ibid., 104.

ments," as Hegel would say.)[5] Another view shared with Hegel: philosophy itself has a historical-diagnostic task. In fact, that basically *is* its task; to determine its "time, comprehended in thought." Another link between them: a theory of justice cannot be separated from concrete social analysis. That is, there is a philosophical reason that Hegel's *Philosophy of Right* is not a treatment of the institutions Hegel thinks constitutive of justice for anyone, anywhere, at any time. It is an analysis of the modern understanding and realization of contract, crime, moral conscience, the modern family, a market economy, and modern political institutions. It is neither an empirical social analysis nor pure normative assessment but some hybrid of both, what Honneth calls a "reconstruction" of the rational core in such historically specific institutions. We must do likewise if we want to philosophize in the spirit of Hegel.[6] (Again a clear problem: If such a rational core is not a timeless ideal, and it clearly is not in Hegel and Honneth, more or less approximated at various times, then what could guide such a reconstruction?) Above all, a final agreement: such freedom does not mean a solitary individual's capacity for self-determination, if that individual is conceived as a self-standing substance, possessing, just by being, a distinct power to initiate action.[7] Rather, the exercise of any such capacity is unintelligible except as the reflection of and dependence on certain prior social relations. In the same way, for example, that the capacity for language is a capacity for a particular kind of social interaction, the capacity for agency must likewise be viewed as, primordially even if not exclusively, a capacity for such a social engagement. This is also made clear by the strikingly unusual fact that Hegel's paradigmatic examples of freedom are not choice, resolve, uncaused causality, or acts of conscience but friendship and love.[8]

5. Many would say, for example, that whether one experiences one's status as recognized as worthy may be an important issue but has nothing to do with freedom.

6. See the account of "normative reconstruction" (Honneth, *Das Recht der Freiheit*, 106, 111). Everything depends on this claim to an inherent, concrete, historical form of rationality. Participation in social institutions, especially the nonoptional ones, like the state and the family, imposes obligations on persons, and these are consistent with such persons being free if and only if these claims are justified in a way that assumes no privilege or unequal status. If the institutions are to be justified by defending their role in human self-realization, that is simply another reason. Our assessment of this can be rational and historically inflected if we try to measure how close to or far from some ideal a historical society is, but that is not the approach Honneth or Hegel takes.

7. Ibid., 90.

8. The basic idea is that one can truly "be oneself" in such a relationship, act as one really is, be accepted and valued for who one truly is, even finally *become* who one really is, only in such

It is also embodied in the formulation that reflects Honneth's deepest agreement with Hegel, that freedom must be understood as "*bei-sich-selbst-Sein im Anderen*," "being-oneself-in-an-other." The idea that being free consists in being in a certain social relation, or unified set of social relations,[9] acting in the proper sense only qua such a participant, and not simply being in the possession of a distinctive power, has been the most controversial aspect of Hegel's theory. To many it seems to confuse several different senses of freedom, and to others it suggests a dangerous norm of "objective" (or "positive") freedom, the dismal reality of which has been all too familiar in the twentieth century.[10]

And all of this is not yet to mention that the structure of Honneth's analysis closely mirrors the structure of Hegel's. Understood in this action-specific differentiated way, freedom must at least be understood as negative freedom, or the freedom from external constraint, noninterference in one's pursuit of preferences, consistent with a like pursuit by others. Entitlement claims, claims of "abstract" or natural right, are most at home in this domain. But it would be hard to understand the value of such freedom if what one had come to prefer was the products of manipulation, coercion, ignorance, or oppression in general. Something about an undistorted reflective capacity to determine for oneself what to do must surely be a component of freedom; "reflective freedom," we can say. The "outer" freedom of negative freedom must be understood together with the securing of the possibility of the "inner" freedom of reflection. And yet, surely one cannot be said to be fully and "actually" free if the results of such self-determination are not also reflected as possibilities in the actual social institutions and practices of one's society. These institutions might not necessarily prevent the realization of one's intentions, but if one must constantly struggle against the "default" presumptions in one's society about what is worthwhile, worthy of cooperative struggle and sacrifice, if one thereby lives a marginal, merely

---

a relationship, and so forth. (Cf., inter alia, ibid., 270–71.) The variations and permutations are complicated, though, especially in their historical variations, as Honneth shows in useful detail at 232–317. Note especially his defense of the persistence of the ideals of friendship in a commercial, competitive age. His defense of the staying power of the ideals of the modern, liberal-bourgeois family is also pretty robust.

9. Ibid., 112.

10. This is a problem, of course, that begins with Rousseau and the "forced to be free" problem, but it has become more familiar with the proliferation in the twentieth century of "people's republics" or the claims for "real" democracy by tyrannical regimes.

tolerated existence, or simply if one must live without any or with very little solidarity with others about such matters, or only with other members of a marginalized group, then one lives a poorer and, Honneth and Hegel want to say, a less free life. One's freedom might not be constrained, and one's reflective determination might not be distorted, but without such solidarity one's freedom cannot be said to have been really realized.

This is a far more positive and substantive account than, for example, Joseph Raz's rights-based argument that no one interested in the possible exercise of freedom can be uninterested in the social conditions that favor its exercise and flourishing;[11] more than Kant's account of our indirect duty to make others' ends our own, and much more substantive and positive than strategic arguments for the rationality of cooperation based on self-interest.[12]

This structure obviously mirrors the structure of abstract right, morality, and ethical life (*Sittlichkeit*) in Hegel's *Philosophy of Right* (his account of "Objective Spirit") and it embodies a Hegelian sentiment of sorts, an avoidance of extremes for the sake of a "dialectical resolution." In this case it would be a kind of "Goldilocks" resolution: not too much emphasis on negative freedom alone, but not too little as well; not too much emphasis on reflective freedom or the call of conscience, but not too little as well. What getting everything "just right" would amount to is then "social freedom," mutually respected noninterference, compatible with reflective self-determination in a way that is genuinely integrative, shared in a social whole.[13]

11. Ibid., 91.

12. See Honneth on "*komplementäre Zielsetzungen*" (ibid., 92). I note the interesting fact that Honneth does not mention the worry of nineteenth-century thinkers like Humboldt, Tocqueville, Kierkegaard, Mill, Nietzsche, and Heidegger that the main problem of modern Western societies will not be atomism, fragmentation, and individualism but "excessive" socialization, a conformity-inducing willingness to set one's goals always in the light of their compatibility, even co-realizability (105), with others'.

13. Ibid., 83. There are important differences of emphasis with Hegel. In Honneth's discussion of the political domain of freedom, he is mostly concerned with the delimitation and understanding of the modern public sphere, the site of democratic will formation, and the changes wrought by modern communicative technologies and so forth. Honneth contrasts Hegel's rather static conception of the will of citizens with Durkheim's and Dewey's more dynamic conception of will formation. But Hegel's most important distinction is between the state and civil society, a distinction that serves for him as a necessary condition of political freedom. See *The Philosophy of Right*, §258 R. (This is the source of Marx's claim that the Hegelian state, just for this reason, must be unreal, a mere mystification.) It is also the source of great skepticism among many about any possible "updating" of Hegel on this issue. The claim is that the state has become

## II. The Hegelian Inheritance: Historicity and Sociality

With such an overview, we can say Honneth inherits from Hegel two foundational ideas that affect almost every other aspect of his project. The first is Hegel's insistence that a theory of a just society and a just political order must be a deeply historically inflected theory, and the second we might call the sociality of freedom thesis.[14] The former sets a clear task. If justice fundamentally means "each to his own" in some sense, where that means, in Hegel and Honneth, what is appropriate or fitting to each as a free, self-determining social being, then we need a "historical" sense to appreciate, first, why that understanding of mutually realized self-determination is the relevant characterization of "each" *now* (and this clearly will involve some controversial claim about normative progress), and second, to understand what *now*, under modern conditions, it might mean for institutions to embody an objective realization of such a status. Honneth clearly agrees with Hegel in rejecting the idea of social and political philosophy as a timeless quest to determine the best human political association once and for all. And, given that we must ask this historical question (what it might mean for institutions to embody an objective realization of such a mutually recognitive status), it is not plausible that in thinking about "the Hegelian option" in political philosophy, we simply have to accept the historical Hegel's ideas about gender and the division of labor within the family, or about "corporations" or about the monarch. Most of these will obviously have little if any resonance in late-modern, technology-dependent, mass consumer societies.[15] So obviously a number of the details of Hegel's account of social institutions will have to be updated and rethought.

However, in the pursuit of this goal, the most serious revision in Honneth's approach concerns issues that go to Hegel's justification of his approach. That is, it goes to the questions: Why should we believe Hegel's

---

little more than the regulator of civil society, and a weak one at that. And is it credible to believe that modern representatives represent anything other than the special interests who got them elected, or that "politics" is anything other than civil war by legal means?

14. I will use the word "historicity" to refer to this requirement, fully aware that as *Geschichtlichkeit* it is something of a term of art in Dilthey and Heidegger. I hope the context will make clear that I do not intend to wander into those thickets. I mean just that the institutional phenomena that Hegel and Honneth are interested in are *essentially* historical.

15. On the differences between the market economy Hegel was familiar with and the modern system of globalized finance capitalism, see Honneth, *Das Recht der Freiheit*, 320–470. The key point he wants to make in Hegel's defense is given on 345–46.

claims about how deeply bound we are to each other? And how can it be that a form of independence, autonomy even, should be understood as the realization of, not limited by, a form of dependence? As noted before, in Hegel's self-understanding, which Honneth rejects, these claims all have a "metaphysical" foundation, and this within Hegel's distinctive approach to such issues, an approach I do not believe has been received in the critical theory tradition. It could be summarized by pointing to Hegel's equating of "logic" with metaphysics, an identity I will discuss shortly.[16] More proximally and in another dimension (the "philosophy of spirit"), the distinctiveness is in view in his treatment of the problem of human being as the problem of *Geist,* or spirit, not, as in classical and early modern philosophy, as the problem of human nature. (Rousseau is the forerunner of all such attempts, with his argument that natural man is unsuitable as a model for social and political man.) Hegelian *Geist* has two implications central to his practical philosophy that one sees inherited by Honneth, but they are not defended in the way I want to claim Hegel wants to defend them. The first could be put by appeal to what Nietzsche would say many years later, that human being is the "still undetermined animal" (*noch nicht festgestellte Tier*).[17] A formulation more in keeping with the metaphysics of German Idealism would be that for *Geist, self-knowledge is self-constituting*. The most comprehensive and most striking formulation by Hegel of this point is from the Berlin version of the *Philosophy of Subjective Spirit.*

> It is of the very nature of spirit to be this absolute liveliness, this process, to proceed forth from naturality, immediacy, to sublate, to quit its naturality, and to come to itself, and to free itself, it being itself only as it comes to itself as such a product of itself; *its actuality being merely that it has made itself into what it is.* . . . It is only as a result of itself that it is spirit.[18]

In other words, wolves do not have to figure out what it is to be a wolf; they just are wolves. On the other hand, what we take ourselves to be is first of

16. Honneth too wants to base his case on what he calls a "social ontology" (*Reification: A New Look at an Old Idea,* 84), but, as I discuss later, his version resembles more the "philosophical anthropology" (Plessner, Gehlen, Scheler, early Heidegger) popular in the early twentieth century than it does Hegel's systematic concerns with the conditions for the intelligibility of being *simpliciter.*

17. *Beyond Good and Evil,* §62.

18. *Philosophy of Subjective Spirit,* trans. Petry, 1:16–17.

all something we must settle on, determine among alternatives, and it is thus an avowal or an expression of a commitment, a pledge about what we shall keep faith with, and not the result of any sort of self-observation. Such commitments can be collectively held as well, something that requires a common struggle to become fully who we take ourselves to be. And in any society there are always also contesting views on what it is to be a human being, and that means what it is to flourish, to live well, as just such a being. No fact of the matter will ever settle the issue. Moreover, basic forms of self-understanding, and so basic forms of human being, change over historical time. The aspiration in Hegel is that in a retrospective analysis of such contestations and attempts across historical time, we can detect a kind of "logic," even a kind of necessity. At least (and it is a massive qualification) within the Western tradition, the history of these attempts makes a certain kind of sense, and the sense it makes has everything to do with the supreme value of freedom. If *Geist* is a distinctive kind by being not a natural but a "self-developing" kind, we could be said to be "learning" collectively the form of life, the institutional form of life especially, suited to such a historical, collectively self-determining being. This means that our analysis of this result is not essentialist or empirical but "reconstructive," a reconstruction in which the meaning of large-scale social and political change is integrated into a view of what, wholly internally, wholly in terms of their own self-understanding, might count as progressive. (As I understand this, and as I understand Honneth's understanding of it, there can be no "guarantee" that such a progressive development will be found.)[19]

Now, to come to the main issue, Honneth wants to agree with something like this basic claim of Hegel's about the historical nature of *Geist* (and the second basic claim that I am about to discuss, the sociality of *Geist*) but, he says, without the "*Geist* metaphysics" (*Geistmetaphysik*) that the historical Hegel relied on to present and defend his system.[20] This would of course depend on what one takes Hegel's "*Geist* metaphysics" to involve. The term is not explained in *Das Recht der Freiheit*. But I want to note at the outset that there are some important issues in Hegel's metaphysics that *can-*

19. Honneth, *Das Recht der Freiheit*, 116 ff.

20. Ibid., 22–23, 107. Honneth has a way of delimiting the concrete norms he wants to assess: those necessary for the reproduction of the institution. Obviously the prior question is whether the practices of habituation and socialization by which specific norms are incorporated can be considered genuine "normative accomplishments" (*normative Leistungen*) as Honneth wants to.

*not* be ignored, revised, or updated if these Hegelian theses about historicity and sociality are to be satisfactorily defended. Like any other part of Hegel, his philosophy of art, say, his theory of objective *Geist* ultimately pulls one far deeper into his project than one might find philosophically prudent. (If Honneth is rejecting not only, say, an immaterialist monism, but also the passage just quoted, then his project is in no interesting sense "Hegelian." Not a tragedy, of course; the question is what one can take and what leave behind in Hegel and still have a defensible position.) In this case, if political and social philosophy *must* be essentially a historical enterprise, if the question of the justice of social and political institutions requires us to consider the participants in such institutions as they are in this historical period, as they are in modern families, in modern educational systems, under conditions of modern labor, as members of mass consumer societies, and so forth, then this is so because we deny that these features are accidental characteristics and that "underneath" such appearances we can find the eternal problems of the human heart, or a fixed and stable human nature. But the contrary assumption is philosophically quite complicated. That assumption is this: to consider a collective subject's self-knowledge or self-understanding as not at all the knowledge of an object, but as self-constituting (wherein there is not available any picture of a subject prior to such self-constitution, but only as constituted). This obviously sounds paradoxical, to say the least. The paradox is already obvious in the formulation itself: human beings cannot just *be* human beings, but must collectively make themselves into the beings they think they ought to be. If that is true, though, who is doing the constituting? If neither they nor we, as critical analysts, revert to an ideal conception of human nature (or, if we do, do so under an illusion that there is such a thing), what could possibly count as doing this well, better or worse, unacceptably or unacceptably? Can there be a "nonideal" social and political theory with some real normative bite?

This problem—how to understand the logic or intelligibility of an essentially "historical being"—precedes any view about Hegel on historical teleology, the end of history, or the Absolute. And Hegel adds a second central element that plays a different role in Honneth. Any such self-constituting being can only be so, according to Hegel, as subject to an order of reason, which order itself is also developmentally or historically understood. Any of the "determinations" of commitments by individuals or groups involve discursive practices of reasoning and justification that involve historically variable critieria. So the problems intensify very quickly, but we need these elements to pursue a normatively critical assessment of contemporary society, and one that is not based on an Aristotelian standard of human flourishing (as in MacIntyre's contemporary reanimation),[21] a Kantian-like norm of pure practical reason, a Rawlsian norm of distinterested contracting, or a Habermasian norm of the ideal communicative situation. I think it is fair to say that critics of Hegel and of Honneth continually return to this point above all others, insisting that Hegelians, critical theorists, and Honneth have confused the logic of education and discovery with the logic of justification, or *Faktizität* with *Geltung*. Why trim our sails in this way, the critics ask, taking on board as constraints the requirements of modern conceptions of romance, marriage, work, and so forth, when it could theoretically be the case that these institutions are already inherently corrupt, pathological, products of unfreedom? If they are not, why not? And if we can show this, why not just concentrate philosophically on the standard or norm we apply to make this differentiation? Isn't that our job as philosophers?

To answer such charges, we need not only an account of the superiority of some set of institutions to what they replaced, and the internal and historically developing notion of rationality that can support such a claim for superiority, but we need a fundamental account of *what sort of a being could be self-transforming in time* in this way. Hegel regularly says that the dominant, authoritative form of account-giving in the modern period, the logic of "the understanding," or *Verstand*, is inadequate to this task, and he would reject as ungrounded and incomplete any account of "Objective Spirit," especially its *necessary* historicity, that was not informed by the right way to *think* about these issues and especially the paradox noted above. This is the issue I will raise in section III below.

I noted before that the deepest level of agreement between Honneth and Hegel concerns not just the historicity but the sociality of the realization of freedom, understood as *bei-sich-selbst-Sein im Anderen*. The best-known feature of this agreement concerns Hegel's theory of recognition in his early works and in the Jena *Phenomenology*. Very superficially, the claim at issue is that an agent can be said to be free only if recognized by others as free, something itself possible only if the agent recognizes as free those who recognize him. Freedom consists in mutual or reciprocal recognition. Why this should be so (must I not first *be* free to be rightly acknowledged as free

21. MacIntyre, *After Virtue*. See also my "MacIntyre's Modernity: On the Third Alternative."

by another?) and what it entails, especially what social and political institutions embody this reciprocity, or better, what contemporary possibilities in our current institutions could be sites of such potential reciprocity, are two of the major questions raised by Honneth throughout his oeuvre.

But again this claim (the *bei-sich-selbst-Sein im Anderen* claim) is not, cannot be, if it is to be consistent with the historicity claim, a claim about a natural, permanent form of human dependence. That would eventually sound like a vague psychological claim about a contingent human need for approval, the dependence of self-esteem on acknowledgment by others, or a general empirical, species-specific fact. The same would be true about a theory that relied on a claim about our basic affective needs. However, this does not mean that the dependence at issue is a contingent feature of human freedom, as a matter of historical fact typical of late-modern Western societies. Instead, I want to say, it reflects Hegel's view about the basic intelligibility of, or again, "the logic of," possible human agency itself, and the implications of that account for human historicity. In the same way that the historicity of social and political philosophy reflects the logical structure of a free, or self-constituting, *Geist*, the "dependence" claim here under discussion reflects a view on the relation between intention, bodily movement, and a social responsiveness necessary for what counts as my reason for acting *actually* so counting, for me as well as for others. This dimension of acting—acting is acting on reasons; the sphere of action is the sphere of giving and demanding reasons among beings whose actions affect what others would otherwise be able to do—is crucial to it being an action, that the bodily movement be "intentional under some description," where "intentional" is, broadly, the content of the answer to the "why" question that Anscombe argued was constitutive of an action as such.[22] The heart of the Hegelian case for some mutuality of recognition is his objection to any purely privately constituted intention, or any private "ownership" of the meaning of an action. The *logic* of intentions, and reasons one gives oneself and others for so intending, cannot work that way, and the sociality of the language necessary to express such intentions does not suffice to account for the necessity of sociality itself. This is admittedly still obscure, and much more needs to be said, but it is important to note that, as with the historicity issue, the issue emerging again concerns the status of some claim about the rationality necessary for actions to count as actions, that is, as realizations

22. G. E. M. Anscombe, *Intention*.

of freedom. I want now only to stress that this does not have anything to do with any metaphysical position that denies contingency, the reality of individual subjects, or the reality of the finite world, or is committed to any immaterialist metaphysical monism. I will try to say more about this, but the idea is: if we keep this dependence on these "logical" matters in view, we get, I want to argue, a different sense of the *sort* of sociohistorical analysis an account of "Objective Spirit" requires. And this is what constitutes "*Geist* metaphysics" proper.

## III. Hegelian Logic as Metaphysics

Now we need some sort of orientation, however crude, within the core of Hegel's theoretical philosophy, his *Science of Logic*. But we should first note, as a matter of context, that there is nothing particularly unusual about such a claim about the dependence of any account of "*rechtlich*," or just, institutions on a "logic." It is in effect the general claim that any account of anything will depend on an overall account of account-giving. Hegel just has unusual ambitions about what a philosophical logic can accomplish. Someone, for example, who believes that, with respect to the relevant kind of account, the only possible practical justification of institutions must be a demonstration of the maximum mutual satisfaction of individual preferences (and who believes this because of views she has about what kind of beings we are), will have thereby already greatly limited the kinds of social and political institutions that can be justified. Someone who believes that the only possible justification must rely on the pure form of practical reason as such will likewise set a frame into which only a few possibilities fit. Someone who believes that practical reason cannot be formalized in any way, that it is necessarily judgmental and experience based, will face the same restrictions. Each of these alternatives also clearly reflects theoretical commitments of some complexity. (Hegel's unusual claim is that such different forms of practical logic are not only compatible with each other but somehow depend on each other for their individual intelligibility, and his account of institutions is a reflection of that commitment.)

Any brief summary of those theoretical ambitions will be quite crude, but I need to distinguish a reading of the centrality of the *Logic* from what I suspect Honneth means by Hegel's *Geist* metaphysics (a substance *Geist*-monism) to make the claim of indispensability I want to defend. Hegel tells us that philosophy concerns "the Absolute," and that the Absolute is "the

Idea." This is often taken to mean that Hegel denies the reality of the sensible world in favor of an immaterial monad, realizing itself in time. The concepts that the *Logic* studies are said to be "moments" in the "realization" of such an Idea's self-realization. I suspect Honneth has something like this in mind. The sketch that follows is an alternative reading.

This can only be a very high-altitude view and will neglect two very important dimensions of Hegel's position. First, Hegel's social and political theory is called by him a "philosophy of Objective Spirit," and to understand that, we would need to understand the systematic structure of Hegel's *Encyclopedia* system, or the relation between *Logic*, the *Philosophy of Nature*, and the *Philosophy of Spirit*. I hope what I will say at least indicates how that relation might be understood. Second, Hegel claims that the concepts treated in the *Logic* delineate what Kant would call a priori "real possibility" and so not merely logical possibility. The forms of thought at this level of fundamentality *are* the forms of being. It would take at least a book to begin to defend this claim, especially in the light of the Kantian suspicion that this is not a possible claim, at least not without a complex "transcendental deduction" to establish it, and even at that with a limited result, only for "phenomena," not "things in themselves."

But even at this altitude there are three difficult elements in particular that are important for his *Rechtsphilosophie*: Hegel's equation of logic with metaphysics; the relation between logic and "actuality";[23] and the self-conscious character of judging and acting.

The ambition of the treatise as a "logic" appears to concern the very possibility of discursive intelligibility, the primary bearer of which in traditional logic is the predicative act. What is in question at such a level of attempted comprehensiveness is, or at least appears to be, something like, at the most general level possible, *an account of all possible ways of making sense*, a scope that would include everything from the form of ethical justifications to the form of empirical judgments to the form of explanation presupposed by the Second Law of Thermodynamics.[24] ("At the *most* general level possible"

23. Honneth is certainly aware of the importance of "*Wirklichkeit*" as a technical term for Hegel (the "*Wirklichkeit der Freiheit*," for example; *Das Recht der Freiheit*, 470), but it does not have the same meaning as that discussed here.

24. The basic claim is that Hegel's *Encyclopedia* is best understood as a theory of *explanatory adequacy*, an enterprise that must presuppose a general account of any possible account-giving. See also chapter 2 of my *Hegel's Practical Philosophy: Rational Agency as Ethical Life*, 36–64. A preliminary account of what the *Logic* as about possible intelligibility, explanatory adequacy,

is an important qualification. Obviously not every attempt to make sense is metaphysics. But at the highest level of generality its questions concern problems that are everywhere presupposed in empirical accounts but that threaten sense: How can two individuals be distinct and yet share a common form? How can a thing change most of its properties and remain the same thing? What distinguishes a mere collection or heap from a unity of parts?) In doing so, we have made sense not of some species-specific feature of human sense-makers, but of the sense the world could make. This is the way Hegel describes his theoretical project elsewhere.

> Metaphysics is nothing but the range of universal thought-determinations, and as it were, the diamond net [*das diamantene Netz*] into which we bring everything to make it intelligible [*verständlich*].[25]

Understood in this way, it is clear that metaphysics, while it has adequacy or satisfaction conditions, does not have the kind of truth conditions that a matter-of-fact assertion has. Determining *when sense has truly been made* is not of the same order of tasks as determining "what caused the fire to start" or "why water freezes."[26] For example, making sense of why there is a practice like art-making, what it means that there is, what sense there could be in it, involves a question that immediately becomes impoverished if we think the question can only mean "What caused human beings to take a distinct pleasure in certain artifacts?" The question rather invites a speculation on something like a "satisfying" account, rather than a factually true one, and clearly one desideratum of any such account has to be that the sense made cohere with other senses made.[27]

It is extremely important that Hegel never says that it is the content of

---

might look like was presented in my *Hegel's Idealism*, 40, on an "account of all account-giving." See also Pinkard, *Hegel's Dialectic: The Explanation of Possibility*.

25. *Philosophy of Nature*, trans. Miller, §246, Addition.

26. Stated in this general form, this reframes a traditional notion of metaphysics. For example: How can we make sense of a thing's remaining what it is throughout great alterations of its properties? Or: How can we make sense of Socrates and Plato both being human beings (what do they share?) and being different individuals? It is important to Hegel that many of the formulations of the classical metaphysical questions are in the form of contradictions or the threat of contradiction; something, that is, that threatens sense.

27. And senses are made, intelligibility is rendered, in Hegel's account. As the quotation just cited notes, candidates for such elucidation are "brought into" such a net of intelligibility-making.

metaphysics, some doctrine of substance, that requires an unusual or new logic for its expression, but that logic *itself*, a theory of thinking properly understood, *is* metaphysics. And it is absurd to attribute to him the position that this is so because reality is actually composed of thoughts, or divinely mental entities.[28]

He also says several times that the *Logic* does not concern thought about any empirical object but concerns what he calls the "actuality" of objects, not their existence or any matter of fact about them. This puts us in sight of our topic in Honneth. For what we want to know is how Hegel understands "the actuality" of the state, of freedom; the actuality of human sociality, or, said colloquially, what the bond of human sociality "actually" is.[29] There is no reason to pay attention to the differences between late-modern families and what Hegel was familiar with unless we have some sort of answer to this question.

If we stand back from Hegel for a moment, we can get some sense of what he means. This kind of issue—actuality, the logos—arises when we ask, for example, if some practice is "actually" religious; smoking peyote, say, or Scientology. We don't doubt that the practice exists and that many facts can be gathered about it; we want to know its "essentiality," *Wert, Sache an sich selbst*, logos, and so forth. Or: we don't doubt that animals exist and have various capacities, many very like ours. We want to know if they are *actually* rights-bearers. We know computers can play chess and win, perhaps one day could even pass Turing tests, but we want to know not whether these *facts* are true but whether the computer is actually *thinking*. A gallery opens, and some objects, clothes strewn around a floor, are displayed. Is it actually art?

These are examples, of course, and are not part of Hegel's *Logic*. (They are examples of Hegel's "*Realphilosophie*" that depend on the meaning of "actuality" as delineated in the *Logic*.) But they help explain Hegel's otherwise bewildering claim that the Concept (in this sense) *gives itself* its own actuality. The claim means: the sort of questions posed above are in no sense empiri-

28. The clearest passage is: "Thus *logic* coincides with *metaphysics*, with the science of *things* grasped in *thoughts*, which used to be taken to express the *essentialities of the things*" (Hegel, *The Encyclopaedia Logic*, trans. Geraets, Suchting, and Harris, §24).

29. A typical formulation: "When thinking is taken as active with regard to objects as the thinking over [*Nachdenken*] of something—then the universal, as the product of this activity—contains the value of the matter [*Wert der Sache*], what is essential [*das Wesentliche*], inner, true" (ibid., §21).

cal questions, answerable by some fact of the matter. If that is so, there is no reason we cannot speak Hegelese and say that thought determines for itself what is actual, gives itself its own actuality. The Concept gives itself its own actuality. The answers to any type of question like those posed above are not empirical (questions also like: What actually *is* thinking, sense-making; any such answer must be "thought's self-determination"). What is exciting about Hegel's project among contemporary alternatives is that, despite what these formulations might suggest, such actualities can be historical actualities; they need not be fixed essences. Indeed what interests him (in the way in which organic beings and artifacts interested Aristotle) is phenomena like art, religion, and politics, which do have histories but whose histories, he thinks, make a kind of logical sense. That sense is their actuality. Neither art nor philosophy nor religion nor political life nor market economies are natural manifestations of the human kind, like eating or mortality. Art is what artists have done and do; philosophy is what philosophers have done and do, and so on. But they cannot be done at all without an implicit reason for doing them in such a way or doing them at all, reasons we can give ourselves and offer to others. And those reasons and the story of their transformations make the sense we can make out of these human practices.

And this involves the most complicated and controversial claim of all. With the issues posed in this way, it means that the self-constitution of *Geist* and its practices over time will depend on an account of the self-constitution of reason, the logic of which, involving strong claims of necessity and unavoidability, is to be provided by the *Science of Logic*. No Hegelian account of the historically achieved rationality of the structure of modern social and political institutions can dispense with such an argument.

In this sense, the topic of the *Philosophy of Right* is the *actuality of freedom*. This is *exclusively* a philosophical question, and we appear to be over our hundred-year temptation to think the question must be about how we use the word, or the necessary and sufficient conditions of the meaning of the word. And the philosophical dimension is necessary, ineliminable, if we are to have a critical perspective on what in modern abstract right, morality, the family, or commercial life contributes to the actualization of freedom and what not. Without this dimension we are trying to construct ad hoc arguments for the claims Hegel makes about such institutions. This is possible, and some have done it very well, but it all runs out very quickly, well before a satisfying account.

This brief suggestion about the role of the *Logic* does not, of course, get us very far, but I hope it indicates a direction that is true to Hegel's intentions and faithful to his unusual claim that his *Logic is* a metaphysics, and differentiates him from the tradition of modern dogmatic metaphysics (special types of objects knowable by pure reason alone), the suspicion I think is behind Honneth's and many others' dismissal of Hegel's theoretical philosophy.

## IV. Hegelian Rationalism and the Hyper-rationalism Objection

The claim is that this is all carried forward into the *Philosophy of Objective Spirit*, and so the claim is that the basic bond of sociality should be understood in terms of the debt we owe others for reasons when our actions affect what they would otherwise have been able to do, and our claim on others for such reasons. The fundamental social bond for Hegel, the one most at issue in issues of justice, is the rational bond.

This can seem unduly "intellectualist" or "rationalist" or cognitivist.[30] One of Honneth's thoughts is that the injustice of societies can consist in a situation in which the needs for "love, esteem, and respect" necessary for the formation of ethically competent subjects are not satisfied. Another is that this sort of rational ability to take up the point of view of the other is based on a deeper and more original *affective* (not rational, or prerational) capacity, systematically distorted in modern reifying societies, and so again is an example of a systematically unjust injury to the human psyche. Another is that mutual recognitive status requires the successful satisfaction of those affective dimensions of our social bond just mentioned, in the appropriate "sphere-specific" domains of freedom: love in the family, esteem in work and trade, respect in one's public and political roles. Another is that successful, institution-bound mutual justifiability is insufficient to fulfill the sort of social freedom necessary for a full or adequate realization of freedom. For that we need a deeper sense of positive cooperation. My pursuit of my goals does not just not interfere with yours but contributes to your pursuit of yours and vice versa. Solidarity, and the sense of meaning and purpose that it provides, must be possible.

Now one might respond here that these issues might be general desiderata of a flourishing society, but that none is properly understood as a matter

30. Cf. Honneth's distinction between "regulative" and "constitutive" "*Handlungsystemen*," and his remarks on Parsons's concept of "relational institutions" (*Das Recht der Freiheit*, 224).

of justice. For one thing, it is not clear what sort of political redress for any of these sorts of wrongs would be possible (on the assumption that they are not "merely" moral wrongs). We cannot—at least beyond issues of abuse and mistreatment—police the level or sort of love in families, cannot create meaningful work by political action, and can only ensure the respect that comes from real equality before the law and equal protection from illegality.

But Honneth is clear in *Das Recht der Freiheit* (or much clearer than he has been)[31] that he does not consider any of these wrongs violations of "rights," and so as redressable by appeal to the state's monopoly on coercion and violence.[32] But they are also not just *any* sort of harms. It is the thesis of his book that they count as failures in the actualization of freedom and *therefore* as serious wrongs of public concern, thereby injustices, not like wrongs such as infidelity in a marriage, or craven, dishonorable self-interest in business dealings, or hypocrisy. Moreover, he is right, in my view, to note in his treatment of *Reification* in his Tanner Lectures, that it is wrong to limit all cases of justice and injustice to questions about *legitimacy*, specifically the legitimacy of the coercive use of state power. We would thereby deprive ourselves of any critique of several "social pathologies" of grave public concern.

The issue raised by this comparison with the historical Hegel is the relation between Honneth's concerns and what might appear the "thinner" dimensions of practical rationality that support Hegel's theory of right and sociality, and ultimately a much larger issue, the role of his logic in any ultimate account of the adequacy of particular practices of justification. There are several things to say in conclusion, at least in brief summary. (We meet here the importance of the third dimension of Hegel's account of logic: the self-conscious character of judgment and action.)

As already indicated, understanding the basic human social bond as a rational one does not mean, at least in Hegel, an explicit invocation of principles or any quasi-theoretical debate about justifiability, any more than

31. See Pippin, "Recognition and Reconciliation in Hegel's Phenomenology," 57–78.

32. Honneth, *Das Recht der Freiheit*, 125–26. See also his remarks, with which I agree, on damage done to clear thinking in political philosophy by the assumption that all its relevant topics are ultimately about juridically enforceable rights. Honneth aligns himself with Hegel, Durkheim, Andreas Wildt, MacIntyre, and Avishai Margalit as explorers in the territory of "*nichtrechtlichen Bedingungen sozialer Gerechtigkeit*" (126). See also the formulation on 221. This does of course raise the question of what sort of political engagement follows from Honneth's position, if it is not the politics of rights enforcement.

the wisdom of the *phronimos* in Aristotle implies that he can formulate a theory about why this or that is of ethical salience or not. We need to recall that Hegel, like Kant, thinks of any judgment or any action as inherently self-conscious, reflexive. (Herewith the third of the elements I mentioned above as necessary in appreciating Hegel's ambition.) The self does not observe itself in action; acting is the consciousness of acting. The point of the assertion of a necessary link between the reflexive nature of judgment and action and the reasons for so judging and acting is to deny that there are two moments involved: the acting, say, and the consciousness of the action as a deed requiring justification. Acting *is* the consciousness of acting, and that means acting is, just qua acting, consciousness of its grounds, and this in the way such grounds are embedded in a social practice of mutual justification.[33] It is just as "logically" impossible in Hegel's broad sense to respond to "Why did you do that?" with "No reason; I just did it" as it is to respond to "Why did that fire start?" with "No reason; it just started." (Or to respond to "Why do you believe the fire was intentionally set?" with "No reason; I just believe it.") Likewise, in initiating and then sustaining an action I obviously know what I am doing and have some sense of why and so can be said to be going about my task "knowingly" without that having to mean that, as the deed unfolds, I keep checking to see if my intention is being fulfilled or if the action still fits the act-description under which I became committed to the intention or if I still regarded it as justified. I can clearly be said to be attentive to all this without being attentive *to* the intention and act-description and evaluation "*as such*" (just as I can be said to have reasons for what I am doing without ever having reasoned). This is all obviously of great importance in appreciating what it means to consider beliefs and actions as subject to the clams of reason.

None of this means that relations of love, esteem, or respect are only possible if justified by an argument, or that in trying to figure out if I love someone, I must assess my reasons for finding the person lovable (on the assumption that if I did, the emotional attachment would be inevitable). That would all be bizarrely self-dissociated. But it *is* to say that loving someone is in fact finding that someone lovable, and that that must be an evaluation of the sort appropriate to relations of love, and, most importantly, it is one that can fail. A betrayal can mean that one's loving trust was unreasonable. Like-

33. These formulations are indebted to Rödl, *Self-Consciousness*. For a fuller discussion, see my "The Significance of Self-Consciousness in Idealist Theories of Logic."

wise esteem and respect cannot be given merely because it would be a good thing in society if there were more esteem and respect. Esteem and respect are appropriate where the object of the attitude is esteemable and respectable, and this for determinate reasons that must be at work in the attitudes. They can be inappropriately or indiscriminately bestowed, or bestowed in a way that degrades them (as when a parent praises extravagantly everything a child does "in order to foster self-esteem"), and these evaluative attitudes imply conditions under which they could not be maintained. None of this needs to be explicit to be real, any more than the fact that my being committed to a proposition also commits me to the denial of every proposition inconsistent with that proposition means I must have all those propositions in mind and deny them for such a commitment to be real. If I weren't so committed, I would not be committed to the original one. That would be a delusion, or a very common mark of self-deceit.

Now, as mentioned, Honneth frequently argues that affective recognitive relations are logically and phenomenologically prior to cognitive or rational assessments, and in that sense that "recognition" precedes "cognition." The claim is that the heart of mutually rational sociality, "taking up the point of view of another," is unintelligible unless we are first able to explain how any would come to care to do so. But it is also true that we wouldn't know *what* we cared about unless the notion of taking up the viewpoint of the other already had some content and some claim on us, and unless it was true that we can find that such care is misplaced (if the other, for example, has no concern with taking up my viewpoint). This suggests that this sort of separation of issues (affective versus cognitive) can be quite misleading. In fact, it is typical of the "philosophy of the understanding" Hegel is working to reject.

Said another way, rendering ourselves intelligible to each other in these normatively charged ways is also rendering ourselves answerable to each other.[34] Virtually anything we do renders us answerable in this way and is inseparable from our self-understanding in intending. This is the social

34. There is no way in this limited context to indicate fully how misleading it would be to think of this issue in strictly "cognitivist" terms. Rendering myself intelligible is (at the same time) rendering myself answerable, and it is also rendering myself vulnerable, raising the issue of trust, being attentive to the issues of dominance and power, and implicating myself in the problems of mutual interpretability. Self- and other-knowledge raises the issue of what Cavell calls "attitudes" to the other, and he does not mean propositional attitudes. See Cavell, "Knowing and Acknowledging," 238–66, and "The Avoidance of Love: A Reading of *King Lear*," 267–356. For

bond, and we will not have a philosophically satisfying account if we are not able to *assess* such attempts at answerability.[35] Admittedly, it is a long, long way from these abstract formulations to the even more abstract claim that in order to distinguish between what are, in some community at some historical time, *taken to be* the normative standards inherent in such evaluative attitudes and, on the other hand, what *actually* (in Hegel's sense of *Wirklichkeit*) *doing* better or worse in holding each other to account would amount to, we need a "logic" of intelligibility and therewith in the practical domain a logic of answerability, something Hegel thinks is itself only developmentally accessible.[36]

My claim has been that the two most important Hegelian inheritances in Honneth's project—the radical historicality and the unavoidable sociality of *Geist*—are linked to a theory of rationality that itself requires that we understand something like the "self-constitution" of rationality over time. That in turn must be understood within Hegel's general account of any possible intelligibility, his *Logic*. This is all obviously preliminary. The promise is that doing so will eventually allow us to understand the otherwise conceptually paradoxical claims about a self-constituting being and a being for whom a certain sort of dependence on others is to be understood as the realization of its independence or autonomy. In particular, the former problem concerns what Hegel, in the *Logic of Essence*, calls the problem of reflection and will ultimately involve a so-called "absolute reflection." And the latter would require a number of elements of Hegel's Logic of the Concept.

Finally, it is important to hold this whole picture in mind not only to get the distinctively Hegelian element in view, but also because without this "frame" Honneth often seems to be depending on a variety of claims

---

the dialectical entanglement of knowing and being known, see my "Passive and Active Skepticism in Nicholas Ray's *In a Lonely Place*."

35. To make these general points about what Honneth inherits from Hegel and what he declines, I am passing over an issue of great importance to both Honneth and Hegel. It is the claim that self-relation and relation-to-others are *inseparable*; self-understanding implicates me in understanding myself from the point of view of the other, to use a Meadean formulation. But this does not mean simply imagining or picturing to myself how the other sees me. It involves both issues of enormous interpretative complexity (the content of what the other thinks of me may not be accessible to the other) and a rational responsiveness to the other's presumed point of view. Her reasons for her view make up the content of that view, are not separable. And vice versa. So a further investigation of this first-and-second-person intertwining will lead us back to our theme.

36. One heroic attempt in this direction: Theunissen, *Sein und Schein: Die kritische Funktion der Hegelschen Logik*.

in so-called philosophical anthropology or developmental psychology, or on a reversion to claims about human nature, reformulated as claims about "social ontology." These seem to include claims about what we supposedly now "know," thanks to Winnicott or various sociological studies, about what people as such "need" or require. This tendency is greatly intensified by, in effect, "medicalizing" various forms of contemporary irrationality as "pathologies." This is not a Hegelian term and would seem to presuppose a notion of health tied to an ahistorical standard. Hegel of course does not deny that human beings have bodies, species-forms with distinctive characteristics, and his own "anthropology" is an important systematic element in his account of the relation between nature and spirit, but it is a transitional account, on the way toward a properly historical account of *Geist*. We need to have Hegel's systematic ambitions in view—all of them structured around the *Logic*—in order to appreciate the limited ambitions of Hegel's account of anthropology, and by contrast the centrality of the concept of the rational "self-constitution" behind his claims in social and political philosophy.

# 6

# Alexander Nehamas's Nietzsche

When Alexander Nehamas's pathbreaking, elegantly conceived and executed book *Nietzsche: Life as Literature* first appeared in 1985, the reception of Nietzsche in the Anglo-American philosophical community was still in its initial, hesitant stages, even after the relative success of Walter Kaufmann's much earlier, 1950 book, *Nietzsche: Philosopher, Psychologist, Antichrist,* and its postwar "decontamination" of Nietzsche after his appropriation by the Nazis.[1] Arthur Danto's 1964 book, *Nietzsche as Philosopher,* was also an important if somewhat isolated event, and there finally began to appear in the seventies less well-known but high-quality secondary literature, like John Wilcox's 1974 book, *Truth and Value in Nietzsche,* and Tracy Strong's 1975 book on Nietzsche and politics, *Friedrich Nietzsche and the Politics of Transfiguration.* And when the Routledge "Arguments of the Philosophers" series brought out Richard Schacht's lengthy 1983 book *Nietzsche,* the idea that Nietzsche, whatever else he was doing in his books, was making philosophical claims and devising ways to defend them was becoming more firmly established. Many of the most successful aspects of Nehamas's interpretation (essentially part 1 of the book) spoke to what was still the early resistance to any philosophical attention to Nietzsche: the facile insistence that his "persepectivism" was a self-refuting relativism, that his attack on truth and the value of truth was equally and hopelessly self-refuting, and that whatever few positive ethical claims there were in Nietzsche celebrated

1. The book was such a sanitizing that it now seems bowdlerizing, Nietzsche de-fanged.

cruelty, elitism, and the exercise of power for its own sake. Nehamas's deft handling of all these putative criticisms was and remains a major legacy of the book, and since I agree with so much of what he says,[2] I will not be discussing them here.

There was, though, another timely aspect of the book as well. By the mideighties, it was widely known that Nietzsche had become an unavoidable figure in Europe—in France, Germany, and Italy especially. Heidegger's lecture courses on Nietzsche in the thirties and forties had been published in the early sixties, and an English translation had appeared in the late seventies. Books by Sarah Kofman, Gilles Deleuze, Jacques Derrida, Jean Granier, Pierre Klossowski, and Karl Löwith had also claimed Nietzsche as a philosopher, but in a much different way than in Anglophone work. The latter tended to be organized in the traditional subdisciplines of professional philosophy and so treated Nietzsche's epistemology, metaphysics, aesthetics, value theory, moral psychology, etc. The European approaches tended to treat very sweeping issues in what might loosely be called accounts of possible meaning in language and thought (or even "the meaning of being") and the possibility of meaningfulness in action, and they portrayed Nietzsche as having much more radical positions, not subsumable in the traditional categories of the profession. Nehamas's book was pathbreaking in many ways but especially because he took such approaches seriously and engaged with many of them directly, mostly disagreeing, but in a genuinely philosophical way, not in the cheaply polemical way still characteristic of reactions to such work.

Moreover, his own approach, with its emphasis on text, textuality, interpretation, and style, was clearly influenced by the European discussion and made available to an Anglophone audience Nehamas's own lapidary and strikingly original variations on the "textuality" theme. Indeed, his book's subtitle seems quite radically "European" in this sense: "Life as Literature," not "Life as like Literature," or "Life as if Literature," or "Literary Models for Life." We shall have occasion to discuss the meaning of the subtitle shortly.

And this was all connected with something until then completely novel in English-language writing on Nietzsche: a very serious attention to the style and form of Nietzsche's books—the hyperbolic, aphoristic, monological character of his published works, ranging from scholarly treatise to

2. With the exception of (what I would regard as) the extreme essentialism about selfhood that Nehamas insists is a major aspect of the Eternal Return doctrine.

polemical pamphlet. Nietzsche's writings, according to Nehamas, were not essays buried inside, and neatly extractable from, rhetorical excesses; they were not, at least not primarily, designed to convince readers by argument and evidence, or at least not by these alone. Instead the work was meant to be *exemplary*; the results of Nietzsche's attempt to make of himself "an unforgettable literary character," a model of a kind of life "made" as a text, a model that might inspire like, but never identical, attempts.[3] But the familiar literary principle of the inseparability of form and content does not just mean that "the Nietzsche character" who was alive "textually" required, in order to do justice to its various dimensions, a variety of literary styles; this inseparability was also crucial in understanding how, for Nehamas, interpretive activity itself should be understood, especially in relation to "what" is interpreted. (That is, there is no such thing as pure, uninterpreted text;[4] an act of interpretation is always displacing another, leading to Nehamas's hermeneutical treatment of "the will to power," understood as a war of contending interpretations.)[5]

And all of this was to be understood in the same way that the Platonic Socrates had become "unforgettable" (although now, in Nietzsche's case, "without the dogmatism"). (Cf. "Both Nietzsche and Socrates are intensely personal thinkers, actively engaged in changing, in one way or another, the moral quality of the life of the people around them."[6]) I think it is fair to say that most writing on Nietzsche in the last twenty-five years has yet to take full account of the difficulties posed for philosophical commentary by the strangeness of Nietzsche's style, and very little of it has reached the level of thoughtfulness on view in *Nietzsche: Life as Literature*.[7]

3. I think this is quite right, but I would suggest that Nietzsche's model here is not so much the drama or the novel as the context for such a character, but Montaigne's opening remarks to the reader in his *Essays*. See my *Nietzsche, Psychology, and First Philosophy*.

4. See Nehamas, *Nietzsche*, 39, for a clear and compelling statement of how this inseparability claim about form and content applies to Nietzsche's own "style" and "content."

5. Cf. ibid., 97: "Many of Nietzsche's readers may find that the reinterpretation of existing structures constitutes a very weak reading of the task of the will to power. But in Nietzsche's own view, reinterpretation is the most powerful theoretical and practical instrument." See 32 on how this applies to Nietzsche's will to power, and so his attempt to make his view of the world and his values "the very world and values in which and by which others live."

6. Ibid., 25.

7. Chapter 1 of Nehamas's book is a compelling defense of the philosophical value of this attention to style. But why then make such heavy use of the unpublished notes, the *Nachlaß*? The context for these remarks, their potential place in a publication, is impossible to determine. For the most part, what Nehamas finds in the *Nachlaß* of relevance to his point is also to

This is not to say that Nehamas did not examine carefully a number of the philosophical commitments held by the character "Nietzsche" who results from the person Nietzsche's lifelong self-narration. I have already mentioned his treatment of perspectivism, truth, and the partiality ("simplification") of any interpretation (and the stake we have in finding ways to ignore our simplifying). And there are distinctive readings of the Eternal Return doctrine (understood to mean that since there is no essential core to any thing or person, then absolutely everything is essential to that thing or person being what or who it is), and the will to power (a thing is the sum of its effects, but how such effects are grouped and organized is a kind of constant interpretive struggle). However, at least for me, the most important part of the book remains its part 2, an extended and subtle interpretation of how Nietzsche understands *the self*, the subject of deeds and thoughts. The claim is that Nietzsche understands the self's relation to its own past deeds, beliefs, aspirations, attitudes, aversions, dispositions, and values as the relation between an artist and her work, specifically an author and her literary work, and more specifically still the author and her narrative literary work. (There is no direct discussion of the category of "literature" in invoking this analogy,[8] but the job Nehamas wants literature and authorship to do in this context appears to mean that the nineteenth-century realist novel and some early versions of the modernist novel are what he has in mind. Proust's *In Search of Lost Time* is most often mentioned as a model.)[9] This

---

be found in one way or another in the published work, but my own view is that one ought to be quite wary of any reliance on these often mysterious notes and fragments.

8. The idea of literature as such, as a distinct mode of collective self-understanding and authorial "creation and discovery," is, it has been argued, a recent innovation in aesthetic categorization, due largely to the *Athenaeum* crowd in Jena, philosophical romanticism generally, and very specific historical conditions. See Lacoue-Labarthe and Nancy, *The Literary Absolute: The Theory of Literature in German Romanticism*. There is also the question of what Nietzsche thought distinctive about literary self-understanding, in its relation, say, to psychology or philosophy or history. For the most part, when Nietzsche focuses explicitly on the aesthetic as such, his position seems to be that such experience is "ecstatic," Dionysian, boundary-dissolving, even that it involves a kind of frenzy, or *Rausch*. I am not aware of anywhere where he directs our attention to narration or says much about the distinctness of realist narrative fiction. No matter; Nehamas is certainly right that what Nietzsche does say seems to have assumptions and implications that can be described or redescribed in the way Nehamas does.

9. See, inter alia, Nehamas, *Nietzsche*, 167–68. While Nietzsche admired Stendhal, he does not so often mention novels; theater and opera (music in general) seem to be his privileged arts. Of poets, Shakespeare and Goethe make the most frequent appearances in his list of admired writers.

is the question I want to raise here. *Is it true that Nietzsche's view is that a subject's relation to itself is to be understood as like the relation between an author and a written text, and is such a view plausible?* (Another admirable aspect of Nehamas's interpretation is that he always asks both sorts of question, and so defends what he takes to be Nietzsche's model for self-identification and self-affirmation.)

The claim is embedded in another broader picture of what we might call Nietzsche's whole project. For Nehamas, that project centrally concerns "writing." His book will show, Nehamas promises early on, that "writing . . . always remains both the main model and the main object of Nietzsche's thinking."[10] Or, as he writes later: "Nietzsche's model for the world, for objects, and for people turns out to be the literary text and its components; his model for our relation to the world turns out to be interpretation."[11] And: "As in the literary case, so in the world, according to Nietzsche, to reinterpret events is to arrange effects and therefore to generate new things. Our 'text' is being composed as we read it, and our readings are new parts of it that will give rise to further ones in the future."[12]

These claims are to be understood as glosses on passages, especially from *The Gay Science*, that certainly do seem to say what Nehamas has them saying. For example, there is the famous passage where Nietzsche claims, "One thing is needful—to 'give style' to one's character—a great and rare art! It is practiced by those who survey all the strengths and weaknesses of their nature and then fit them into an artistic plan until every one of them appears as art and reason and even weaknesses delight the eye."[13] And there is this: "We should learn from artists while being wiser than they are in other matters. For with them this subtle power (of arranging, of making things beautiful) usually comes to an end where art ends and life begins; but we want to be the poets of our life—first of all in the smallest, most everyday matters."[14]

With remarks like these Nietzsche, who was of course not that well informed about the modern or post-Kantian German tradition, nevertheless is staking out a claim on the issue that was the most pressing and complex for them—*the proper account of the self's relation to itself*, both in *all* experi-

10. Ibid., 29.
11. Ibid., 91.
12. Ibid.
13. Nietzsche, *The Gay Science*, trans. Nauckhoff, 290.
14. Ibid., 299.

ence and action, and in explicit claims to self-knowledge or, we might say most broadly, self-identification, the positive result of some self-assessment. (In many ways this last issue, the issue of possible *self-affirmation,* is the master issue in Nietzsche, the one that Nehamas is encouraging us to think of as the issue of "writing oneself into existence" as a kind of "author" or "poet" of one's own life, and so it is the one I will be concentrating on.) Kant had shifted this question of self-awareness from its Cartesian formulations, rejected the relevance of the question of the "nature of *res cogitans,*" and treated the question of the relation between a subject and its own experiences and deeds in a way that forced the question of the very intelligibility or the "logic" of this self-relation to the forefront. Many post-Kantians were interested in the inadequacy of a so-called reflective model of that relation, any kind of inner observation or introspection model. Subjects were not related to themselves as subjects were to objects, and neither apperception nor self-knowledge could be understood as the product of observation, inference, or any form of intellectual intuition. So what was it for the subject to be about itself in various modalities of attentiveness?

Two aspects of Nehamas's Nietzsche echo developments in that tradition. First, such a self, as the object of some identification and affirmation, had to be understood as a product or result, and this meant, paradoxically, a result of itself. To be a self is to be in effect carrying oneself forward, unifying and sustaining such unity. This is a paradox—how could the self be both producer and product?—that Nehamas himself raises as relevant and we will return to shortly. Second, self-knowledge, since in no sense reportorial, has to be understood as self-constituting. (Nehamas has Nietzsche in the thick of this issue by having him insist that it is only in "creating" a self that I "discover" mine, and that both notions are equally necessary.) Coming to any such point of potential self-identification and affirmation—quite possibly multiple identities to be affirmed, such as Christian, teacher, father, patriot, poet, whatever—must be understood as more like coming to make avowals or pledges and so as necessarily provisional, unstable, "testable" by deeds, and ever reinterpretable as situations change, and especially as one finds out something about the level and intensity and propriety and perhaps the very meaning of one's avowed commitments.[15]

15. See Nehamas's citation (*Nietzsche,* 173) of Nietzsche, *The Will to Power,* trans. Kaufmann, 552, and Nietzsche's distinction between a "truth" about oneself as a "determining," not "a becoming conscious of something that is in itself firm and determined." See also 158 on the

This is, in my view, all to the good and an exciting line of interpretation. But it requires two qualifications, and I am uncertain about the implications of the qualifications. The two powerfully Nehamasian passages cited above from *The Gay Science* appear to remain in a distinctly aesthetic register. That is, at *Gay Science* 299, when Nietzsche talks about the "subtle power" that unites and arranges, he tells us that such a power is the power to "make things beautiful." And in the earlier passage, *Gay Science* 290, the point of the arranging is said, quite broadly, to be "what delights the eye," and the passage goes on to make clear that what is to be avoided is "the ugly." This would suggest something that, from his subtitle and some of his stronger formulations, one might also reasonably infer to be a certain aestheticism about life attributed by Nehamas to Nietzsche and affirmed in both their names, as if the highest values were purely aesthetic values.

Despite the passages just cited, though, this would not sound much like Nietzsche, who, after *The Birth of Tragedy*, spoke often of his distrust of artists and their values, and the ideal of the beautiful does not even resonate very deeply in his own account of art, which tends to emphasize the disruptive, the sublime, and the intoxicating. There is not much to give us reason to think Nietzsche thought there was anything particularly valuable in narrating one's life and presenting oneself to the world in a way that would "delight the eye," hide the ugly, or look beautiful.[16] Even his early notion of an "aesthetic justification of existence" does not trade much on traditional aesthetic properties of Greek tragedies and focuses instead on tragedy as if it were a distinct ethical category, a worldview of compelling power. And while there might be something "Greek" and so perhaps valuable for Nietzsche in assessing others and their deeds aesthetically (on the very broad *kalos k'agathos* standard, the echo of which is in his *gut/schlecht* distinction from *On the Genealogy of Morality*), it is hard to believe that all the fuss Nietzsche made about nihilism, the death of God, last men, bows that have lost their tension, herd society, and so forth should have, as its appropriate response, beautiful self-narrating pieces of art (a.k.a. persons).

Moreover, despite what still seem to me somewhat confusing signals from Nehamas about this (like his bold subtitle, and the apparent implica-

---

"fluidity" of "personality" for the *Übermensch*, and 182 on identifying ourselves differently at different times.

16. This may be why he says that he follows the artists only so far, that we must be wiser than they are "in other matters." But that just raises the question both for Nietzsche and for Nehamas of what the corresponding value *is* in "life narration" if it is not the beautiful.

tions of the very notion of "trying to make of one's life a work of art"), this would also not be the way Nehamas understands the bearing of these aesthetic notions on Nietzsche's views about the all-important Socratic question: how one ought to live. This is somewhat clearer (at least it became clearer to me) in a later article of his, published in 1995, in the *Cambridge Companion to Nietzsche*. Responding to the charge that he has Nietzsche aestheticize life (a charge made by me in a book called *Modernism as a Philosophical Problem*), he says this in discussing two clear possibilities about the role of aesthetics in Nietzsche:

> It may mean that the choice of a particular mode of behavior is *like* an artistic decision concerning, say, the adoption of a particular style. But it may also mean that the choice of a model of behavior is *itself* an aesthetic decision, focusing only on the aesthetic features of the course of action in question. The first alternative concerns the basis on which choices and decisions are made: It holds that artistic decisions provide the model for all action. The latter refers to the very content of the decision itself: It holds that all decisions are straightforwardly artistic. And though the two interpretations are probably interconnected, my own view is that the former is more likely to be correct.[17]

Fair enough; point taken. It is true that Nehamas mostly says such things as "Nietzsche's *model* for the world, for objects and for people turns out the be the literary text and its components."[18] Model, then; not *life as text itself*, in that radical "French" sense we are all now so tired of. But what then replaces the strictly (and unsatisfactory) aesthetic values that govern the self-narrational act Nehamas has Nietzsche requiring for any even provisionally stable identity? What counts as the basis of the affirmation, if and when it is possible? Nehamas emphasizes the attempt to find and make harmony, unity, coherence—these are the values to be observed in the narration—and this in the service of a supreme value, the value "freedom." That is: "Freedom of the will so construed is not the absence of causal determination but a harmony among all of a person's preference schemes. It is a state in which desire follows thought, and action follows desire, without tension or struggle, and in which the distinction between choice and constraint may

17. Nehamas, "Nietzsche, Modernity, Aestheticism," 333.
18. Nehamas, *Nietzsche*, 90.

well be thought to disappear."[19] The question raised by this claim is simple: Do we know why for Nietzsche the highest human aspiration should be a free life in this sense? Do we know that this is in fact his view, and that this is his view of freedom? Would we not have to say that such a claim is "undertheorized" by Nietzsche?[20]

There are three further problems in any such picture of the *Great Desideratum* in any attempt to narrate the details (*all* the details, down to the most minor) as fitting together in a coherent whole, and all three are honestly mentioned by Nehamas. I am just not sure where he wants to go with them. There is first the fact that Nietzsche does not so much praise harmony and unity, but instead a state of maximum if also controlled *conflict* of internal states and memories and evaluations! His heroes in this regard, Shakespeare and Goethe, were great because they contained such multitudes within themselves somehow, contradictions in commitments and evaluations that they did not reconcile but in some way "mastered." That was their greatness. Such epic figures are said to have instincts "that conflict powerfully," or even "bore all the conflicting tendencies of the age,"[21] and yet they managed to create a "totality" without resolving or reconciling these instincts. At least I see no independent indication that a pacific ideal of harmony and order is necessary for such a totality, and there are these indications that some sort of rule over warring estates is the political model Nietzsche has in mind; a kind of truce, not a peace treaty.

Second, the notion of freedom as, to say it backward, non-self-alienation, an identification with oneself, and an experience of my deeds as genuinely mine, especially because of a seamless harmony between thought and action, all understood and affirmed as such by me and integrable in a whole that makes some sense to me as a whole, is not a novel idea in Nietzsche. This notion of freedom has its fullest development in Hegel, but with one crucial difference, and from the perspective of that difference, it looks

19. Ibid., 187.

20. See also Nehamas's citation (*Nietzsche*, 190–91, 195) of Nietzsche, *The Will to Power*, 617, and *Twilight of the Idols* 1.9, the remarks on the issue of freedom, and the remarks on "perfect unity and freedom" (the model achieved by literary characters). On the other hand, there are passages where Nehamas suggests a more pragmatic basis for this unifying-interpreting. "The apparent world, Nietzsche believes, is not a world that appears to be and is distinct from reality but simply the world as it appears to any being that needs to survive in it and that therefore must arrange it selectively for its own purposes" (45).

21. Nehamas, *Nietzsche*, 188.

like there is something badly missing in Nehamas's Nietzsche. For Hegel's is still a rational agency account of freedom. I can experience my deeds as mine in understanding *why* I am doing what I am doing, and that "why" answer is a *reason*. The inevitability of such a justificatory relation to what I do stems from the fact of our finitude: from the fact that what I do inevitably affects, alters, or perhaps prevents what others would otherwise have been able to do, and so prompts either a direct struggle or an exchange of putative reasons. Hegel has a historicized "social practice" view of at least practical reason, the entertaining, offering, or rejecting of considerations that count as justifications at a time and to a community. But I mean only to say in this context that Hegel's harmony of the soul, unity as hierarchy among conflicting impulses and desires, has a rational and social structure. And this in the simplest sense: I am tempted to do X but can understand that X's benefiting me would harm S, and it merely benefiting me could not count to S as an acceptable reason. So, at some historical point in the development of rational institutions, I do not count it as an acceptable reason and in that sense rule or master it; I am even in some sense reconciled to it; I understand it and why it cannot be acted on.

In Nietzsche's view of the matter, when, for example, I do not find myself wanting what I have come to consider worth wanting, or I find myself wanting badly what I also regard as despicable, or simply do not do what I think I must, or am pulled in two directions and cannot decide, then the question is: In *what* way, by appeal to *what*, guided by *what* consideration, do I attempt to unify what I have done, what I believe and what I feel? How are we to understand the process of unifying and ordering, if not guided by some aesthetic ideal ("the beautiful" or an aesthetic-organic notion of harmony, as in Schiller's account of *Bildung*) and if not adjudicable by any appeal to reason? The ideal of narrative coherence in a novel is a bit of a help here, but not much. When such a narration is successful, we appreciate how a character who did *that* would think *this*, or one who wanted *that* would end up declining *this*, and whose development makes sense in that way too. But in the narration of an actual life, either life is being treated *as* literature, and we have our aestheticism problem again; or literature, writing, is only "a model," but if the strictly aesthetic principle of unification is not the one relevant "for life," what would correspond to it?[22]

22. If the answer is something like *whatever makes possible an integration and unity that allows me to "identify" with all such components and so achieve freedom*, and there is no general rule

There is a consequence of this problem that Nehamas also points to, and it too seems to me to lead to more profound qualifications on the life-as-literature theme than he acknowledges.

> Nietzsche, of course, constantly emphasizes the importance of evaluating oneself only by one's own standards. Nevertheless, especially since he does not believe that we have any special access to knowledge of ourselves, such questions are finally decided from the outside. This outside, which includes looking at one's own past, may consist of a very select public, of an audience that perhaps does not yet exist. Still the distinction between the fact and the feeling of unity must be pressed and maintained. Zarathustra taunts the sun when he asks what its happiness would be were it not for those for whom it shines. . . . Similarly it takes spectators for unity to be made manifest and therefore for it to be there. Nietzsche in particular . . . may be totally at the mercy of his readers.[23]

This seems to me quite right, but how could such profound reciprocal dependence (which again brings Hegel to mind and the unavoidable goal of mutuality of recognition) be articulated further in Nietzschean terms? His anxiety about herd morality and modern conformism means that he has to tread very carefully around any such acknowledgment of this level of deep dependence (that is, a dependence on others for the standard of success for everything of importance in Nehamas's "achievement" notion of self-identity and his literary model of that work of achievement). Nietzsche's own portrayal, in literary terms, no less, of such dependence is a portrayal of failure; for example, Zarathustra's relation to his disciples. (In fact, Zarathustra never does find such an "outside" audience.) And if we have "no special access to knowledge of ourselves" (so little that we depend on others for confirmation of the achievement of an authentic unified self-identity), then it is unlikely we will ever be able to claim any "special access" into the true characters of others, no way to ensure they are in fact the appropriate audience, whatever "appropriate audience" turns out to mean. And this is all not

for how to do this, then the fact that some "I" at a time and from a perspective does the integrating and unifying also raises the question of how "I" in an another register could understand why I did the integrating and unifying in that way, as does the question of the difference between thinking I have effected this unity and really effecting it, the next question raised in the text below. For the former issue, see the discussion below of whether such a task is "vicious."

23. Nehamas, *Nietzsche*, 186.

to mention the problems that arise when we acknowledge, as we must, that the values and standards any such "audience" would apply are inevitably historical and variable. When Orestes accepts that it is his fate to murder his mother, Clytemnestra, in Aeschylus's *Oresteia*, his explanations to the Chorus and his own resolution of the conflict he experiences between this religious duty and his filial duties all depend on religious notions of fate and the gods unique to that community then. What sort of audience could we expect to be available in the mass societies of modern commercial republics, even if we concede that it must be a tiny, elite fragment—and why wouldn't we be just as liable to self-deceit and simple error in picking or accepting such an audience? Perhaps the point is that we cannot ever be sure of any of this, and must instead find a way of living with a constant anxiety about the possibility of our own self-deceit, never sure if "the feeling of unity" achieved represents the achievement of any genuine unity.

This issue is connected with what I said was the third qualification that arises from this picture of a self-relation as an author-text relation, and it is also one that Nehamas mentions. It begins to be apparent in the paradoxical air of the Nietzschean injunction "Become who you are." Who else could you become? And what would it mean to *have become* who you are, given that Nietzsche denies any substantial, true, or essential self, even if the result of becoming? But this is not the form of the most serious paradox. The issue Nietzsche is concerned with clearly has to do with something like an ego-ideal, base-level or grounding commitments, a kind of mastering self-image by reference to which what else one does and believes can come to make a kind of sense. In *this* sense one can certainly be enjoined to become the actual person one ideally claims to be, or one can be accused of being or not being in any process of becoming whoever it is one takes oneself to be or to be becoming. And Nietzsche has no problem conceding that, whatever ego-ideal or fixed point of reference is necessary for such a narrational and purposive activity, it can change, as one finds out what it is to be such a person, or as one comes to see that one's narrating one's life is an episode in a life that comes to have another meaning from yet another point of view on oneself, as narrator as well as narrated. In fact, acceptance of such instability is largely why another of Nietzsche's life-values has the form it does, constant "self-overcoming."

This means that fidelity to oneself is not faith-keeping with a fixed inner essence but largely a matter of action and, especially, interpretation. Again the "having" of such an ideal is an avowal, not a discovery; and becoming who one avows one is, is a matter of acting in a way that expresses or realizes that ideal. And there is no point where one has "attained" such an ideal. It is only ever provisionally true that one truly acts in the light of it. Perhaps one simply has not yet encountered the one situation that shows one to be a fraud; perhaps in the process of acting in the light of it one finds it to be much different in what it requires than one has anticipated. Perhaps nothing that one does in its name is acknowledged by anyone else, even one's most like-minded audience, as consistent with its avowal.

Hence the truly paradoxical situation. Nehamas follows Nietzsche in using language like an author creating himself, unifying events of the past, narrating the events, finding an interpretation that would reveal how everything in one's past is "what one is," and so forth, all as if a distinct subject is consciously dealing with objects of attention "before" his or her mind as intentional objects, available for one interpretation or place in a narration or other, as the subject "decides."[24] This is a natural and almost unavoidable way of putting the issues, even though the subject's separation of and distinguishing of itself from itself remains puzzling, and even though Nehamas is fully aware that Nietzsche wanted to deny any real distinction between the subject and its thoughts and the doer and its deeds, claimed that there was no "subject" behind such thoughts and no agent or doer behind the deeds. Nehamas cites a couple of times the famous birds of prey/little lambs passage from *On the Genealogy of Morality*, I, §13, which says just that. And Nehamas accepts all the implications of this denial: no mental acts functioning as causes of bodily movements, no distinct faculty of the will, no punctuated moments of decision, no substances and attributes, no agents and effects, and a commitment to "long, complicated events with neither obvious beginnings nor clear ends."[25]

But what then does the "poet" in the "poet of our own lives," or the "author" in authoring our own narrative, refer to? At one point Nehamas suggests the following. (In this passage the language shifts from a more or less romantic notion of a creative, active source of unity, an author, to one where such subjectivity is, let us say, more "dispersed" and even "event like.") "Dominant habits and traits, as long as they are dominant, assume

24. See, for example, the grammar of typical claims at ibid., 136, how one "gives meaning, organization and value to the world," or that one "has shaped oneself into an object so organized that every single part of it is equally essential."

25. Ibid., 77.

the role of the subject; in terms of our metaphor, they assume the role of the leader. It is such traits that speak with the voice of the self when they are manifested in action. Their own coherence and unity allow them to become the subject that, at least for a while, says 'I.' "[26]

He goes on to note that for Nietzsche, there are a variety of "habits" and "character traits" that vie for dominance, such that "we identify ourselves differently over time," and that therefore "the unity of the self, which therefore also constitutes its identity, is not something given but something achieved, not a beginning but a goal."[27] But, again, *who* does the achieving? The sort of language just cited suggests that being a subject is a matter of being subject to, rather than subject of, dominant inclinations, passions, and drives, which group, arise, and subside as something like themselves subjectless events, but if left at this impression, any unity (subordination of counter instincts and drives) would be in effect something that contingently *happens,* not so much something I could be said to *do* or to achieve. And the unity would be hard to understand since the main engine of that unification, "interpretation," is not and cannot be something that happens to me, but is something I reflectively do.

Nehamas frequently suggests another sort of model for all this, Proust's narrator, writing himself into existence as a character by narrating coherently the events of his past life. But there are problems here too. In the first place, the old Marcel's flashback memories are involuntary, and so the train of associated memories is not something he "does."[28] For another, Marcel's narration of his own past is an element of *another* narration, the narration written by Proust, the novelist, who is not the novel's narrator.[29] And this is an odd feature of any self-narration: that one's narrating self is not only the subject of the narrating in the way just described but immediately becomes an element *in* the narration, an event like any other in a life history, always eluding any attempt to narrate from some distinct "subject" position.

26. Ibid., 181.

27. Ibid.

28. This would, though, be more consistent with the less "subject-directed" passages just cited.

29. Muller, *Les voix narratives dans la "Recherché du temps perdu,"* can identify seven different "Marcels" in the text; Landy, in *Proust, Philosophy and Fiction,* five. I would at least insist on three, the becoming-Marcel Marcel, the old, remembering Marcel, and the author Marcel Proust. So while "Marcel Proust" did write the words cited in Nehamas's epigram, it is the character "Marcel"—not Proust—who "writes" them.

How and why one narrates as one does is an event like any other that must be both inside and outside the narrative line.

And this is noted by Nehamas: "To make a perfectly unified character out of all that one has done, as Nietzsche wants, may involve us in a vicious effort: we may have to be writing our autobiography as we are living our life, and we would also have to be writing about writing that autobiography, and to be writing in turn about that, and so on and so on without end."[30] Exactly; but is this a "vicious effort" or not? Proust's *book*, while technically unfinished, has a last novel and formal closure. Marcel appears to find what he was searching for: lost time, and so understands why he became a writer, why he could not earlier, and what it means to have become a writer. Of course even *that* occurs "inside" the character Marcel's self-narration, and so his belief that he has found "the" past is quite possibly, once interpreted by the reader, another of the illusions he has entertained throughout, about Swann, Odette, Albertine, the Verdurins, and so forth.[31] But we don't survive the closure of our own *lives*; when "the book" ends, so do we, and we are not there to put the ending together with the rest.

Nehamas's response to this issue introduces a distinction that I find puzzling. He quotes Nietzsche encouraging us to ignore the *actual* or living artist when considering the work. Nietzsche says that artists are only the precondition of the work, the soil out of which it grows (an organic metaphor somewhat at odds with the picture of a poet making a poem or someone becoming the poet of her own life). And Nehamas asks, again with a clear, silent reference to Proust: "What, then, if the work itself, in its totality, results in the construction of a character whose biography it turns out to be?"[32] His answer to this question appears to be: it is this created character who is important; we need attention to another character, the living character who created this character, only for the actual biography of Nietzsche the person, not the one of significance in historical memory. But then we would not have "Life *as* Literature." The subtitle should read: "Literature *Instead of* Life." Likewise at the end of the book, we find this distinction between life and literature again, even more strongly put. In mentioning Nietzsche's praise of cruelty and his general illiberal sentiments (all of

30. Nehamas, *Nietzsche*, 198.

31. Cf. the scene in the last novel when Marcel discovers, in Gilberte's house, a copy of the Goncourts' journal and sees that the Verdurins, whom he has come to hold in mild contempt, were actually thought by the Goncourts (beloved by Marcel) to be brilliant.

32. Nehamas, *Nietzsche*, 199.

which are interwoven throughout Nietzsche's texts), Nehamas denies that these are reasons to dismiss him. "On the contrary, they are reasons why we should continue to read him and why we should admire him even as we disagree with him. In engaging with his works, we are not engaging with the miserable little man who wrote them but with the philosopher who emerges from them, the magnificent character these texts constitute and manifest, the agent, who, as the will to power holds, is nothing but his effects—that is, his writings."[33]

"Miserable little man" is the phrase that catches one's eye. I would have thought that much of the force of Nehamas's interpretation would be to reduce any such difference between the "real" Nietzsche and this putative "character"; that there is no *real Nietzsche* except *as* narrated, created, made. If the "Nietzsche" that the miserable little man created is not also miserable (or, I suppose, little), then he is a kind of fantasy of the real Nietzsche, not what his life amounts to or means, and it is hard to see what could be satisfying about such a fantasy, or what it might have to do with leading a free life.

Finally, this whole issue—let us say, Nehamas's picture of a creatively interpreting, narrating, world-making Nietzschean subject[34]—touches on a very large problem that I only have space to note. I mentioned at the outset that the state of Nietzsche studies in 1985 consisted of early, sometimes rather clumsy attempts at the professional categorization of Nietzsche's positions and the early reception of European, especially post-Heideggerian readings. The Anglophone context over the last decade or so has obviously been much influenced by attempts to naturalize—or "neuralize," one might even say—philosophy, ethics, aesthetics, politics, even literary studies. In this context, what clearly appears to be Nietzsche's skepticism about the possibility of an autonomous, reflective, deliberating, or even interpreting subject and a self-causing, individually responsible agent has become quite prominent. Comparisons with Darwin and Freud are much more common now than comparisons with Shakespeare and Proust.

Now, no one can deny that Nietzsche is interested in *some* sort of difference between, on the one hand, "the way things *look* to a consciously deliberating and acting subject" and so "the reasons such a subject gives herself," or "the interpretations she comes up with," and, on the other hand, "the

33. Ibid., 286.

34. Cf. "The world we construct, Nietzsche repeatedly insists, is absolutely necessary, and we could not live without it; for it is as real as can be" (ibid., 95).

(putative) *real* explanation for the appeal of such reasons and the attractiveness of such interpretations," explanatory factors normally not accessible by the subject/agent. And Nietzsche does refer to these "factors" as "instincts" or "drives." But I take Nehamas to be committed to something like the unavoidability, let us say, of "the interpretive stance," even when Nietzsche is referring to what appears to be his fundamental drive. I mean first such passages as "that everything that occurs in the organic world consists of *overpowering, dominating,* and, in their turn, overpowering and dominating consist of re-interpretation, adjustment."[35] Or: "But every purpose and use is just a *sign* that the will to power has achieved mastery over something less powerful, and has impressed upon it its own idea [*Sinn*] of a use function; and the whole history of a 'thing,' an organ, a tradition can to this extent be a continuous chain of signs, continually revealing new interpretations and adaptations."[36]

Second, my sense of what is at stake in the "difference" mentioned above concerns how one understands the possibility of any intentional content in any such "factor" (instinct, drive) and therewith the proper role of such "not conscious" factors in the psychological explanation of belief formation or action. The idea (of the unavoidability of the interpretive stance) would be the denial that there could be any such thing as preinterpreted content to any such drive or impulse, at least any that could play an explanatory role. This seems to me to be an implication of, or perhaps what is asserted by, Nehamas's claim that Nietzsche's view is "that the 'mental acts' of thinking and desiring (to take these as representative of all the rest) are indissolubly connected with their contents, which in turn are indissolubly connected with the contents of other thoughts, desires, and of course actions."[37] I take it he does not mean causally connected.[38] Any explanatorily relevant motivation cannot be understood as something like a somatic force, in the way that a brain injury or a drug could be said to be responsible for a change in thought or behavior. Any such motivationally relevant factor has a sense and significance and weight for the subject (even, and here the great complexity, "for the subject" in a way not consciously attended to by the subject) in a way that cannot be isolated from the way anything and everything

35. Nietzsche, *On the Genealogy of Morality*, II, §12, trans. Diethe, 51.

36. Ibid.

37. Nehamas, *Nietzsche*, 178.

38. Cf. ibid., 89–90, on the difference between causal and interpretive holism.

makes sense for such an agent. Moreover, no one experiences an urge and "then" interprets it as an urge to do X. There is no urge except as an urge to do X (hence Nehamas's claim about "indissoluble connections"), where X means what it means for a subject at a time. And as we have already seen, the "inseparable" interpreting activity can be as blind to itself about its *own* motivation as any explicit self-evaluation.

There is also no question that Nietzsche thinks various aspects of this motivational economy can fall out of conscious attentiveness and be "hidden" from such attentiveness. Nehamas notes that we find ways to ignore how much simplification and exclusion goes on in our perspectival interpretations, and he notes how prominent the appeal to self-deceit is in Nietzsche's account.[39] The slaves in revolt were motivated by ressentiment, but their "conscious" self-interpretation was that they were motivated by moral righteousness. Ressentiment, though, did not well up and "cause" them to revolt. Such ressentiment had its object within (and only within) a self-interpretation in which such a reaction, even an unconscious reaction, would make sense. (An understanding of their own humiliating weakness and their refusal to resist, in this case. Absent such an interpretation of what is happening to them, no ressentiment.) But they also found a way to deny that motivational content; they "kept" it out of consciousness and invented another interpretation. How this actually works in Nietzsche is as complicated as any account of the possibility of self-deceit, but he seems to think the phenomenon is far more prominent and powerful than acknowledged, and it certainly allows Nehamas to be as sensitive to the power and importance of "what lies outside consciousness" in Nietzsche's genealogy as anyone would want.

Finally, if we consider everything said so far, the picture that emerges is not so much a romantic picture of a creative genius, producing, by means of the force of his imagination alone, credible self-narrations. As Nehamas himself indicates frequently, virtually no one succeeds in being the poet of his own life. However creative we may be, we cannot secure our interpretations, reassure ourselves about them, ward off suspicions about self-deceit,

39. The logical structure of this simplification is a knotty philosophical problem itself. In discussing the "will to ignorance," for example, Nehamas writes that this will "must turn upon itself and become the will not to know that one is failing to know many things in the process of coming to know one" (ibid., 69). So one wills to know, wills to simplify and exclude in this willing, and then wills not to know that one is in effect willing not to know. A neat trick.

properly understand the right way to react to others' responses to them. We never reach any stable point of view in such a process, never simply become who we are. And this is reflected in Nietzsche's own fate. There are far more and far more incommensurable "Nietzsches" among his audience than there are "Socrateses." He is indeed, as Nehamas puts it so well, "the first modernist at the same time that he is the last romantic."[40]

40. Ibid., 234.

# 7

# Bernard Williams on Nietzsche on the Greeks

## I

In his 1993 Sather Lectures, *Shame and Necessity*, Bernard Williams made clear what many had long surmised: his debt to the thought of Nietzsche and especially his debt to Nietzsche's views on the prephilosophic or "tragic" Greeks. There are many specific references to Nietzsche in Williams's book, and he clearly viewed Nietzsche as his most important ally in attacking the institution he held in such low regard that he associated it with slavery, using the same epithet, "the peculiar institution," that had been prominent in discussions of slavery. However, the institution that both Williams and Nietzsche seemed to consider not just wrong-headed but pernicious and completely unworthy of human allegiance was "morality." Neither of them, of course, meant thereby to be championing complete amoralism, or a complete indifference to considerations about how human life might best be lived.[1] Their target was the Christian inheritance and its legacy (most apparent in the modern moral philosophy of Kant), with its notions of duty and self-sacrifice, its asceticism, and its fixation on motivational purity. So for

I am grateful to Mark Jenkins, Glenn Most, and Candace Vogler for conversations about the topics in this chapter.

1. In the sense, for both, of how "*I* might best live," not how "anyone at all, at any time, might best live."

both, a pre-Christian culture in which an alternative picture of human life and human ideals could be found, one that nevertheless maintained some great claim on the Western—that is, our—imaginary, was very important.[2]

Moreover, neither was all that impressed with the results for ethical life of the turn to philosophy accomplished by Socrates and Plato. (Williams's position on Aristotle is more complicated because he so admires Aristotle's attention to moral luck. But Williams still rejects a "teleological ethics.")[3] Nietzsche seemed to hold Socrates and philosophy responsible for the end of the superior ethical perspective of "Greek tragic culture," and, together with Nietzsche, Williams thought it one of the greatest "con jobs" in history that Socrates convinced courageous, prudent people that because they could not tell him what courage or prudence was, they didn't know what they were doing, and so could not have really been courageous or prudent. One of Williams's most famous and controversial thoughts is a Nietzschean one: that "self-consciousness kills ethics," or "reflection can destroy [ethical] knowledge."[4] In one of the most important conclusions of *Ethics and the Limits of Philosophy,* Williams makes clear that he means by such claims *philosophical* reflection, as if what ethical life needs is a theory, a rational grounding. It does not. Within ethical life there is of course reflective deliberation, but its content is much more psychologically interrogatory for Williams, just as it is in Nietzsche: What do I really want? What are my motives? What is it actually that I am doing? What would this action mean to another? And without signing on to Nietzsche's nihilism diagnosis, Williams makes the Nietzschean point that what modern ethical life needs is a kind of "*confidence,*" not something that can be achieved by philosophy, and something that the "pervasive presence" of reflection in our age can promote if it is undertaken "from strength" and not "from weakness of self-deception and dogmatism." That "strength," "weakness," "self-deception," and "dogmatism" are meant in a Nietzschean voice is confirmed by the next sentence. "Confidence is not the same as optimism; it could rest on what Nietzsche called the pessimism of strength."[5] This is of course a term Nietzsche uses for the tragic culture of the Greeks.

2. "It is not a paradox that in these very new circumstances very old philosophies may have more to offer than moderately new ones, and a historical story could be told to show why this is so." Williams, *Ethics and the Limits of Philosophy,* 198.

3. Ibid., 48.

4. Ibid., 148. See also 155 on "more ethical knowledge" in the "less reflective past."

5. Williams, *Ethics and the Limits of Philosophy,* 171.

Now, Williams did not agree with Nietzsche on the supposed "innocence" of the Greeks or their tragic poets, their status as child to our adult, and he did not agree that they displayed openly a kind of brutality or realism about power self-deceptively and pathologically continued but disguised in the Christian moral tradition. But he says that Nietzsche offered us "more than this line of thought," and that it is a deeper set of Nietzschean ideas that he wants to take up: namely, "joining in a radical way the questions of how we understand the Greeks and of how we understand ourselves."[6] The substance that emerges from this joining is very clear. It amounts to Williams's withering attack on the "progressivists" like Snell and Adkins who are out to show that the epic and tragic poets either completely lacked or grasped only very primitively the notions of agentive causation, intention, responsibility, and interiority that we now realize we need for an adequate account of agency and responsibility.[7] On the contrary, Williams argues, the epic and tragic poets had all the concepts they needed to make the relevant distinctions. What we have and they don't is simply a body of bad philosophy, the philosophy necessary to support the morality institution. By seeing ourselves in the Greek poets and not just in the Greek philosophers, we can start to free ourselves from the morality delusions. Williams argues for this relevance by pointing out often that if the progressivists were right, then our experience of such literature would be of some strange, heartless, cruel, barely intelligible foreign tribe, almost unrecognizable as "one of us," objects of study, rather than of engagement. But we *are* gripped and moved in ways that belie the distance the progressivists want to create. In a paradoxical but telling phrase, he notes that there is a difference between "what we [actually] think" and "what we merely think we think"[8] about normative matters, and the experience of Greek literature can make this distinction vividly clear.

But perhaps the deepest level of sympathy between Nietzsche and Williams arises out of his common cause with Nietzsche on our current historical fate in late modernity, what we have to face now, what we cannot avoid. The proper study of Greek literature can help us understand and face such

6. Williams, *Shame and Necessity*, 10.

7. Not being a classicist, I am unsure of the status of Williams's targets in his attack. I am told that it is widely accepted that this scholarship is dated and has been superseded, and even told that Williams is going beyond beating dead horses. He is digging them up to beat them again. I have no view on the matter.

8. Williams, *Shame and Necessity*, 7.

a fate, just as Nietzsche insisted, especially at the beginning of his career in *The Birth of Tragedy*. Nietzsche's name is not mentioned in the following passage, one of the most stirring and sweeping in *Shame and Necessity*, but there is no mistaking his profound influence. It is such a fine broadside that I will permit myself to quote it in full.

> We are in an ethical condition that lies not only beyond Christianity but beyond its Kantian and Hegelian legacies. We have an ambivalent sense of what human beings have achieved, and have hopes for how they might live (in particular, in the form of a still powerful ideal that they should live without lies). We know that the world was not made for us, or we for the world, that our history tells no purposive story, and that there is no position outside the world or outside history from which we might hope to authenticate our activities. We have to acknowledge the hideous costs of many human achievements that we value, including this reflective sense itself, and recognize that there is no redemptive Hegelian history or universal Leibnizean cost-benefit analysis to show that it will all come out well enough in the end. In important ways, we are, in our ethical situation, more like human beings in antiquity than any other Western people have been in the meantime. More particularly, we are like those who, from the fifth century and earlier, have left us traces of a consciousness that had not yet been touched by Plato's and Aristotle's attempts to make our ethical relations to the world fully intelligible.[9]

Indeed the passage is *so* redolent of Nietzschean sensibilities that it prompts the same sort of prudent, understandable recoil that many have had to Nietzsche on such topics as "nihilism." One rarely finds contemporary philosophers making such startling pronouncements, with this "Nietzschean" language of whole historical epochs closing or opening. Can we really be said to be *beyond* the Christian era? To be beyond the Kantian and Hegelian legacies? What could that mean? Just *who* is beyond *what*? Nor do we hear such confident finality of judgment. History tells *no* purposive story whatsoever? Claims like Hegel's about the progressive realization of human freedom are *wholly* worthless? Such heterodox suggestions about the founders of our philosophical tradition are also rare: that, from the start, Plato and

9. Ibid., 166.

Aristotle muddied waters that had been not only clearer but more humanly nourishing.

## II

But the fact that the two philosophers had the same institution in their critical sights, that the rhetoric of their criticism went well beyond standard philosophical disagreement, and that their sense of the fate of late modernity in the Western, Northern industrialized world invoked the same epochal, grand gestures of failure and radical revaluation, also disguises some sharp differences between them, differences that are actually quite important and, when understood, help make clearer that the final import of the critique of morality in Williams's two most important books, *Ethics and the Limits of Philosophy* and *Shame and Necessity*, is actually (and surprisingly, given the rhetoric) quite limited, quite a bit more limited than Nietzsche's. This difference between them will then help explain some differences in their respective appeals to epic and tragic Greek poets. At least that is what I will try to argue.

There is first of all a difference of emphasis in their respective accounts of "post-Greek" styles of thought about normative matters, influenced so massively as it is by "morality." For both, the Socratic question is the unavoidable and paramount one: How ought one to live? For Nietzsche this seems to be primarily a calling of oneself to account, a self-evaluation that has a prominent psychological dimension, one especially urgent given the modern prevalence of self-deceit: What do I really want, really love? What really motivates me? What am I willing to do in the light of such aspirations? How much under the shadow of *what others want me to want* do I stand? An insistence on a kind of existential authenticity is very prominent, one possible by virtue of one's having achieved a great degree of independence from others. The process of self-fashioning is just that, an individual's *self*-fashioning. As Philippa Foot and Jürgen Habermas and Tracy Strong and Alexander Nehamas have all argued in influential commentaries, there is an unmistakable aesthetic dimension to such an attempt, one that can often look uncomfortably indifferent to the effects of one's attempts on others. (I say this seems to be what Nietzsche means because we still do not have an authoritative interpretation—or even standard disagreements about what the interpretive options are—of the very strange but obviously crucial text where the nature and limits of human dependence and independence are worked out in some way: *Thus Spoke Zarathustra*. The central drama in that story revolves around Zarathustra's changing and complex relation to his public and his disciples, or, one could say, Zarathustra's rhetorical "politics.")[10]

On the other hand, Williams takes for granted that questions about how one should live, as the central ethical questions, immediately and unavoidably raise questions about the effects of whatever I propose doing *on others*. Counting such considerations as possible reasons to do or forbear from doing something simply constitutes ethical thought, even for positions like ethical egoism.[11] No question about how one ought to live can get very far without conceding that any human life must be a social existence and so that at some significant level the question of how I ought to live is inseparable from the question of how *we* ought to live, in what ways we are bound to each other and how we ought to acknowledge this fact.[12] So he states clearly this difference from Nietzsche at the beginning of *Shame and Necessity*, claiming it a great limitation of Nietzsche's thought that "he did not move to any view that offered a coherent politics"[13] and just thereby his relevance for contemporary societies is limited.

And there are other differences even more important. Williams has essentially two main complaints against the morality institution, two problems he wants to use Greek literature to counter. The first concerns its model of moral agency and human responsibility. That is, morality tries to *limit* human responsibility, by which Williams mostly means culpability, to what is done *intentionally*, and the strictness of this limitation comes with a correspondingly harsh emphasis on a kind of absolute blame as the appropriate reactive attitude. (If the individual is responsible at all only because he could always have done otherwise, then he and he alone, as a distinct individual causing a unique set of bodily movements, is *absolutely* responsible.) Accordingly, the proper mode of agent regret is guilt, a kind of self-punishment that is potentially unending, it being forever unclear when any such self-punishing attitude is "enough."

10. See the discussion in my introduction to *Thus Spoke Zarathustra*.

11. Williams, *Ethics and the Limits of Philosophy*, 12–13.

12. See Williams's extensive defense of the appropriateness of a concern with shame in ethical matters, or of a concern with the opinions of others (*Shame and Necessity*, 82 ff.). Also relevant: his interesting speculation about book 2 of Plato's *Republic* and his suspicion that the man described there, so well known for injustice but believing himself to be just, might very well be a "deluded crank" (99).

13. Ibid., 10.

Williams's genealogy of such a moral self-understanding is interestingly different from Nietzsche's. For Nietzsche, it is understandable that those suffering under near-complete domination by others—Jews and later Christians under the power of Roman masters, for example—would devise a framework under which the masters' egoism was intentional, caused by those masters alone, and which could have been otherwise but for their selfish decisions, and so was wholly attributable to them, blamable, just as the slaves' own failure to revolt was likewise a decision, an intentional indifference to suffering in this world for the sake of heavenly reward and moral rectitude. This also involves for Nietzsche a pathetic self-inflation of the volitional powers of the individual, all as a compensatory strategy for really being of such weak or slavish character or nature.

Williams, however, in an analysis that involves some of his most important ideas, notes that while the effect of the adoption of the moral notion of responsibility can seem like the self-inflation described by Nietzsche (Williams sounds this note whenever he is criticizing the morality system's stress on the voluntary, its insistence that I am bound only by what I bind myself to),[14] it is actually a way of greatly *limiting* the responsibility of the agent, or *protecting* the agent's self-image from the effects of chance or luck. If I am responsible for what I intentionally do, then I am *only* responsible for what I *intentionally* do, and not for what I bring about but unintentionally. The harm I inadvertently do (except in cases like negligence) has nothing to do with me, and I may, in effect, walk away "untainted" by such ill effects. Accordingly, I can profess bewilderment at what Oedipus puts himself through, all that suffering. He didn't intentionally kill his father, after all, but the haughty stranger on the road to Locris. For Williams, if we try to understand why we do *not* react with such bewilderment to Oedipus (or to Agamemnon or to Ajax) but rather with understanding and sympathy, we will begin to understand that what we think we think about the burden of moral luck is not actually what we think.

The moral picture of agency also involves a sweeping denigration of any self-interested or desire-based human motives (at least it does according to Williams), in favor of a rationalistic criterion, one that adopts a universal point of view. This is Williams's second major concern, what he calls

14. This is a thesis Williams wants to reject, holding instead that the social roles we simply happen to occupy (like son or brother or American) can provide reasons for our actions without our having "chosen" such roles.

morality's insistence on, aspiration for, motivational "purity."[15] Since Williams famously argued that there could only be "internal reasons" for action, considerations related to my "motivational set," such as a standard for worthiness in acting was a mere fantasy, and conceding that did not at all mean that, therefore, all human action was basely self-regarding, outside anything that could be called "the ethical."

Nietzsche also had such a concern, but his worry about morality's picture of agency is much more radical than Williams's, and that will lead us to the real substance of their differences and from there to differences in their treatment of the Greeks. But it is also relevant to note first that Nietzsche also had far more substantive concerns with the morality institution than Williams. While the agreement just noted explains their common suspicions about individual responsibility and about asceticism and self-denial, one never finds in Williams Nietzsche's unremitting denigration of the actual Christian virtues and their secular counterparts: humility, pity, brotherly love, forgiveness of enemies, peaceableness, charity, tolerance, gratitude, benevolence, altruism, selflessness. All such traits are for Nietzsche expressive of a slavish cast of mind, and all make the achievement of anything truly worthwhile much less likely. Most importantly, Nietzsche's criticisms culminate in what he thinks all such character defects ultimately require: an egalitarianism that is not merely political (although Nietzsche certainly expressed himself clearly about that political dimension) but that supports the notion of the absolute moral equality or moral worth of every individual just as such. Williams, on the other hand, was clearly some version of an egalitarian liberal democrat. ("Some version" because his preference was not for a liberalism of rights or a liberalism of self-realization but what he called a "liberalism of skepticism and fear.")[16]

## III

I said before that what Williams wanted out of his contrast between Greek literature and the morality system (and sometimes between Greek literature and philosophical theory itself) was limited, or at least much more limited than Nietzsche's contrast. What I meant, aside from the fact that

15. Williams, *Ethics and the Limits of Philosophy*, 55.

16. As in his collection *In the Beginning Was the Deed*. See my discussion in Pippin, review of *In the Beginning Was the Deed*, by Bernard Williams.

Williams was an egalitarian liberal democrat, was this. Williams thinks there would be something inhumanly cold about an indifference to the effects of what I did, even if I did not act intentionally, and so, he argues, Greek literature can help us see something that we have been using the morality system to try to forget: that we bear the burden of what we have done and its consequences, even if we did not act intentionally. Morality cannot shield us from the burdens of moral luck. Oedipus is of course the prominent example. But Williams clearly does not think Oedipus is to be held accountable *in the same way* as a man who meant to kill his father and so intentionally killed his father. (Oedipus certainly does not think so, and his last long speech in *Oedipus at Colonus* would suggest that the phrase Williams likes—"I suffered those deeds more than I did them"—could be interpreted to mean "I simply suffered them, I *did not do* them, and what suffering I bear because of them, all of it, is a great cosmic injustice.") The phrase that sums up Williams's whole position is "We know that in the story of one's life there is an authority exercised by what one has done, and not merely by what one has intentionally done."[17] But this "authority" is *not* the authority of what one has intentionally done, and the mark of the difference is what response others are entitled to have. In the nonintentional case, blame by others is not appropriate, for example, and the audience certainly does not react as they would if they had seen a parricide. Here is Williams's formulation.

> But one thing it [tragedy] expresses is that the significance of someone's life and its relation to society may be such that someone needs to recognize and express his responsibility for actions when no one else would have the right to make a claim for damages, or be in a position to.[18]

But if this is so, then Williams must be using the term "responsibility" ambiguously, in one sense for intentional actions and in another sense for unintentional. One commentator has suggested we distinguish simple "accountability" from "culpability," and that is a good suggestion.[19] But if *this* is so, then no great frontal assault on the model of agency in the morality system is being mounted. Its central link between the intentional and the fully culpable is maintained, not challenged, by Williams, and a kind of qualification

17. Williams, *Shame and Necessity*, 69.
18. Ibid., 74.
19. Witt, "Tragic Error and Agent Responsibility."

or footnote is added: unintentional effects nonetheless can hugely alter a life, and their burden must be borne (that is, regret is appropriate), even if not in the way blameworthy actions and results must be borne. If we are able to show that an agent's ignorance was culpable or the product of reckless indifference, then we are able to qualify the notion again, distinguish strict unintentionality from a culpable form, and again preserve the central intuition. Williams is quite right to show that all these distinctions and an appreciation of their importance are alive and well in epic and tragic poetry, contra the progressivists, but the philosophical payoff is not high.

It is a little higher with Williams's attack on the notions of unconditionality, obligation, the denigration of the role of desire in action, and the strict link between purity of motivation and praiseworthiness. His neo-Humean account is made at great length and with much subtlety in *Ethics and the Limits of Philosophy*. But a major element of the critique—the denial that obligations are always and everywhere all-trumping considerations in ethical deliberation—is not an argument that relies on any deep alteration in the underlying issue at stake in Williams's attack: the right way to understand the connection between an agent and her deed, what she must bear, what she owes, from having acted, rather than because of what happened to her. Moreover, a good deal of what morality wants to encourage and what criticize is preserved in Williams's own voice, something Stephen Darwall pointed out.

> Williams himself believes we should recognize obligations (he refuses to call them "moral") and correlative rights that one "cannot ignore without blame." Like almost any moralist, he says that obligation "is grounded in the basic issue of what people should be able to rely on." And he includes under this rubric the traditional negative obligations and obligations to aid when the need is "immediate." How does this differ in substance from the status that moral obligations are ordinarily thought to have?[20]

So Williams does not deny that one is obligated to do what one promised to do, and he is obviously willing to countenance some universal absolute proscriptions (it is never permissible to torture children for one's amusement). He wants only to abandon appeals to strict unconditionality, to deny that all

20. Darwall, "Abolishing Morality," 82. This passage is quoted in a valuable article by Clark, "On the Rejection of Morality," 114.

obligations derive from higher obligations, and that only another obligation can override an obligation. But given that the Kantian metaphysics needed to support these claims is worth discarding anyway, again the payoff for our understanding of morality and agency (as opposed to seeing what is wrong with Kant or Hare or Smart) is not high.

## IV

This is the context in which I would like to discuss the central question raised above. That question was how to understand the relation between an agent and her deeds, and therewith how to hold such an agent "to account" for what she has done. We have already seen that, compared with Nietzsche, Williams's embrace of " 'the tragic culture of the Greeks' versus Christian morality" is quite limited in scope, not terribly substantive, consistent with a liberal egalitarianism, and concerned mostly with how we should understand the burden of unintended consequences. In *Ethics and the Limits of Philosophy*, he prosecutes his case mostly against the arguments of several philosophers, as if these arguments amounted to something like the "essence" of the morality institution. In *Shame and Necessity*, he deals mostly with the "progressivists," as if refuting them with his sensitive and often brilliant interpretations of Greek texts would clear the air and allow us to see something close to the fact that Christianity is mostly "the longest and most painful route from paganism back to paganism."[21] The question for Williams now is whether he is right that, in effect, we can "see" in epic and tragic poetry *everything* we need to do justice to relatively unproblematic intuitions about this relation. I don't think we can; I think Nietzsche knew that too, and that this is related to some of the differences between Nietzsche and Williams.

The first thing to note is that Williams's approach to this issue is naturalist and broadly compatibilist but not very ambitious metaphysically. He is happy to admit that human beings are "metaphysically free," but he insists "this news is less exciting than it might sound."[22] His full formulation of the issue is the following.

21. Williams, *Shame and Necessity*, 12. This is a variation of the well-known Polish joke that communism is the longest road from capitalism back to capitalism. Williams says, of course, that this is *not* what he is saying about Christianity, but he is clearly quite taken with the thought. I think it fair to say that it is what he is *tempted* to say.

22. Ibid., 152.

> Human beings are metaphysically free in the negative sense that there is nothing in the structure of the universe that denies their power to intend, to decide, to act, indeed to take and receive responsibility in the fundamental and intelligible sense that we found . . . already in Homer.[23]

He goes on to say that "the real obstacles to our freedom . . . are not metaphysical but psychological, social, and political."[24] Despite the recent flurry of attention to the putative metaphysical underpinnings of Nietzsche's project, I think that this is basically a Nietzschean thought too, with the emphasis on the "psychological" limits to freedom.

The only notion of a causal relation between agent and deeds that Williams thinks he needs (rightly, I believe) is what we might call a forensic notion of causality; the relation relevant to the law, for example. Assigning legal responsibility does not require metaphysics. When the law seeks to determine "Who *did* it?" they don't mean to ask whether a noumenal subject or neurological processes or the closed set of the physical events in the history of the universe should be said to have ultimately caused the movement. They want to know whether it was the butler or the mistress who shot Jones, and they need to establish that whoever did it was not coerced or crazy, and did not mistakenly shoot Jones, thinking he was an intruder. All the deliberative faculties required for such a forensic notion are fully on view in Greek literature, Williams shows, as is the distinction between intentional and unintentional (as in the case of Telemachus at the end of the *Odyssey,* a case Williams dwells on to make this point). But this is a very standard picture of a singular agent with the mental capacity to reflect before acting, deliberate, form intentions, and bring about bodily movements.

Nietzsche's picture is quite different, and the difference indicates how much farther away from the so-called Christian picture he wants us to be, compared to Williams. The canonical formulation is, quite typically, couched in a figurative language that makes restatement in traditional philosophic terms risky. I will only have time to stress one salient aspect. Here is the formulation, from *On the Genealogy of Morality.*

> And just as the common people separate lightning from its flash, and take the latter to be a deed, something performed by a subject, which is

23. Ibid.
24. Ibid.

> called lightning, popular morality separates strength from the manifestation of strength, as though there were an indifferent substratum behind the strong person which had the freedom to manifest strength or not. But there is no such substratum; there is no "being" behind the deed, its effect and what becomes of it; the "doer" is invented as an afterthought,—the deed is everything.[25]

Williams is aware of this passage and notes correctly that despite appearances, given so much of what Nietzsche says about human actions, motivation, the kinds of creatures we have "made" ourselves into, self-deceit, and so forth, it cannot make what Williams calls the "uninviting" claim that "we never really do anything, that no events are actions."[26] But he says little about how to interpret the position positively.

What is interesting about the passage is that even though Nietzsche is denying that there is any doer or substratum-agent, *separable* from the deed, he does not say that there are only bodily movements, that there is no difference between my raising my arm and my arm going up.[27] He says instead that, in effect, the doer is *in* the deed, or, as the tradition inspired by Herder and stretching through Hegel to Wittgenstein would put it, the doer is "expressed" in the deed. Agents can ex ante formulate all sorts of intentions and commitments, even sincerely, but when it comes time to act, they find, by what they are actually willing to do, that they were in reality not committed, or not as strongly committed, to the action as they would have ex ante insisted. And Nietzsche shows no inclination to explain such occurrences by appeal to "weakness of the will." Like Williams, he thinks that such a notion of the will, as understood by Christianity—a volitional "engine" needed, distinct from the passions and the intellect, in order to explain, as in St. Paul, that "I do the very thing I hate"—is a moralized faculty, that is, one that is created in the service of some moral picture of the soul, one that would not be necessary but for these moral purposes. When we don't do what we avowed we would do, we do not weakly fail to follow through; we simply discover what we are actually committed to. This does in fact entail quite a counterintuitive claim: that we only can properly ascribe intentions to

25. Nietzsche, *On the Genealogy of Morality*, I, §13, trans. Diethe, 26.

26. Williams, "Nietzsche's Minimalist Moral Psychology," 241.

27. I argue for this interpretation in Pippin, *Nietzsche, Psychology, and First Philosophy*, chap. 4.

ourselves post hoc, after actually acting. But that is exactly what Nietzsche means by insisting that "the deed is everything," *das Thun ist alles.*

Of course, in nearly all instances, what we do properly corresponds to what we avow, but the "failed" cases reveal, for Nietzsche, something of the general picture of the soul needed. And that picture is an expressivist one (or one might say an "actualization" one, where the intention is coming to be realized, at work, in the doing), not one in which discrete mental states like intentions cause bodily movements. The picture is much more like an author or sculptor who only finds *in the attempt* to express a provisional idea what in fact the idea could be, as externalized or expressed. Such provisionality in our avowals is crucial to the picture; otherwise we would fall back into the lightning-flash or doer-deed model in another way. Ex ante intentions or ideas "then" get expressed in deeds or objects, and we would have made no progress beyond the standard picture. But as just indicated, while actions require such ex ante avowals (Nietzsche never denies this; we must be able to say what we are doing), they are always provisional, contradictable or underminable by what we are actually willing to do or say.

Ultimately this different model for action means that our whole picture of self-knowledge must be much different than the intuitively powerful one: a "turn inward" and an inner reflection in a search for true motives, a relation between a self and some sort of object, an inner self. And there are many other things to be worked out for this expressivist picture to be plausible, but there are two points of relevance to Williams that I would like to stress.

First, although he does not draw out explicitly any of the above implications from the *Genealogy* passage, it is very clear that he has some (but not all) of the same suspicions about "*akrasia*" theories, and even some of the same willingness to reject "ex ante" models of intentional action. I mean his example in the second chapter of *Shame and Necessity* about a man having an affair, who ends the affair but finds himself wavering, finding occasions still to meet the lover. Williams notes that in effect, what settles what he really intended to do is with whom he ends up. (Or: *Das Thun ist alles.*)

> But if in the end he and his wife separate, and he goes to live with his lover, it may be that those episodes will count not as akratic, but rather as intimations of what were going to prove his truly stronger reasons. It is an illusion to suppose that there had to be at the time of those episodes a particular kind of psychological event that occurred if things turned out in

> one of those ways, and not if they turned out in the other; yet *akrasia*, to the extent that it offers a psychological explanation, is supposed to explain an event. We have reason to say that *akrasia* is not so much a psychological concept as (in the broad sense) an ethical one, an element that serves to provide an ethically significant narrative.[28]

There is an implication of this way of looking at things that Williams also accepts, but having gone this far with Nietzsche, it will return us to the general question of whether we can find everything in Greek epic and tragic poetry that we need to account for this implication. The issue comes out clearest in Nietzsche's remarks on the issue so crucial to Williams's analysis in *Shame and Necessity* of agent regret and the variety of forms it can take. The passage is again from *On the Genealogy of Morality*, in the second section, paragraph 15. Nietzsche refers to a passage in Spinoza, where Spinoza is himself, having also rejected the picture of a separable "causal center of agency," wondering what to say about the "*morsus conscientiae*," the bite of conscience, or agent regret. If I, being I, could not have acted otherwise, whence such regret? Nietzsche notes that Spinoza had in effect "reinvented" this conscience and had not abandoned it.

> "The opposite of *gaudium*," he finally said to himself,—"a sadness accompanied by the recollection of the past event which turned out contrary to expectation" . . . "something has gone unexpectedly wrong here," not "I ought not to have done that."[29]

Finding out that I was not actually who I had taken myself to be, and the sadness that accompanied this, is the right way to understand such regret. Now, in the Socratic preemptive objections to what would be the Aristotelian notion of *akrasia*, Socrates also treats the deeds as the measure of what a person truly believes to be good for him, no matter what he avows. But a disconnect between the avowal and the deed is taken to be a sign of ignorance. If someone does not do what he avows to be good for him, then he does not truly believe the rejected action or end would have been good, and he obviously mistakenly pursues something else, and in this, he is simply wrong.

Given this picture, Nietzsche, though, is much less interested in figuring

28. Williams, *Shame and Necessity*, 45.

29. Nietzsche, *On the Genealogy of Morality*, II, §15, trans. Diethe, 56.

out how to hold people to account, at least as compared to Williams. Nietzsche wants to expose the "falseness" in human self-avowals and ascriptions, not so much blame them, shame them, or even justify a way to find them accountable, and his framework for correctly explaining why people actually act the way they do is so much larger than the individual agent that, apart from discussing the social institution of how we hold people to their promises and thereby train each other to hold ourselves to our promises, he is not much interested in how we assign such accountability, treats the issue always as a matter of varying practices, given various, contingent general needs at a time, and does not seek any foundation for such practices. Indeed, so little interested is he that one might say that from a Nietzschean perspective, Williams seems more interested in *expanding* the essentially Christian notion of individual responsibility, *insisting that we must also bear the burdens as individuals of what we unintentionally do*!

But the implication of the passages we have been looking at—and this is massively borne out by Nietzsche's entire critique of Christianity—is that we need a different and more complicated picture of the soul to account for what Nietzsche is after and what Williams wants to follow: the contested phenomenon of self-deceit, genuinely knowing something about oneself, but finding a way—however hard it has always been for philosophers to account for it—of "hiding" it from oneself, or in Sartre's famous image "fleeing myself," something always deeply paradoxical (I am always still there, wherever I flee to). When I find out that I am not who I took myself to be, it is not as if I discover I am something like a different person. For me to have been motivated to do what I actually did, I have to be in some sense aware of what end I am trying to accomplish, but "aware" of it in a self-deceived way. Nietzsche's whole account of Christianity is based on a claim that the motivation of Christians to be Christians is actually what he calls "ressentiment" against the powerful, not a genuine commitment to humility and charitableness. The latter may be what they tell themselves, but what they do and say (especially their depiction of the suffering of the damned, for example) reveals their true motivations, motivations that could only motivate if some intentional in-order-to structure were in place, but "self-hidden in some way." And, as noted before, Williams is certainly no skeptic about self-deceit. It is profoundly central to his own project as well. Just recall, from that florid, long passage about the end of the Christian era that I quoted earlier, that Williams's greatest aspiration or "hope" was that human beings could live *without lies* (not without insecurity, or in peace or even with justice), and he makes clear in many places, particularly in his attack on Christianity and in his last book on truthfulness, that he does not just mean the lies we tell each other, but more importantly the lies we tell ourselves. (This is particularly clear in one of Williams's finest pieces of writing, chapter 8 of *Truth and Truthfulness,* his Trillingesque account "From Sincerity to Authenticity." More on that in a moment.)

## V

The point of this brief, inadequate summary of Nietzsche's attack on conventional post-Christian models of agency was to note the centrality of self-deceit in that expressivist account, and how supremely difficult it is to avoid self-deceit. Now, an extremely interesting question, but one far too large to address here, is: Just when in the Western tradition did self-deceit become an identifiable problem? For our purposes, though, the question is a bit smaller but no less contestable: Is it a phenomenon, a way of explaining a character, an account of the structure of the soul, that one can find in the Greek literature Williams is defending? One thing one can say at least: it is not a phenomenon Williams himself ever identifies as such or even indirectly in the Greek literature he considers. In fact, there is a kind of gaping disconnect between the way he treats the historical progressivists in *Shame and Necessity,* where he writes as if he thinks *all* claims that the prephilosophical Greeks are missing some understanding of ourselves crucial to an adequate account were based on the "distortions" of the morality system, and in his last book, *Truth and Truthfulness,* where he is much friendlier to exactly that notion of something lacking, although he does not draw out any implications from this for his earlier account.

In some sense the contrast in question is routine, conventional. In Aeschylus's *Oresteia,* Orestes is faced with equally horrific alternatives—either to avenge his father's murder by murdering his mother, or not to do so and thus to directly disobey the command of Apollo—but it certainly never occurs to Orestes to question his own motives, to ask himself whether his own surface explanation of his motives is true, nor to wonder whether what he thinks he is commanded by a god to do might be his own motivated projection. It is often rightly said the classical tragedies assume a kind of necessary ignorance on the part of tragic heroes, an ignorance made all the more painful for the audience in their knowledge of what the hero cannot know, in what is intimated by the Chorus and by the inevitable prophet or soothsayer, who is never, perhaps can never be, believed. But the point at issue is that the relevant state in question is ignorance; a result of hybris or finitude or whatever, but ignorance. The contrast between Orestes and the Orestes-like Hamlet is thus profound. Hamlet is forever wondering about all of these things, and even about the status of his father's supposed "ghost." (So the Hegelian contrast between ancient and modern tragedy seems confirmed: Orestes knows what he must do and why, but those requirements are "objectively" incompatible; Hamlet's tragedy is that he is in doubt about what is actually required and especially in doubt, subjectively, about himself.) But what is surprising is that when Williams treats such issues in chapter 8 of *Truth and Truthfulness,* he admits (with a qualification, as if he realizes how important is the concession) *that such an issue could not have arisen without Christianity* and the anxiety generated by Christian morality's insistence on honesty about oneself, on the pervasiveness of self-deceit, on the threat of falseness in one's sense of one's own rectitude, and so on the necessity of a lifelong and very difficult project of self-inquiry new to the Western tradition. (Socrates's understanding of the oracle's command, "Know thyself," had little to do with Hamlet's problem, but rather with the requirement to know what it is to be a human being and so how best to live, best for anyone, anywhere and anytime.) Consider how he describes his sense of the problem of understanding the ideals of sincerity and authenticity in modernity.

> The history in question certainly has something to do with Christian traditions of self-inquiry, and it is tempting to speculate that the rise of authenticity—besides its connection with the weakening of fixed social identities . . . —was shaped by the Protestant rejection of auricular confession. The priest could absolve me on the basis of what he took to be my best efforts at sincerity, and reassure me that I had done enough. When I was alone before a silent God, it might well seem that only an absolute sincerity would do, a total confrontation with myself.[30]

Aside from an overemphasis on Protestantism (the issue in question is also a burning one for Augustine, say, or Pascal), this seems to me exactly the right intimation, that the whole notion of interiority itself and our access to our very selves had become a much different issue in the philosophy and literature of the West because of both the altered historical world ("the

30. Williams, *Truth and Truthfulness,* 301n1.

weakening of fixed social identities") and the influence of Christianity and its requirements of its adherents. Williams is right to insist on the fact that the emphasis on sincerity and authenticity, and the potential failure of attempts at both, is an "invention" that requires a historical genealogy, not a philosophical assessment. But in *Shame and Necessity,* such a sentiment is not prominent, and he uniformly treats the morality institution as something like a philosophical and hermeneutic *mistake,* one we have fortunately grown out of, and not as a response, in the way Hegel would understand, to inadequate and incomplete forms of self-understanding, inadequacies visible in tragedies like *Antigone.* And Williams treats the "progressivist" classicists by rightly attacking the shallowness of their interpretations and the philosophical crudity of their concepts of agency and reflection, but he does not note that, for all of that, they were onto *something* in their general sense that the classical understanding of the *soul's relation to itself* "lacked" something, something other than moralized and so unnecessary notions.

In his own account of the origin and fate of sincerity as an ideal in Rousseau, Williams begins with an episode, likely *the* pivotal episode, in Rousseau's *Confessions,* and it is clear from his descriptions that it is hardly an episode that could conceivably have appeared in a Homeric epic. Rousseau reports that he stole a ribbon and, when the theft was detected, immediately accused a fellow employee, Marianne, of having taken it. He is believed, and she is dismissed without a reference. Rousseau reports that he was haunted by this episode his whole life, and is clearly especially haunted by his being unable to give a clear explanation of why he did this. (Marianne had been a good friend to Jean-Jacques.) At times he tries to use a more "classical" or traditional explanation, that he was overcome by shame and fear of being found out, a way of saying in effect that he did not, in any robust sense, fully "do" the deed; something, his passions, interrupted and clouded his normal reasoning. But he is not satisfied with this and in an amazing confession tries to argue that he acted *because* of his friendship with Marianne. He had intended all along to give the ribbon to her, and for that reason her name was the first that sprang to his lips. Williams rightly calls Rousseau's bizarre appeal to his benevolence a "touching achievement of self-deception."[31]

In going on to discuss Diderot, Williams draws very wide conclusions from his analysis, and again it is striking how historicist his perspective is. He argues that Rameau in *Rameau's Nephew* could be seen as an "extreme

31. Ibid., 176.

enactment of what modern culture involves, a self-consciousness which can no longer feel unreflectively at home in its social environment."[32] And later he notes that any attempt to place such a high value on sincerity, such as Rousseau's, will lead, in our world, the new world of modern self-understanding, "inevitably . . . to self-deception."[33]

## VI

Two brief concluding remarks. First, the Hegelian sentiments of *Truth and Truthfulness* actually correspond more with the more consistently genealogical approach taken by Nietzsche when considering both the relation of the Christian self-understanding to the ancient, and the achievements and limitations of such a revolution. For example: "The history of mankind would be far too stupid a thing if it had not had the spirit of the powerless injected into it."[34] And:

> It was on the foundation of this *essentially dangerous* form of human existence, the priestly form, that man first became an *interesting animal* and that the human soul first acquired *depth* in a higher sense and became *evil*—and these are the two basic forms of man's superiority, hitherto, over other beasts.[35]

Second, there is perhaps some irony in the fact that if Williams had lived to follow through the more historical-genealogical approach—that is, what is clearly the Hegelian approach he had adopted in *Truth and Truthfulness*—and in its light had reviewed and revised *Shame and Necessity*'s language of mistakes, distortions, and evasions, in favor of his later appreciation of what is *gained* with the Christian distrust of putative self-knowledge, his results would have been considerably more Nietzschean than they already are.

32. Ibid., 190.
33. Ibid., 199.
34. Nietzsche, *On the Genealogy of Morality*, I, §7, trans. Diethe (with changes), 17.
35. Ibid., I, §6, 16.

# 8

# Heidegger on Nietzsche on Nihilism

## I

The phenomenon that both Nietzsche and Heidegger refer to as "nihilism" is often understood as a historical event, an episode in late-modern Western culture.[1] The event is taken to be a widespread collapse of confidence in what Nietzsche calls our "highest values," especially religious and moral values, at least among the educated classes in the latter half of the nineteenth century. These highest values have, according to Nietzsche, somehow "devalued themselves."[2]

Heidegger, however, in his influential series of lectures on Nietzsche in the 1930s, correctly noted that Nietzsche himself did not treat the phe-

1. Heidegger's lectures on Nietzsche were published by him in a redacted form in two volumes in 1961, which have now been reissued again in the *Gesamtausgabe*, volumes 6.1 and 6.2. I will cite the English translation first, Heidegger, *Nietzsche, Vols. 1, 2, 3 and 4*, trans. Krell, followed by references to the 1961 edition, Heidegger, *Nietzsche, Bd. I–II*. See Heidegger's summary of the original coinage and use of the term by Friedrich Jacobi, especially in his letter to Fichte where he poses as the natural contrary of Idealism what he calls Nihilism (or "Chimerism"). Heidegger, *Nietzsche, Vol. 4*, 3; *Nietzsche, Bd. 2*, 31. Heidegger goes on in this first lecture to note the uses of the word in Turgenev, Jean Paul, and Dostoevsky's forward to his Pushkin lectures in 1880.

2. Nietzsche's account is strongly and surprisingly dialectical. It was the cultivation of "truthfulness" (*Wahrhaftigkeit*) about motivation required by Christianity and Christian morality that eventually produced *too much* truthfulness about the "low" origins of the "high." Nietzsche, *The Will to Power*, trans. Kaufmann, 10; *Der Wille zur Macht*, 11.

nomenon of nihilism as a *mere* historical event.[3] The phrase "the highest values *devalue themselves*" (*die obersten Werte sich entwerten*)[4] already indicates that. Devaluation does not just happen. Heidegger elaborates:

> In Nietzsche's view nihilism is not a *Weltanschauung* that occurs at some time and place or another; it is rather the basic character of what happens in Occidental history [*Grundcharakter des Geschehens in der abendländlichen Geschichte*]. Nihilism is at work [*am Werk*] even—and especially—there where it is not advocated as doctrine or demand, there where ostensibly its opposite prevails. Nihilism means that the uppermost values devalue themselves. This means that whatever realities and laws set the standard in Christendom, in morality since Hellenistic times, and in philosophy since Plato, lose their binding force [*verbindliche Kraft*], and for Nietzsche that always means creative [*schöpferische*] force.[5]

As the passage indicates, there *is* an event (a loss of "binding force"), but it is not a contingent moment, like the moral disintegration that a plague or disaster can cause. Indeed, the "event" or the fate of Western history as a whole is itself at issue. (Clearly, the scope and ambition of this claim are mindboggling.) That sort of event character is captured in its magnitude by the famous phrase announced in *The Gay Science*, "God is dead," which Heidegger summarizes in an unusual way: "The Christian God has lost his power [*Macht*] over beings [*über das Seiende*] and over the destiny [*Bestimmung*] of man."[6] He puts it this way:

> "Christian God" also stands for the "transcendent" [*Übersinnliche*] in general in its various meanings—for "ideals" and "norms," "principles" and "rules," "ends" and "values," which are set "above" beings, in order to give

3. "The devaluation of values does not end with a gradual becoming worthless of values, like a rivulet that trickles into the sand." Heidegger, *Nietzsche, Vol. 4*, 44; Heidegger, *Nietzsche, Bd. 2*, 82.

4. Heidegger relies very heavily on the *Nachlaß* collected as *The Will to Power*. Many scholars have shown how risky this is, even how perverse (since Heidegger rarely deals in detail with Nietzsche's published works). Here he is relying on *Will to Power*, §2: "What does nihilism mean?—That the highest values devalue themselves. The aim [*Ziel*] is lacking; the answer to the 'Why?' is lacking" (Nietzsche, *The Will to Power*, trans. Kaufmann, 9, translation altered; *Der Wille zur Macht*, 10).

5. Heidegger, *Nietzsche, Vol. 1*, 26; *Nietzsche, Bd. 1*, 35.

6. Heidegger, *Nietzsche, Vol. 4*, 4, translation altered; *Nietzsche, Bd. 2*, 33.

> being as a whole a purpose, an order, and—as it is succinctly expressed—"meaning" [*Sinn*]. Nihilism is that historical process whereby the dominance of the "transcendent" becomes null and void, so that all being loses its worth and meaning. Nihilism is the history of beings [*die Geschichte des Seienden*], through which the death of the Christian God comes slowly but inexorably to light.[7]

On the other hand, Nietzsche and Heidegger do not treat the crisis of nihilism as primarily an intellectual crisis, a problem of credible belief (although it is clearly also that). There has been no devastating argument or philosophical critique that has provoked such cultural collapse. The situation is not described as analogous to a scientific crisis—for example, the result of anomalies, experimental inconsistencies, effective refutations, and arguments that generate skepticism about and finally rejection of a scientific claim. In Nietzsche's case, he often treats the phenomenon of nihilism not as a crisis of belief or will, but as some sort of pathology of human desire: either a collapse of desire altogether (in indifference or boredom, a lack of concern with what might be worth wanting), or a growing self-deceit about what it is we really desire, or a self-abasing reduction in the ambition of what is wanted. A frequent image here is of "bows" that have lost their "tension," as in, from *Zarathustra*, "Alas, the time approaches when man will no longer launch the arrow of his longing beyond the human, and the string of his bow will have forgotten how to whir,"[8] and the striking claim from *The Gay Science* that "neediness is needed [*Not ist nötig*]!"[9] That is, we now find nothing truly needful, nothing important worth wanting, worth sacrificing for.

With this in mind, I want to show two things in the following: first, that Heidegger is right in trying to understand Nietzsche in terms of his own early existential phenomenology (e.g., *Being and Time*), but, second, that he

7. Ibid.; translation altered.

8. Nietzsche, *Thus Spoke Zarathustra*, trans. Del Caro, 9, translation altered; *Also Sprach Zarathustra*, Bd. 4, 19.

9. Nietzsche, *The Gay Science*, trans. Nauckhoff, §56, 64; *Die fröhliche Wissenschaft*, Bd. 3, 418. In *On the Genealogy of Morality*, §12, in commenting on the "stunting and leveling of European man," he again suggests that nihilism is some kind of affective disorder, a fatigue or failure of desire. "The sight of man now makes us tired—what is nihilism today if not that? . . . We are tired of man" (trans. Diethe, 25). In the *Nachlaß*, Nietzsche characterizes nihilism in a wide variety of ways, at one point saying that nihilism amounts to, all at once, "the repudiation of value, meaning, and desirability" (Nietzsche, *The Will to Power*, trans. Kaufmann, 7; *Der Wille zur Macht*, 7). I am grateful to Ken Gemes for some clarifying correspondence about this issue.

goes wrong when, after the 1936 lectures and especially after 1940, he turns against Nietzsche and his own position when he accuses Nietzsche (and so his early thought) of still being part of the Western metaphysical tradition (a tradition that inevitably leads to nihilism). Said another way, this later charge misses something crucial and quite radical about Nietzsche, when Heidegger attributes to Nietzsche a "metaphysics" of "the will to power."[10]

## II

In Heidegger's case, there are already indications of a similar understanding of the nihilism diagnosis when he says that the highest values have lost their "binding force," and that being loses worth and "*meaning*." In Heidegger and in general, meaningfulness (in the sense of what he calls *Bedeutsamkeit*) is not sustained by beliefs about what is or should be meaningful. (Meaning, in a sense we need to consider more closely, is either found, or present, or experienced, or not.) A crisis in "meaning" is thus relatively independent of, deeper than, and presupposed by arguments, evidence, and so forth. A practice that had made sense, an institution that had made sense, comes to seem senseless, something that can happen without a critique or an attack. And Heidegger had already said something striking about Nietzsche on nihilism that is relevant to this point. It slides by unremarked on, but it is immediately paradoxical. He had claimed that, far from being a matter of what can be believed or not, "Nihilism is at work even—and especially—there where it is not advocated as doctrine or demand, there where ostensibly its opposite prevails." Nihilism is thus the sort of phenomenon that can appear, can be "at work," even if unnoticed. But how can people suffer *unknowingly* from the devaluation of their highest values? What could "at work" mean?

Even more paradoxically, Heidegger notes that nihilism is at work "where ostensibly its *opposite* prevails." Intense, fervent *dedication to a purported highest value* (not the failure of desire but some sort of pathological intensification) must "now," after "the death of God," *also* count as nihilism

10. Sluga, "Heidegger's Nietzsche," dates Heidegger's turn against his own position, and therewith against Nietzsche, or toward a more critical evaluation of Nietzsche, from his *Introduction to Metaphysics* (1935) and from his writing "On the Origin of the Work of Art" (1935–37), 105–7. Sluga's article is indispensable in understanding the various factors, persons, and events that influenced Heidegger's shifting emphases in the lectures. I am concentrating here on the nihilism issue, but there are many other subjects at issue between them, helpfully noted and glossed by Sluga.

at work. It might be that in many situations, class allegiance, say, becomes profoundly more important, perhaps fanatically so, just because of a growing suspicion of its irrelevance.[11] Some sort of self-deceit and overcompensation is at work.[12] But again, believing fervently in something that has no real ground of belief, or in a situation where more and more people are unable to see such a ground, does not look like any breakdown in "meaning." Where is the "nihilism at work"?

However paradoxically put, though, Heidegger is responding to Nietzsche's own formulations. When Nietzsche "stages" the announcement that "God is dead" in *The Gay Science,* presenting a minidrama of a crazy man and his auditors, the response that the crazy man, *der tolle Mensch,* receives to his first announcement, that he seeks God, is mockery and indifference, not anxiety or despair or reassertions of God's existence or some other basis for transcendent value (something objectively valuable, in itself, not because value has been conferred on it). Regarding the search for God, they say:

> Has he [God] got lost? asked one. Did he lose his way like a child? asked another. Or is he hiding? Is he afraid of us? Has he gone on a voyage? emigrated?—Thus they yelled and laughed.[13]

The proclamation that God is dead is met with silence. It is not as if no one believes the madman; they just don't care.

Moreover, Zarathustra's audience in the Prologue to *Thus Spoke Zarathustra* is mocking and indifferent as well, as if the most prominent and disturbing manifestation of nihilism is the absence of any manifestation, and instead such large-scale indifference and self-satisfaction.[14] Throughout *Thus Spoke Zarathustra,* those "down below" whom Zarathustra comes to enlighten are "the last men," potentially "last" because in their stupefied self-satisfaction they barely possess and are likely to lose what Zarathustra

11. See, for example, Kazuo Ishiguro, *The Remains of the Day.*

12. The question of reconciling Nietzsche's frequent claims about the necessity of illusion with his praise of an "intellectual conscience" and his insistence on exposing self-deceit is a complicated issue. See Pippin, *Nietzsche, Psychology, and First Philosophy,* chap. 5, "The Psychological Problem of Self-Deception."

13. Nietzsche, *The Gay Science,* trans. Nauckhoff, §125, 119; *Die fröhliche Wissenschaft,* 480–81.

14. See the account of "pale atheists" in Nietzsche, *On the Genealogy of Morality,* III, §24, trans. Diethe, 110–113.

treats as the distinctive human capacity, esteeming (*schätzen*), or valuing, or at least the ability to value the highest values.

Now, it is true that this may all be because of some sort of historical time delay. This delay may be the reason why the devaluation of the highest values does not *yet* "show up" in the everyday world. The madman puts it this way:

> "I have come too early," he said then; "my time is not yet. This tremendous event is still on its way, still wandering; it has not yet reached the ears of men. Lightning and thunder require time; the light of the stars requires time; deeds, though done, still require time to be seen and heard. This deed is still more distant from them than most distant stars—and yet they have done it themselves."[15]

But Nietzsche here poses his own (and largely unremarked on) paradox: if the time lag explanation were true, how could the crazy man emphasize that the death of God is a "deed," and *we all have done it*? The deed may be "more distant than most distant stars," but "*they have done it themselves*." (The problem of self-deceit arises again.) More generally, what could it mean to say that "the highest values *have devalued themselves*"? It would seem to amount to a claim that some far-seeing individuals—the madman, Zarathustra, Nietzsche himself—have seen that commitment to such values, at least by their lights, is not credible or is in some way now unavailable (in what they demand of us, we find the demand to be empty, baseless), and that it is inevitable that eventually nearly everyone else will realize this too. But Nietzsche does not credit such higher types with such a discovery. The highest values have devalued themselves. Some internal dynamic in the playing out of the implications of Christian morality, for example, made it unavoidable that such values would lose their "binding" or "creative" force. (Nietzsche seems to mean, for example, his account of how the Christian emphasis on honesty about one's motives would eventually have to reveal that in the significant cases these motives are, by Christian lights, base.) They were "our values," all of us, and they have become unavailable, however much we all seek to flee in self-deceit from this event.

15. Nietzsche, *The Gay Science*, trans. Nauckhoff, §125, 120; *Die fröhliche Wissenschaft*, 481–82.

Further, the implication of Nietzsche's formulations is not that all value has devalued itself; only the highest values, and that is an important qualification. After all, *action as such* is unintelligible without value *of some sort*. The bodily movements that make up action count as actions only if intentional. Action necessarily *is* an agent's consciousness of action. An action is not an event that goes on whether we are conscious of it or not. In such a case, there might be bodily movements, but if I am not conscious of doing it, it is not a doing. There would not be action. And since one has practical knowledge of one's acting not by observation or inference, but by *being* the agent who acts, just by being conscious of acting, one unavoidably is conscious of why, why it is at least better to do this (at least better for me) than to do nothing or to do something else. To be subject to this "why" question is to be implicated in some commitment to value, the value "behind" this action, here and now. This is partly why agents can still act intelligibly, even if no part of any answer they might give themselves to such a "why" question has anything to do with "highest values," just "lower values." *That* might be a manifestation of nihilism, that we no longer "launch the arrow of . . . longing beyond the human" (where "beyond the human" refers to something "higher" than the "human" or prosaic bourgeois values we find defended by Hobbes, Locke, Hume, Mill, Rawls, and so forth). That is, the fact that many do not interpret this *as* a great loss or lack, that they are not affected by the fact that where there once were "the highest values" there is now, for them, "nothing," is such a reduction in aspiration that it counts as something worse than mere nihilism: the *embrace* of such nihilism. One can sincerely seek some set of valued goals without realizing what one has "settled for," and so one can unknowingly have accepted the devaluation of the highest values, can in that sense be an unwitting nihilist.

These are the issues I would like to explore further. They all need to be understood within some interpretation of what might be at stake in Nietzsche's diagnosis of nihilism, and Heidegger's version of that diagnosis. With such a simplified summary, we seem left according to Heidegger and Heidegger's Nietzsche (certainly a recognizable Nietzsche) with a situation in which a self-aware elite has at least come to "experience" the self-devaluation of the highest values (even if they have not caused it), although the nature of that experience is not clear. It is not a mere contingent event, something that merely happens to them. It is not an intellectual crisis, some philosophical insufficiency in the ground of some valuation. It is something like a failure of desire, but a failure also paradoxically manifest in an intensification of desire and in a redirection of its direction, "lower."

## III

As indicated earlier, aspects of Heidegger's approach to these issues help a great deal to clarify Nietzsche's understanding of and diagnosis of nihilism. Yet when Heidegger in effect "turns on" Nietzsche (something more and more prominent as the lectures unfold from 1936 on), that is, when he accuses him of nihilism, or links him to a subjectivistic metaphysics and so implicates him in the modern technological "enframing" of the question of the meaning of Being, he both distorts Nietzsche and misses an opportunity to make better use of Nietzsche's diagnosis in addressing the central points at issue. This is famously connected to Heidegger's "turning on" his own position in the late 1920s, his phenomenological account of *Being and Time*. I think that Heidegger's misreading of Nietzsche is connected to his misunderstanding of those issues, but I cannot make that case here. We will have to be content with a snapshot of Heidegger's development on the question of the meaning of Being as it surfaces in his Nietzsche interpretation in his six lecture courses on Nietzsche.

The lectures cover an extraordinarily large amount of material, and there is no space to discuss some of the most interesting questions, but for our purposes we need to examine three issues. The first has already been signaled by the passage cited above from the 1940 lecture on European nihilism.

> "Christian God" also stands for the "transcendent" [*Übersinnliche*] in general in its various meanings—for "ideals" and "norms," "principles" and "rules," "ends" and "values," which are set "above" beings, in order to give being as a whole a purpose, an order, and—as it is succinctly expressed—"meaning" [. . . *einen Sinn zu geben*].[16]

The fact that Heidegger summarizes the highest values that he lists as, most comprehensively, what "*gives meaning*" introduces the fundamental ques-

16. Heidegger, *Nietzsche, Vol. 4*, 4, translation altered; *Nietzsche, Bd. 2*, 33. In the first, more diagnostic part of the *Nachlaß* organized as *The Will to Power*, Nietzsche frequently links nihilism to meaning and the loss of meaning, as in §12A, §25, §36, and §55.

tion of his entire career, since the lectures make clear that he wants to interpret Nietzsche as addressing (if incompletely) the most fundamental question of meaning, "the meaning of Being." (Although Heidegger will turn against his own formulations about the meaning of Being, I note that he is still using such formulations as late as 1940.) We will then need to understand, second, what Heidegger means by the claim that for Nietzsche the meaning of Being is "the will to power" and, third, why Heidegger thinks that *that* claim reveals Nietzsche's implication in the metaphysical tradition whose culmination (*Vollendung*) is the very nihilism at issue for both of them, and the stance of predatory subjectivity now unleashed on the earth.

The first point to be made is already controversial, the claim that Heidegger's famous *Seinsfrage*, question of Being, is a *meaning question*, a question about the meaning of being. But in the lectures he leaves little doubt that this is the fundamental question. Consider this dispositive passage from the first lectures in 1936–37, "The Will to Power as Art." It addresses two of the questions just posed.

> The expression "will to power" designates the basic character of beings; any being which is, insofar as it is, is will to power. The expression stipulates the character that beings have as beings. But that is not at all an answer to the first question of philosophy, its proper question; rather, it answers only the final preliminary question. For anyone who at the end of Western philosophy can and must still question philosophically, the decisive question is no longer merely "What basic character do beings manifest?" or "How may the Being of beings be characterized?" but "What is this 'Being' itself?" The decisive question is that of "the meaning of Being" [*Es ist die Frage nach dem Sinn des Seins*], not merely that of the Being of beings. "Meaning" [*Sinn*] is thereby clearly delineated conceptually as that from which and on the grounds of which Being in general can become manifest as such and can come into truth.[17]

Although Heidegger had already, by 1929, begun to move away from the phenomenological approach of *Being and Time* (1927), and had pretty much rejected it by 1933, this sort of formulation about meaning as the central issue does not change. A typical formulation from *Being and Time*:

17. Heidegger, *Nietzsche, Vol. 1*, 18; *Nietzsche, Bd. 1*, 26.

> Basically all ontology . . . remains blind and perverted from its ownmost aim, if it has not already first clarified the meaning of Being and conceived this clarification as its fundamental task.[18]

In that work Heidegger had proposed, as a preliminary way into the meaning of Being *simpliciter*, a phenomenological investigation of ordinary meaningfulness in our worldly dealings and in our self-relation, where "phenomenological" roughly means what it is like for us, for a human being—which Heidegger calls "*Dasein*"—to be out and about "understandingly" in the everyday world. "Meaningfulness" in that sense just means the unproblematic, immediate, unthematic intelligibility of what we deal with in our ongoing tasks and projects. This kind of intelligibility is just "familiarity," of the unreflective sort. Heidegger's main opponent in such an account is a kind of representationalism, which holds that such familiarity is a result of the having of representations or beliefs about objects, representations that bestow meaning by our conscious attentiveness to what things are for, how they are used, what successful use consists in, and so forth. This view is, Heidegger claims, phenomenologically false and ultimately creates an unnecessary and unsolvable skepticism about the relation between representations and the world. By contrast, meaningfulness, familiarity, the unproblematic intelligibility of entities in the world, is a matter of our engaged, unthematic, skillful coping; of competence or know-how, correctly using the hammer, not "following" a representation of how it is to be used. *Dasein* is always already "in-the-world," does not originally or primordially represent objects in the world as objects of conscious intending.

*Dasein*'s intelligibility to itself is a different matter, but also not a matter of representation. *Dasein* is the only being for whom the meaning of its being is "at issue." Wolves don't have to determine what it means to be a wolf; they just are wolves. But the meaning of the being of *Dasein* is "to be," possibility, a distinct modality of being Heidegger calls "existence." (There is no fact of the matter or of nature that will settle what it is to be *Dasein*, always uniquely my *Dasein*. At his most extreme in making this point, Heidegger claims that *Dasein* is the "null basis of a nullity.")[19] This opens onto quite a complicated set of issues, but the problem in this context is the Heideggerian "meaning of meaning," what we need to understand that claim

18. Heidegger, *Being and Time*, trans. Macquarrie and Robinson, 31; *Sein und Zeit*, 11.

19. Heidegger, *Being and Time*, trans. Macquarrie and Robinson, 331; *Sein und Zeit*, 285.

about the meaning of Being in the Nietzsche lecture. A passage from *Being and Time* gives us a hint.

> But in significance itself [*Bedeutsamkeit*], with which *Dasein* is always familiar, there lurks the ontological condition which makes it possible for *Dasein*, as something which understands and interprets, to disclose such things as "significations"; upon these, in turn, is founded the Being of words and of language.[20]

The hint in the passage is that Heidegger is aware that the question of the meaning of Being, the meaning of *Dasein*'s being, or the meaning of encountered beings, has a dual significance. There is "*Bedeutsamkeit*," and there is "the Being of words and language," and the claim is that the possibility of the latter is founded on the former. There is, that is, the linguistic notion of meaning, and the question is "What does the word 'Being' or the concept of Being mean, signify?" Or "What do we mean by '*Dasein*'?" When the question is "Do you understand what a hammer is?" it could be taken to mean "Do you understand what the word 'hammer' means?" But there is also a much broader notion of meaning, something like the "meaningfulness" that Heidegger designates as *Bedeutsamkeit*, translated above by "significance." Questions about meaning in this sense would be "What did it mean that she didn't show up for Thanksgiving?" or "What is the meaning of this!?" or a claim like "I didn't understand the meaning of that activity." Or "After that, I found going to church meaningless." This practical sense often refers to the goal or very "point" of some saying or doing. In this sense, understanding what objects around me mean is understanding how they fit into some structure of significance. They have a point within some more general purpose or end, itself intelligible in the light of higher-order goals. And so I understand the meaning of the lectern, the classroom, the building, the university, my way to school, by being able to navigate unproblematically, and even for the most part unthinkingly, in such a familiar world. If, instead of a lectern, I one day stepped up to a child's wading pool in the front of the class, I would not understand what its presence would mean, what to do.

As noted, in the quotation above Heidegger says that the Being of words and language, what it is *to be* signifying language, significant speech,

20. Heidegger, *Being and Time*, trans. Macquarrie and Robinson, 121; *Sein und Zeit*, 87.

is "founded" on significance, meaningfulness in this practical sense, and that is a much more controversial claim. In the simplest example, the point he is making is relevant when we say in a certain context that we do not understand what someone meant by saying what she did, do not know how to respond to some speech act. The context can indicate that we do not mean that we do not understand the literal or lexical meaning of what she said; we do not understand what she meant *by* saying what she said. We might say: we cannot see what the point was of her saying that then. It is in this context that we can say that we have to understand such an issue within the broader scope of the problem of practical meaningfulness or *Bedeutsamkeit,* the structure of implicit, presupposed purposiveness that is a necessary condition for this familiarity, the primordial level of everyday significance that Heidegger is investigating. That is the context in which the notion of a "point" to any linguistic usage is relevant; or, let us say, the context of "*mattering*." Literal meaning would not be isolatable from this sort of context, goes the claim; language would be said to occur always already in a practical context like this, often not prominent (say, in science textbooks or lectures) but always presupposed (textbooks and lectures have their point), often quite prominent (in cases of confusion or misunderstanding). Everything we do, including speaking to or writing for each other, must be understood to occur in this purposive context, the context of mattering, revealing by what we do and say, and what we do not do and say, what matters and what does not, and thereby what makes sense and what does not.

Again I should stress that Heidegger would come to see, is coming to see in the pages we are considering, that this formulation about the question of Being (as a question about the meaning or intelligibility of Being) still "measures" what could be in the light of what we could find meaningful and intelligible. That is still implicated in the subjectivity and metaphysics that must terminate in nihilism. (The Greek maxim that begins philosophy, "To be is to be intelligible," is also its original sin.) And he will strive into ever more unusual formulations (*Gelassenheit,* a *Denken* that is a *Danken,* and so forth) to avoid such commitments. But his approach to Nietzsche in the thirties is still profitably understood in terms of language typical of the early, or perhaps the late-early, Heidegger.

So *Dasein*'s primary mode of intelligibly being-in-the-world is not representational or spectatorial, observational, but always practical, intelligible in terms of what has come to matter, in some hierarchy of significances. Accordingly, Heidegger insists, *Dasein*'s primary relation to the world in its intelligibility, in our understanding involvement, is not "knowledge." It is rather determined by what Heidegger says is the very "being" of *Dasein*, what he calls "care," *Sorge*, which we might also translate as "mattering." Things and persons are intelligible, can be said to make familiar sense, in the light of what has come to matter or not. This entails that that basic relation to the world, always a matter of mattering, becomes a problem of knowledge only when this engaged involvement breaks down in some way, requires attention to what he calls the merely "present-at-hand" qualities of the objects. Here is a summary:

> Proximally, this Being-already-alongside is not just a fixed staring at something that is purely present-at-hand. Being-in-the-world, as concern, is fascinated by the world with which it is concerned. If knowing is to be possible as a way of determining the nature of the present-at-hand by observing it, then there must first be a deficiency in our having-to-do with the world concernfully.[21]

If the question of the meaning of *Dasein's* being can be understood this way—*Dasein*'s intelligibility to itself is a matter of its "care," what is significant, what matters—then it might be possible to understand what Heidegger might mean by the question of *the meaning of Being* itself in a similar way. The question does not mean "What is there?" (The answer to that, as has been observed, is easy: everything.) It is not "What do we mean when we say that anything exists?" As just indicated, such an abstract noun would not exclude anything; and for that reason, according to Aristotle, there is no highest common genus. It does not mean "Why is there something rather than nothing?" That presupposes we already know "what it means" for something to exist. But if we follow this practical sense of "means," then we can roughly say that the question concerns the significance of there being anything at all, a horizon of the general significance of anything at all—the way in which we understand how the meaning of our own being "fits in" with there being anything at all—always already presupposed and taken for granted in our dealings with entities. It is something like the most comprehensive orientation in anything being able to matter; it is where our nested series of "in-order-to's" and "for-the-sake-of which's" ultimately point, even if obscurely and unthematically.

21. Heidegger, *Being and Time*, trans. Macquarrie and Robinson, 88; *Sein und Zeit*, 61.

At this point we go a long way toward understanding the deeper point in Heidegger's whole project if we simply note, with this material before us, that what has come to "matter" to us is not in any significant sense ever "up to us." There may well be many things that we wish did not matter to us, that we know in some sense are insignificant. But they *do* matter. We may never avow such concerns and never act on them, but they *have* come to matter; they are what matters to us despite ourselves. We also can suspect that what we avow and do may actually matter to us for reasons other than the reasoned-out reasons we think we are acting on. And there may be many activities or ideals or goals that we convince ourselves ought to matter to us a great deal, and we may act to achieve some, but we can do so without such issues ever really mattering to us. (Something else is mattering, perhaps, like our reputation.) This is something Heidegger calls the "thrownness" of human existence (*Geworfenheit*), and it is a point of perhaps the deepest affinity with Nietzsche's own skepticism about our ordinary sense of the scope of conscious control and direction. But since we cannot simply decide what matters on the basis of some reflection on what ought to matter, how do we explain, at the individual or social or even civilizational level, what has come to matter? With this in mind, we can appreciate the radicality of Heidegger's basic early claim, the innovation responsible for the tremendous influence of *Being and Time* over the rest of the century. Such practical teleology is not a specific domain of intelligibility (just the way things "fall into" their unthematic and familiar places as we carry out a task, or don't and obtrude as mere "present-at-hand" objects). That sort of familiarity and that aspect of our being-in-the-world is, rather, "fundamental," is the horizon for *all* possible meaningfulness, in the original, prediscursive, unthematized sense suggested by Heidegger. *Everything* else, representational sense, for example, is derivative. (To say everything at once, this is one way, a pretty good way, of understanding "psychology," as Nietzsche understands it, to be "first philosophy.")

If we understand Nietzsche's diagnosis of nihilism in these terms, then we can see that his view is in practice very like what the early Heidegger was suggesting: an *interpretive* account of basic mattering, where such mattering is itself treated as condition of sense, significance, meaning. This would be Nietzsche's "interrogation of the meaning of Being." He calls these sources of mattering "highest values," but that can misleadingly suggest that individuals bestow value in intentional acts of valuation. His practice suggests rather that what actually matters in a practice or institution is often hidden, requiring the same sort of interpretive work to get at that is called for in understanding complex political struggles or ambitious novels or plays. (The value language is as misleading as inferring from his skepticism about conscious determination of these values that they are determined by forces like "drives" or "instincts" "behind our backs." The way "what really matters" in doing something requires interpretive work need not be the opening to an appeal to causal accounts, about which Nietzsche expresses great skepticism. They can be hidden, unavailable, and determinative even if still "inside" the psychological or existential.) So, for example, according to Nietzsche, after Socrates (and all that he embodies and represents), "knowing the truth" had come very much to matter—matter too much for our own good, Nietzsche wants to say; too much was expected of it. It mattered *above all*, as if nothing could matter unless we could know why it ought to matter, as if this were how anything could really matter. With the impossibility of ever providing such grounds, mattering looked as contingent and arbitrary as taste. Given the Christian and Platonic expectations, that result had to look like nihilism.

## IV

At least this is what Nietzsche would look like from the perspective established by Heidegger around the time of *Being and Time*. But it is at this point that Heidegger's deepening criticism of Nietzsche (and actually of his own position in *Being and Time*)[22] is relevant. For Heidegger claims that Nietzsche has a sweeping "metaphysical answer" to the question of ultimate mattering, his own version of a response to the meaning-of-Being question: the "will to power." To be precise, according to Heidegger, this answer is not one that addresses his own understanding of the basic question, but it is a penultimate or preliminary answer. Nietzsche is giving a metaphysical answer, one that tries to provide the "fundamental character" of all being, what would be more properly understood as the horizon of common or shared significance established by the realization of what there basically is, and what could thereby matter. This is the kind of answer, with its impli-

22. For Heidegger's own association of *Being and Time* with the criticism he is making of Nietzsche, see Heidegger, *Nietzsche, Vol. 4*, 141; *Nietzsche, Bd. 2*, 194. The association is correct, but, I am claiming, his critique of what amounts to the perspective of the priority and autonomy of "the human experience of the human" in any question about what I am calling "mattering" is misplaced.

cations for *Bedeutsamkeit,* with which we are familiar in philosophy, and among the familiar alternatives—atoms in the void, extended and thinking substance, Berkeley's ideas, *ens creatum,* a pantheistic God—Nietzsche's answer in this list is supposed to be: the will to power.

Heidegger does not make the mistake of thinking that Nietzsche is trying to say that all of being should be understood as in some sort of struggle for supremacy, dominance, or survival. His interpretation in the lectures of the will to power is as metaphysical as he says it is. It is an account of ceaseless, purposeless becoming. Nothing can be said to be stable or secure; to be resistant, one could say, to the unlimited "power" of change, chance, contingency. *That* power is all powerful; it is the will to power as the "basic character of Being." According to Heidegger, Nietzsche takes his bearings from such a "metaphysics," and on its basis proposes a "revaluation of the highest values." This is, for Heidegger, a repetition of the cardinal error of the Western philosophical tradition. Here is an example of how Heidegger gets from his metaphysical reading to his indictment.

> What is being contested is decided in advance: power itself, which requires no aims. It is aimless, just as the whole of beings is value-less. Such aimlessness pertains to the metaphysical essence of power. If one can speak of aim here at all, then the "aim" is the aimlessness of man's absolute dominance over the earth. The man of such dominance is the Over-man.[23]

I note that Heidegger does not help us understand why he thinks this view of "aimlessness" would then require "human domination of the earth." It would not exclude it as a possible response, but why would it require it? But this is only the first of the problems of reading Nietzsche this way.

Here is a full statement of the criticism.

> Consequently, in spite of all his insights, he could not recognize the hidden essence of nihilism, because right from the outset, solely on the basis of valuative thought, he conceived of nihilism as a process of the devaluation of the uppermost values. Nietzsche had to conceive of nihilism that

23. Heidegger, *Nietzsche, Vol. 4,* 82; *Nietzsche, Bd. 2,* 125.

> way because in remaining on the path and within the realm of Western metaphysics, he thought it to its conclusion.[24]

Heidegger is saying: Nietzsche is captured by what he opposes. He sees that where there had been hoped-for presence and ground—nature, natural hierarchy, the ends of our life-form, God's will, our basic passions—there had turned out to be nothing stable, a chaotic void. *This void must be filled.* But for Heidegger, attempting to fill it at all, especially by some human self-assertion, is itself an expression of nihilism (a forgetting of our passivity with respect to, dependence on, what could matter, the meaning of Being). Hence Nietzsche is associated with what Heidegger regards from the thirties on as the most dangerous expression of this "nihilistic" response to nihilism.

> The securing of supreme and absolute self-development of all the capacities of mankind for absolute dominion over the entire earth is the secret goad [*geheime Stachel*] that prods modern man again and again to new resurgences, a goad that forces him into commitments that secure for him the surety of his actions and the certainty of his aims.[25]

So Nietzsche is after all charged with being still a "philosopher of subjectivity" and "representation"; he is "a Cartesian." But the *subjectum* is now simply the body, and we have not overcome nihilism.

I have been trying to suggest that this is a forced and unfounded reading of Nietzsche. Nietzsche is much better read in the terms of *Being and Time,* with the same refusal to see what he is doing as mere anthropology, or empirical psychology, concerned above all with how anything could matter (where that has to mean matter for us, even if hidden from us), and how mattering is a condition for the possibility of intelligibility. We all inherit the web of matterings, and so meanings, by the light of which we navigate the everyday world (the world that matters to us, the world of politics, friendship, romance, war, death), and Nietzsche's attention to how an ideal or practice could come to matter and cease to matter (his genealogy) does justice to both the hiddenness of such mattering and its possible disclosure.

24. Heidegger, *Being and Time,* trans. Macquarrie and Robinson, 22; *Sein und Zeit,* 54.

25. Heidegger, *Being and Time,* trans. Macquarrie and Robinson, 99; *Sein und Zeit,* 145.

Heidegger's case that Nietzsche is to be understood as a metaphysician, that his metaphysics is a will-to-power metaphysics, and that it is linked to the nihilistic implications of the entire metaphysical tradition, that he is the last metaphysician, was extraordinarily influential in the twentieth century, first on postwar French philosophy, and through those thinkers on literary theory and cultural studies. I have tried to suggest that it is a forced and tendentious reading, one that prohibits Heidegger from appreciating the irrelevance of metaphysics for a project very like the renewal of philosophy Heidegger himself attempted in *Being and Time*. Indeed, Heidegger can only build any case for all of this being based on "metaphysics" by concentrating almost exclusively on the *Nachlaß*, ignoring the published works, and forcing Nietzsche to play a role in the drama for which he is supremely unsuited. Ironically it is Heidegger's own hermeneutical framework from 1927 (which he explicitly disowns in the 1940 lecture) that is of great use in explaining Nietzsche's project.

Anyone making such claims is obviously required to extend such an interpretation and provide a reading of the notions of will to power, eternal recurrence, *amor fati*, and other terms that have come to be treated as technical terms of art in Nietzschean philosophy. (One form of such an extension is to ague that they are badly misinterpreted if understood as technical terms of art.) That cannot be done here.

A final comment. Just as a widespread forgetfulness about *Dasein*'s own being at issue for itself, an evasion of that burden, and a consoling normality in being "lost" in the world of *das Man*, the They, can help account for how this "tranquilizing" normalcy, the nonappearance of nihilism, is an instance of nihilism, the loss of meaning (*Dasein* is living as if it is not *Dasein*, a being whose being is always at issue); just as a fervent attachment to an ideal can be an instance of self-deceived desperation, a flight from a possible collapse of meaning, and so a nihilistic symptom; just as a settling for the "lower values" of tranquility, comfort, and consumption could be other signs of a self-deceived flight from oneself: Nietzsche can be viewed as in many ways, at least when compared with Heidegger of the twenties, more Heideggerian than the philosophical master of Messkirch himself. "Metaphysics" is of no importance for such an account. Or: some version of metaphysics could be of importance, but only on some understanding of the possibility of its having come to matter prior to, and so independent of any consolation in, metaphysics.

# 9

# Leo Strauss's Nietzsche

## I

In the three seminars that Strauss taught on Nietzsche, in the discussion of him in *Natural Right and History* and other published works, and in the one piece that he wrote devoted exclusively to one book by Nietzsche, the article on *Beyond Good and Evil* (*BGE*) published in the journal *Interpretation* in 1973, right before his death, Strauss treated Nietzsche as the most important political thinker since Rousseau, and as a philosopher; indeed, one of the great philosophers, to be mentioned in the same breath as Plato.[1]

Enlisting Nietzsche in the small army of great philosophers is not straightforward, especially because of the way Strauss himself placed Nietzsche historically. That is, Nietzsche is assigned a major role in "the crisis of our time," the crisis of modern natural right, as Strauss diagnoses it. In fact, Nietzsche is the beginning of the "third wave" of Strauss's three waves in that crisis. Rejecting the ancient natural-right doctrine and its Christian natural-law descendants, modern natural right in its first wave is oriented from the most powerful human passions and desires, especially the fear of sudden, violent death and the desire for commodious self-preservation, and not from the natural ends of the human life-form (the exercise of reason

1. He realizes that this assertion itself creates something like a distinct category of "political thinker," since anything like a political program based on Nietzsche's individualist orientation is impossible.

in common in pursuit of the common and individual good, happiness). In the philosophy of Locke and Hobbes, this meant a doctrine giving pride of place to rights and claims of noninterference, rather than to duties, as in antiquity.[2] The second wave is attributed to Rousseau (the first crisis) and those whom Strauss regards as his German followers, Kant and Hegel. For a variety of reasons, nature came to be understood as unavailable to serve even this limited standard (its main importance in Rousseau is its unavailability for social man),[3] reason takes the place of nature, and freedom, understood as the acknowledgment of the authority of reason, is the source of right. However, since, for Rousseau, man in his natural state is not rational, reason is acquired, and the ground is also laid for eventually viewing all the distinctly human aspects of life, including the shape that an appeal to reason might take, as the products of history. Nietzsche, in the third wave, is the first to realize the catastrophic consequences of this development. He embodies this crisis and so embodies the beginning of the crisis of nihilism. Reason, after Kant's critique and Hegel's treatment of history, comes to be seen as incapable of providing such a foundation for social and political life, and the contingency of its various forms ensures a widely accepted historical relativism. But, according to Strauss, historical relativism is deeply enervating as a social phenomenon. As a truth it is unavoidable (given the implications of the modern revolution in philosophy), but human life is not possible on the basis of such a truth. That is the crisis.

Strauss has written that Nietzsche so "dominated and charmed" him between the ages of twenty-two and thirty that "I literally believed everything I understood of him."[4] Much of this evaluation is still clear in the discussion of Nietzsche in *Natural Right and History*. There the source of the problem Nietzsche has seen so clearly is not so much historicism's relativism but its "theoretical attitude," also typified by modern natural science and its philosophical apologists (the separators of fact from value). These theoretical, scientific, and philosophical enterprises cultivate a value-neutral, objective perspective. This prevents them from understanding human "life" as the distinct ontological kind it is, because such a life is unintelligible (as lived)

2. See Leo Strauss, "The Three Waves of Modernity," 88–89. This has as its consequence that all political problems are in essence technical problems (90).

3. Man in the state of nature is "subhuman," so such nature cannot serve as a standard or guide. Ibid., 90.

4. Strauss, "Letter to Löwith," in Lampert, *Leo Strauss and Nietzsche*, 5.

without "commitment" (and not understandable at all except *from* the lived perspective). So Strauss argues this way:

> Since the theoretical analysis has its basis outside of life, it will never be able to understand life. The theoretical analysis of life is noncommittal and fatal to commitment, but life means commitment.[5]

If life is to be possible, Nietzsche is thus left, Strauss claims, with the options of esotericism about theoretical results, writing only for the few, keeping the truth from the many (in Strauss's view, Plato's option; on the surface, but only on the surface, not the immoderate Nietzsche's), or the denial of the possibility of theory's self-understanding, viewing it instead as a product of life, or fate.

This prepares us for understanding what is typical of Strauss's characterizations of Nietzsche, above all in the essay on *Beyond Good and Evil*. That is, we find there unusually indirect characterizations, unexpected references, and a puzzling caution. In *Natural Right and History*, the momentum of these sentences just quoted suggests that we are heading straight for Nietzsche's position, the latter of the two possibilities sketched, the "unboundedness" of the perspective of life; that is, the claim that every aspiration to theory or to reason always already reflects a pretheoretical "commitment." And that certainly does sound like the received view of Nietzsche, and may already be taken to be a manifestation of Nietzsche's view of the fundamentality of "the will to power" as explicans. But even in *Natural Right and History*, Strauss shifts our attention and only says, "*If not Nietzsche himself*, at any rate his successors adopted the second alternative."[6] Why make this qualification if there is not a substantial question as to whether Nietzsche ever actually held the view? Even in the footnote, in which Strauss seems to retract this caution and *does* include Nietzsche within the theoretical attitude of the historical school,[7] Strauss quotes three passages from two Platonic dialogues[8] and cites "On the Use and Abuse of History for Life,"

5. Strauss, *Natural Right and History*, 26.

6. Ibid.

7. And if this is so, why be so originally cautious with that "if not Nietzsche himself"?

8. We are asked to consider Nietzsche's sympathy with Callicles on the one hand, and his preference for the "tragic life," not "the theoretical life," on the other. The *Gorgias* passage cited deals with Callicles's fickleness, his willingness to say what is pleasing, and it is not clear if Strauss is pointing to the need to say sometimes something other than what one believes, or if

saying that Nietzsche there clearly adopts "what one may consider the fundamental premise of the historical school."[9]

Strauss's seventeen-page essay on *Beyond Good and Evil* explores this issue and several more. It is an extremely complicated essay, and every paragraph raises questions like the ones just posed, with (typically) very little affirmed in the author's own voice, and replete with references to sources that seem to have little to do with Nietzsche. Moreover, it has three extreme peculiarities, especially for a scholar as careful with texts as Strauss. First, there is hardly any discussion of *BGE*'s opening blasts at Plato, the "dog-

---

he means to suggest that that Heideggerean "unboundedness of the perspective of life," fatalistic position in effect amounts to this unprincipled, sophistic shiftiness, Rameau's-nephew-like; whatever the age requires. It appears to be the latter, since the second passage from the *Gorgias* accuses tragic poetry of flattery. The *Laws* passage is much the same, and the imputation seems to be that anyone convinced of the basic premise of the historicist school must consider himself not merely the child but the servant of his time. This problem is mentioned by Strauss in §30, 201, as regards philosophical rule. That is, he suggests it ("servant of the time") is the problem that must be avoided, and from the context (and the next paragraph) it is clear that he is suggesting that, for any true historicist, it cannot be. That leaves the question of whether Nietzsche is a "true" historicist open. The issue surfaces again as Strauss contrasts Hegel and Nietzsche, this time as a contrast between being a son of one's time (Hegel's *Lectures on the History of Philosophy* are cited) and a stepson (Nietzsche's *Schopenhauer as Educator* is cited). A stepson is not by nature connected with his paternity, and this plays a role in Strauss's concluding discussion of "*vornehme Natur*," when he emphasizes that such a nature *is* so connected (to his biological parents), thus silently distinguishing the philosopher from a noble type.

9. Strauss, *Natural Right and History*, 26n9. Not "what *is* the premise of the historical school"? And "may one consider it" that way because it is a premise that the school itself, or Nietzsche himself, would not recognize? And are we to consider only the premise? Not the implications? The passage Strauss cites is not at all as clear-cut as he suggests. Nietzsche is, on the one hand, criticizing the pretense of "objectivity" and indifference on the part of historians, and he insists that where the "highest and rarest" (*Höchste und Seltenste*) in human life is at stake, such a pretense of indifference is "outrageous" (*empörend*). But this denial of a fact-value distinction is a major thesis of *Natural Right and History* itself! Nietzsche goes on to say that one should not pretend to be just to the past unless one is willing to take on the task of a just man (*wenn er nicht zu dem fürchtbaren Berufe des Gerechten geweiht seid*), and while he says that ages and generations as such should not presume to be able to judge the past, *a great individual can*. The principle is simply "like to like" (*Gleiches durch Gleiches*). None of this justifies attributing to Nietzsche the "premise of the historical school." Most of what Nietzsche says on the page of the Insel edition that Strauss cites (73) is in fact very close if not identical to Strauss on the impossibility of a value-neutral perspective on human affairs, including the past. This is not to say that Nietzsche does not elsewhere talk about how any age needs to exist in a "cloud" of illusions, or that he does not at other places attack any notion of objectivity in history, but it is fascinating that Strauss cites *this* passage (Nietzsche, *Vom Nutzen und Nachteil der Historie für das Leben*, 73).

matic" philosophy Plato is responsible for, and the "perspectivism" Nietzsche encouraged by contrast. These are passed over mostly in silence.[10] (There is a bit, to be discussed below, but not a full engagement.) In a way typical of Strauss, this itself may already suggest that the traditional view of Nietzsche as the arch anti-Platonist might be superficial.

Second, in the fifteenth paragraph of the essay, in the midst of a discussion of Nietzsche's treatment of religion, quite an important topic in the essay, coming to what Strauss even calls the "nerve of Nietzsche's 'theology'" (a topic not at all familiar in Nietzsche studies but at the heart of this essay), Strauss, in a kind of stunning withdrawal from the field, says that this "nerve" is something "of which I have not spoken and shall not speak since I have no access to it."[11] He refers us to an article by Karl Reinhardt published first in 1935 on one of Nietzsche's late *Dionysos-Dithyramben*. (And of course the obvious question is, if Strauss has "no access" to this issue, how would he know that Reinhardt's treatment of it is "worthy"?)[12] And finally, *BGE* ends with a poem, "From High Mountains: Aftersong," that Strauss completely ignores, does not even mention. So Strauss ignores

10. I mean what appear to be the major "claims" of the first chapter: questioning the value of truth; insisting on the priority of "instinct" over "consciousness"; treating "truth" as a matter of what is life-enhancing; the apparent prioritizing of a "physio-psychological approach" over a philosophical one; the skepticism about distinguishing "text" from "interpretation"; the claim that thought comes when "it" wills, not when I will; and so forth.

11. Strauss, "Note on the Plan of Nietzsche's *Beyond Good and Evil*," in Lampert, *Leo Strauss and Nietzsche*, §15, 195. Heinrich Meier has pointed out to me that this sounds very much like Socrates's "false modesty" about the gods in the *Apology*. And there is certainly the same sort of irony in Strauss's pretense that religious matters are beyond him, beyond what he can understand. The practical implication of the remark is not so much "I can't understand such things" as it is "I can't understand how anyone could believe such things."

12. This is noted by Lampert, *Leo Strauss and Nietzsche*, 57, but he offers no interpretation of Strauss's withdrawal. Strauss cannot be saying: "Nietzsche claims a lot of things based on some vision he had of Dionysos and Ariadne. I don't know what to say to visions." Strauss is fully aware that there is no revealed religion in Nietzsche. What he might mean is suggested by his own comment on §45 of *BGE*, where Nietzsche in effect says that one cannot truly understand the religious believer unless he can find a way "inside" such a point of view, and he can't do that except *as a true believer*, so cannot stand inside and outside at the same time. This is the same sort of language as "I have no access" to the nerve of Nietzsche's theology (i.e., *I am not a believer*). Of course, whenever Strauss expresses reluctance to express a view about religion, it is possible that there could be all sorts of reasons for the reluctance, but he does not mention that Nietzsche goes on in §45 to insist he *will* nevertheless do what he suggests cannot be done. Strauss seems to be doing the same, and yet again we have this complex and indirect association with that "other Nietzsche."

much of its beginning, the heart of its anti-Platonism, says he has no "access" to the deepest issue in Nietzsche's religiosity, and ignores the textual ending, where Nietzsche presents himself not as a philosopher but as a poet. We can be sure that all this is not because of an oversight. Again in a way typical of Strauss, this may suggest that the right category for Nietzsche might not be philosopher (rival as such to Plato) or poet but has something to do with religiosity. Among the other oddities, one might also add that the strange last sentence of the essay, written in German—*Die vornehme Natur ersetzt die göttliche Natur*—clearly appears as if a quotation from an original text, but is actually the culmination of Strauss's interpretation of Nietzsche; that is, his interpretation of the "text-interpretation" issue in Nietzsche. So we end with another reminder of the importance of Nietzsche's struggle with, perhaps entanglement in, religion.[13]

It is possible to isolate three very large topics in the essay, interconnected in various ways. There is first that relationship just mentioned between Plato and Nietzsche. We often take for granted a standard view of that relationship, one in which Plato is the paradigmatic realist philosopher, someone who believes that reason can detect an order in nature that can ground claims about social and political life (the heart of the claim of natural right), and Nietzsche is among the first who philosophize "after" such first philosophy is over, after that paradigmatic Platonic tradition has lost all credibility among thoughtful and influential people. Strauss does not frame the issue this way, at least not prominently, in this essay. In the "three wave" analysis, and in a blistering passage at the end of the essay "What Is Political Philosophy?," he does. In the latter he treats Nietzsche not as a philosopher but as a political rhetorician. Nietzsche "preached the sacred right of 'merciless extinction' of large masses of men," he was guilty of political irresponsibility, and made his readers "loathe democracy."[14] In the *BGE* essay,

13. See Reinhardt, *Nietzsches Klage der Ariadne*, 330, on the problem of a "text that interprets itself as an Interpretation."

14. Strauss, "What Is Political Philosophy?," 54–55. Lampert comments that there is no such passage where Nietzsche encourages this. Richard Velkley has suggested to me that Strauss may be thinking of the passage on *The Birth of Tragedy* in *Ecce Homo*, where Nietzsche, looking forward a century, and assuming success in his "attack [*Attentat*] on two thousand years of anti-nature and the desecration of mankind [*Menschenschändung*]," notes that undertaking "the greatest of all tasks," "the breeding of humanity to higher levels [*Höherzüchtung der Menschheit*]," will require "the merciless destruction of everything degenerate and parasitic [*die schonungslose Vernichtung alles Entartenden und Parasitischen*]." That phrase, *schonungslose Vernichtung*, does indeed suggest this passage. But the context of the passage is the cultivation of a life-

the relationship is presented in such a complex, multilevel way, it is hard to conclude anything about Strauss's view, but there is not much resonance with these excoriations and almost no hint of Nietzsche's putative indirect responsibility for fascism.[15] In this context Strauss says "philosophy is surely the primary theme of *Beyond Good and Evil*,"[16] and that is his main focus, not Nietzsche's historical responsibility.

There is, second, the problem of religion, where this includes the competition between philosophy and religion and Nietzsche's own putative religiosity, and then there is the largest issue, the status of nature and therewith the complementary problem of history.

So, three peculiarities and three main issues. Being able to say anything about issues of this magnitude will be difficult. The heart of the matter, I want to show, consists in both the opposition staged between Plato and Nietzsche and then, in various ways, the weakening, even ironicizing, of this opposition. But nothing is possible without some serious attention to Strauss's manner of presentation. Before climbing into those higher altitudes, a very close look at how he begins his essay, the first four paragraphs, can indicate the interpretive difficulty.

---

affirming way of life, and the necessity he notes is the destruction of "everything" (*alles*) degenerate and parasitic (and "degenerate" and "parasitic" are used as nouns, not adjectives); that is, whatever practices or "things" that are life-denying, and in *that* sense degenerate and parasitic, will have to be destroyed. This (*Vernichtung*) is admittedly an ominous word, and Nietzsche's rhetoric should not be sanitized, but it is a mistranslation to suggest that Nietzsche is talking about exterminating people. And there is no mention in the *Ecce Homo* passage of any "sacred right," nor is there anywhere else known to me.

15. Almost. The only indication of this theme in the essay is in paragraph 25, where Strauss himself is discussing Nietzsche's views on the "superior morality of leaders" and inserts the German word "Führer." This is peculiar because the passage in *BGE* he is discussing, §202, does not use that word, and Strauss quotes no passage where the word is used. In each of the three lecture courses, Strauss made sure his students understood that Nietzsche would have despised everything the Nazis stood for, but he also made a point of saying that Nietzsche's influence was not irrelevant to the factors that paved the way for the National Socialist movement. A typical example from his publications is at the end of the "Three Waves" essay. Strauss says that Nietzsche is "as little responsible for fascism as Rousseau is responsible for Jacobinism. This means, however, that he is just as much responsible for fascism as Rousseau was for Jacobinism" (98). How responsible is *that*? In the next paragraph, he says that the "political implication of the third wave [Nietzsche's wave] proved to be fascism." One could agree with that but consistently believe it was not true of Nietzsche, properly understood, as opposed to the Nietzsche of historical influence.

16. Strauss, "Note on the Plan," §5, 190.

## II

The essay begins not with an introductory remark about Nietzsche but with an autobiographical remark about Strauss himself. He says he always found *BGE* "the most beautiful of Nietzsche's books." Now, we are to hear very soon in the same paragraph what seems like a rare direct criticism of Nietzsche in this essay: that Plato as an individual disappears behind his books, points beyond himself, whereas Nietzsche points to himself everywhere, to, Strauss says, "Mr. Nietzsche." The glib informality of that phrase is odd for two reasons: both for the informality, which is unique in the essay, and because Strauss himself had begun everything *by pointing to himself*. Why should we care which book *he* finds most beautiful? *Is it beautiful?* is all that should interest us, if even that. (If the work is a work of philosophy, why shouldn't the important assessment be about its truth?) Does this mean that Strauss himself will write here more like Nietzsche and less like Plato? Why?[17]

I want to suggest that the answer to this question is affirmative, and that the strategy has something to do with Strauss's expressing Nietzsche's ideas (or the ideas of a certain historically influential Nietzsche) in a way that manifests, mostly implicitly, a kind of implicit self-undermining of that traditional view.[18] Nietzsche the antireligious atheist, as performed by Strauss, turns out to be a transitional phase and, as a kind of foretaste of the philosopher of the future, he turns into a theologian of some sort.

"Most beautiful," though, he reminds us, is not the same as "most profound." To explain what he means, Strauss suggests an example "which is perhaps not too far-fetched," again that comparison with Plato. Plato, we

17. Strauss's rather indirect search for a "platonizing Nietzsche" implies key elements of Strauss's Platonic conception of philosophy: it is the highest and best form of human life; it is interminable, but not because of skepticism or human finitude; its chief rival and chief political problem is religion; such a life cannot be taught, and one cannot be argued into it; its possibility has prephilosophical "conditions." This theme at the heart of the essay, Plato-Nietzsche, ultimately tells us as much about Strauss's view of Plato as of Nietzsche.

18. One could also say (although it would introduce a huge complication) that in Strauss's ironic commentary, we see that Nietzsche the anti-Platonist keeps subtly turning into some sort of a Platonist (a uniquely Straussian Platonist) as Strauss expounds his views. Or at least this is partly what is going on. The question of what it means to describe Nietzsche as some sort of Platonist *malgré lui* could be answered in any number of ways. As just noted, it could show us something about what Strauss thinks it is to be a Platonist, which for Strauss does not seem to have a lot to do with the existence of abstract objects, the problem of nonbeing, or the separability of the soul and its relation to the body. It could even amount to Nietzsche showing us the implications of positions he experiments with, and this not to reject them.

are told, had no use for categories like "most beautiful" or "most profound," whereas Nietzsche does tell us what books he preferred, *Dawn of Morning* and *The Gay Science*, and this because they were the "most personal." Again the implicit suggestion is that this is a betrayal of philosophy (or of Platonic philosophy, anyway), that we should be concerned with the profound, not our preferences, but again, Nietzsche appears to be criticized for having views about his books that are the same sorts of views Strauss himself begins the essay by expressing.

Moreover, as Strauss surely knows, what is "far-fetched" in what he is doing is not the example, but the use of Plato as some sort of measure for Nietzsche's project at all, as if the Platonic measure is relevant, given that *BGE* begins by criticizing Plato for the great "dogmatic" error of inventing "the pure mind" and "the good in itself." But Strauss goes even further in this association. He recalls Nietzsche's remark from *Ecce Homo* that, whereas his *Thus Spoke Zarathustra* was "far-sighted," "inspired" and "dithyrambic," *BGE* is concerned with what is closest to us, timely, and all around us. This then, Nietzsche reports, required a different form: the graceful subtlety as regards form, as regards intentions, and as regards the "art of silence." From this *alone* Strauss concludes:

> In other words, in *BGE*, in the only book published by Nietzsche, in the contemporary preface to which he presents himself as the antagonist of Plato, he "platonizes" as regards the "form" more than anywhere else.[19]

"Platonizes" again suggests that Nietzsche's self-characterization as anti-Platonist may obscure elements of his own Platonism. But here this platonizing is said to be evinced just by virtue of being subtle, intending to look at human life "closer up" than *Zarathustra*, and holding some things back, believing they are better left, or better understood, unsaid. There seems to be some (very faint) suggestion that Nietzsche's concern with the beauty of his forms (to return to the opening remarks by Strauss) is a kind of tip-of-the-iceberg revelation, and that the iceberg is something of crucial importance in the essay—Nietzsche's affirmative attitude toward all of life, his "yes-saying." If there is, say, a natural hierarchy, an order of rank, if human life, even in its tragedy, is beautiful, if Nietzsche entertains such considerations, then Nietzsche can be associated with Plato and against Christianity

19. Strauss, "Note on the Plan," §3, 188–89.

(even if perhaps not as a philosopher): *the whole is basically good, lovable,* the origin perhaps of Nietzsche's famous *amor fati.* It is also the first instance of that argument form (or perhaps theatrical strategy) used by Strauss: it can be "shown" in many other places too that Nietzsche "platonizes" (in this case, affirms for Platonic reasons) in spite of himself, or in spite of his official persona, at least with respect to this very sweeping issue.

The next paragraph is one of the most complicated in the book. Strauss's essay as announced is about the "plan" of *BGE,* its basic structure. He will soon tell us what others have noticed, that the basic structure appears to be a grouping of the first three chapters on philosophy and religion, an Interlude (4) of aphorisms, and the remaining five chapters on morals and politics. We are to think about the relation between philosophy and religion (especially "who rules whom," the "Athens-Jerusalem" problem so important to Strauss)[20] and especially about the "ruling" relation between first principles in philosophy versus religion, and the implications of both possibilities for morality and politics.

But in his first remarks in his own voice, in §4, he does not mention this structure and directs us instead to the Preface, where Plato is criticized for inventing "the pure mind" and the "good in itself" and then to the penultimate and ultimate paragraphs of (the prose portion of) the book. This, beginning and end, is the first structure we are shown, and the link that should make them part of the same structure is difficult to understand. The inner logic goes like this: according to Nietzsche, Plato's invention was an error; so there is no pure mind, no good in itself. Diotima's view would then follow (although Diotima is not mentioned by Nietzsche): there is no wisdom for human beings (the suppressed premise: wisdom requires a pure mind and the good in itself; more precisely, apparently, the possession of a pure mind and satisfaction with the good in itself amounts to wisdom), and so the gods would be wise and would not philosophize. But when Nietzsche discusses Dionysos in the penultimate paragraph,[21] he claims that the gods *do*

20. As an illustration of the belonging together of philosophy and religion, Strauss cites Hegel on the difference between "absolute spirit" (philosophy, religion, and art) and "Objective Spirit," Hegel's social and political philosophy (Strauss, "Note on the Plan," §6, 190). But Strauss must have realized that if the comparison is to Hegel, the question that Strauss raises immediately as the natural one, "the fundamental alternative," the rule of religion over philosophy or vice versa, is completely foreign to Hegel, for whom religion, philosophy, and art are complementary and compatible modes of knowledge of the Absolute. So why cite Hegel?

21. Nitezsche, *Beyond Good and Evil,* §295.

philosophize. (Strauss calls Dionysos a "super Socrates";[22] Nietzsche does not.) But, Strauss reminds us, Plato is not Diotima, and it is possible that *his* view was different from hers and he too thought the gods philosophize.[23] Finally, Strauss points us to the final paragraph in *BGE*, where Nietzsche notes the difference between written or painted thoughts and their originals. Strauss notes that this reminds us of Plato's Seventh Letter (he does not mention the *Phaedrus*) on the "weakness of the *logos*" and concludes this long excursus with "The purity of mind as Plato conceives of it, does not necessarily establish the strength of the *logos*."[24]

I said that Strauss ignores the main issue in Nietzsche's critique of Plato: dogmatism. That is not exactly right. This way of framing the beginning and end structure of Nietzsche's book is a silent comment on and rejection of that criticism. Plato, Strauss implies, realized the possibility *that even the gods philosophize*. That is, philosophical problems are such that even the gods cannot solve them, and so must still be interested in the quality of disputations. Nietzsche was wrong to connect dogmatism with the invention of the pure mind and the good in itself. Plato doubted "the strength of the *logos*," appreciated the permanent unavailability of wisdom, pure mind or no, and so shares more with Dionysos than Nietzsche realized, or let on. That is why that god can be called a "super Socrates," after that great zetetic. So, Strauss is again implying, we can ignore the dogmatism critique and concentrate on what unites Nietzsche and Plato.[25] The critique is all surface rhetoric and intimates another instance of Nietzsche, Platonist *malgré lui*. Or a Nietzsche who has his own reasons for presenting Plato as an arch dogmatist.[26]

22. This is in itself a striking indication of Strauss's view of Socrates.

23. Strauss quotes *Sophist* 216b5–6, where Theodorus claims there are gods who philosophize and refute bad opinions in humans, and *Theaetetus* 151d1–2, where Socrates complains about women who get angry when he takes their foolish opinions away; they do not understand he does this in kindness, in imitation of gods, who would never be unkind to humans (!), implying gods do take away such opinions, or can. They philosophize.

24. Strauss, "Note on the Plan," §4, 189.

25. Expressed too telegraphically: they agree that philosophy is not a body of doctrines, but a way of life, one that never escapes a dissatisfaction with any resolution of "the fundamental problems," Strauss's interpretation of the Platonic Ideas.

26. The tendency in the remarks, however elliptical, is, yet again, to suggest the unavoidability of "Platonism" or rationalism as a kind of unintended irony. See "Note on the Plan," §26, 199, where Strauss tries to show that Nietzsche's praise of cruelty, apparently a celebration of an irrational aggressive instinct, is actually *a rational strategy*. The praise of cruelty is "only the indispensable and therefore reasonable corrective to the irrational glorification of compassion." It is

## III

The core of what Strauss wants to say about Nietzsche on the elusive topic that keeps reappearing in the essay, religion and, much more controversially, Nietzsche's own religiosity, is derived from a reflection on *BGE* §37, and its preparation in §36. As we shall see in this section, he is out to show that the deflating implications of the will-to-power claim can be combined with, nevertheless, an affirmation of existence (all of it, eternally) only *by means of* the language of religious mythology.

§36 is the most concentrated and explicit passage in all of Nietzsche concerning his "doctrine" of the "will to power." Strauss realizes a doctrinal attribution would be hasty. He speaks of Nietzsche's "bewitching playfulness" and the "character of his proposition" as "problematic, tentative, tempting, hypothetical." Then we have §37, in reaction to the claim that the "world seen from the inside," in its "intelligible character," "would just be this 'will to power' and nothing else."

> "What? Doesn't that mean, to use a popular idiom: God is refuted but the devil [*der Teufel*] is not—?" On the contrary! On the contrary, my friends! And who the devil [*zum Teufel*] is forcing you to use popular idioms [*populär zu reden*]?[27]

The question asks: If the world is will to power, if understood minimally as some sort of chaotic collision of various kinds of forces, with struggles for some sort of ascendancy (and how could we possibly follow Strauss's line of thought here without at least a provisional interpretation of this doctrine, which Strauss does not give us), then haven't we replaced the credibility of any divine order with a mere absence of order, or a malignant order, aka "the devil"? Nietzsche himself makes a satanic curse (*zum Teufel*), as if to mock the invocation of the devil as a characterization of the will to power. But Strauss suggests that Nietzsche is not dismissing the question but answering it.[28] One could say that Nietzsche both dismisses the question as a mere "popular" and distorting formulation, and answers it in a fashion, "On the

---

by no means clear that Strauss means this as a criticism of Nietzsche; it could rather be an excavation of Nietzsche's intended strategy, and so a qualification of his presumed irrationalism.

27. Nietzsche, *Beyond Good and Evil*, §37, 36.

28. "On the contrary" could mean not that "God is *not* refuted, but advocated for" but "there is no God, no devil; the question is absurd." I think this latter is what Nietzsche meant.

contrary." (This could mean either that God is not refuted or that *both* God and the devil are refuted.)

But Strauss goes much further and says something quite surprising, in fact the heart of the essay: "The doctrine of the will to power—the whole doctrine of *Beyond Good and Evil*—is in a manner a vindication of God."[29] Lampert reports that that extraordinary phrase, "a vindication of God," is repeated five times in the essay. In support, Strauss directs us to §150, §295, and #7 of the Preface to *On the Genealogy of Morality*. This is somewhat peculiar, because Nietzsche had just used that phrase, *advocatus dei*, in §34, which Strauss does not mention. And there it is a term of *criticism*, not at all a self-characterization, used against those who think the "erroneousness" of the world, its untrustworthiness, should be attributed to us, our finite and fallible thinking and inferring. And §150 is mysterious, saying only that just as a hero turns everything around him into tragedy, God turns everything around him into "what? Perhaps 'world'?"[30] The other two references, however, introduce the question that runs throughout the essay, only rarely visible as such: the meaning of Nietzsche's references to, expressions of debt and allegiance to, Dionysos.

One such place is in paragraph 11, where Strauss suggests that what Nietzsche means to say is that modern atheism is just a transitional phase, necessary for the "free minds" of the second chapter of *BGE*, but not for the philosophers of the future. He attributes to Nietzsche the idea that "a certain kind of non-atheism [a typically cautious and indirect formulation; what is "non-atheism"?] belongs to the philosopher of the future who will again worship the god Dionysos or will again be, as an Epicurean might say, a *dionysokolax*."[31]

29. Strauss, "Note on the Plan," §9, 192.

30. Its mysteriousness does not mean it is unimportant for Strauss. He refers to it twice more, and interprets it to be a claim by Nietzsche that, in his view, there cannot be a world without God at its center (ibid., §13, 195). He does not consider the possibility that Nietzsche is, as he appears to be, quoting someone who believes that, not avowing it himself.

31. Ibid., §11, 193. This is an extraordinary example of Strauss's rhetorical complexity. He is suggesting in all apparent seriousness that the philosophers of the future will embody a new kind of religiosity; they will worship Dionysos. But *then* he refers to *BGE* §7, and cites Epicurus's joke-criticism of philosophers, that they are all *Dionysokolax*. But he does not tell us that *Dionysokolakes* are flatterers of Dionysos—or as Nietzsche more crudely translates it, *Speichellecker*, a boot-licker or brown-noser. They, adherents to Dionysos, are false: actors or poseurs. Strauss seems to be making the same point as he did (indirectly) in the citations of the *Gorgias* and *Laws* (see note 8 above). It is of course of the utmost importance that Strauss cites Nietzsche's reference to Epicurus, that Nietzsche is well aware that worshippers of Dionysos could also be

Such a suggestion raises two obvious questions. The first is how we are to understand the possibility that the disclosure of the world as "will to power and nothing else," which Strauss characterizes as equivalent to the "fact that human life is utterly meaningless and lacking support," could possibly yield to, even lead to, serve as "indispensable transition" to, "the most unbounded Yes: the eternal Yes-saying to everything that was and is." Strauss realizes that this is to ask the question about Zarathustra's teaching, the Eternal Return of the same, and so to ask how this universal affirmation of *everything* past, present, and future can be compatible with, indeed follow from, the disclosure that all is will to power and nothing else.

Strauss's response is abrupt and telling. He insists that willing the Nothing as eternity *cannot* be in itself affirmative. The world is not affirmable, beloved, *by being loved or affirmed*. If, as it appears we must, we say it must *be* lovable to be beloved, "would we not become guilty of a relapse into Platonism, into the teaching of 'the good in itself'?" (There is that "malgré lui" or "indirect Platonic affirmation" argument form again.) Some sort of realization about the meaning of the will to power is supposed to effect this transition, and the most one can infer from what Strauss says is a vague hint that the very "intelligibility" of the world as will to power permits some sort of affirmation. The whole is, at least, comprehensible; we must, as Nietzsche says, "love" its necessity; that at least makes it accessible to us, knowable, in its necessity. *Amor fati*.

But the second issue raised by this analysis is now relevant. What are we talking about? Worshipping Dionysos? An affirmation of religiosity? A post-atheistic "theology"? At first glance, it would appear that Strauss is guilty of crudely literalizing what are essentially literary tropes; as if Nietzsche seriously thought that everyone must wait around for a Persian prophet named Zarathustra to show up, or that he thought there exists a pagan god named Dionysos whom we would be well advised to worship.

Interestingly enough—and it is the most interesting aspect of the essay, just by the ellipsis—*this* is the main topic of the Karl Reinhardt essay "Nietzsches Klage der Ariadne," published in 1935, about issues (actually this issue, the relation between religious imagery and religiosity) that Strauss says he has no "access" to. The essay raises directly the question about whether all

called sycophantic flatterers of the god. In *Ecce Homo*, Nietzsche calls himself "*Jünger des Philosophen Dionysos*" (§2, trans. Norman, 258).

this Dionysos talk is meant as a "Symbol" of the new man Nietzsche proposed and prophesied, or whether it was meant "in a literal sense [*im wörtlichen Sinn*] as about a god of the future, a promise, a justification of suffering." And Reinhardt concludes that the latter is the case.

The "Klage der Ariadne" is the seventh of nine *Dionysos-Dithyramben.* For the greater part, Reinhardt's essay is a scholarly account of the development of Nietzsche's poetry up until the very end, the *Dithyramben* of 1889. His main claim is that the character of Nietzsche's poems and songs changed drastically after the "Zarathustra year" of 1883, and that there are still more interesting changes, changes, given many of the same phrases, from the "songs" in *Zarathustra* (especially the "magician's") to the *Dithyramben,* where some reappear. He is especially interested in the changing of gender in these phrases, from masculine to feminine,[32] and with trying to show that Nietzsche came to understand his personal drama throughout the phases of his writing as the "basic drama (*Ur-Drama*) of existence itself,"[33] especially the relationship between denying and affirming, self-sacrificing and self-conquering. And the core of *that* drama turns out to be quite relevant to where we are left hanging by Strauss: a form of affirmation that is not based on reason, not in that sense justified, not based on knowledge of any order or inverted order to the world. Reinhardt sends us to passages like §229 in *BGE* that speak directly to Strauss's question about the religious affirmation of the will to power he finds in Nietzsche, but, again, Nietzsche's formulation is not in standard discursive prose and so has an overdetermined meaning: "The 'wild animal' has not been killed off at all. It is alive and well. It has just become—divine." This, however mysterious, *is* the divinization that Strauss questioned, and Reinhardt supplies evidence that Nietzsche means the will to power as if it were a claim one would find in the mysterious divinizing prose of the pre-Socratics about an elemental force: water, fire, eros, pneuma, nous. Reinhardt thus goes even further than

32. Reinhardt connects this with the Preface to *BGE,* which begins with the supposition that truth is a woman and philosophers up to now clumsy lovers. In the terms of *Natural Right and History,* this is a way of claiming that what emerges from one as "theory" is always already the "expression" of commitment, can never be an independent reflection on such commitments (except as the expression of another pretheoretical commitment). A commitment to the truth, love of the truth, cannot be based on any reasoning about what one should be committed to, any more than love of a woman could "follow" from a reflection on who ought to be loved.

33. Reinhardt, *Nietzsches Klage der Ariadne,* 319.

Strauss's suggestions, beyond theology to sacred mysteries, a *Mysterienspiel.*[34] Nietzsche himself has made of himself not a work of art, a poem of sorts (as many passages seem to imply and some commentators assert), but *a religious myth,* the only way that the relation between active and passive in affirming and failing to affirm can be comprehended, if "comprehended" is even the right word anymore.[35]

Strauss is considerably more open about this claim in the essay (or more precisely, in the lecture) "Existentialism," given originally in Chicago in 1956 and published in 1995 in *Interpretation.* There he had simply said, concerning the difference between the Platonic philosopher and the Nietzschean:

> Nietzsche's philosopher of the future is an heir to the Bible. He is an heir to that deepening of the soul, which has been effected by the biblical belief in a God that is holy. The philosopher of the future as distinguished from the classical philosophers will be concerned with the holy. *His philosophizing will be intrinsically religious.*[36]

But why (for both Strauss and Reinhardt) single out the religious imagery alone as genuinely religious?[37] Nietzsche does not literally (*im wörtlichen Sinn*) believe that truth is a woman, that Baubo exists, that tragedy committed suicide, that we murdered God, that there are daemons like Life and Wisdom, that we should worry that our bows have lost their tension, that evolution's stages were camel, lion, and child, any more than Plato believed there were chariots pulled by Eros and Thymos. Surely the relationship be-

34. Ibid., 324.

35. The other reference to Reinhardt's collection, the last page of a eulogy for Walter Otto, is the culmination of an account of Otto's distinction in treating the Greek gods as no other philologist had or would, as "real," and so not even as objects of "belief." He says that Otto's central premise is simply "*Die Götter* sind." And he praises Otto's understanding of Greek religion as a matter "*des objektiven Erkenntnis*" (ibid., 378). The last remarks that Strauss mentions claim Otto as the only true successor to Hölderlin's treatment of the gods, which is an indirect (to say the least) way for Strauss to characterize how we are to understand Nietzsche's treatment of Dionysos (379).

36. Strauss, "Existentialism," 315 (my emphasis). Given the exclusivity of the Athens-Jerusalem alternative in Strauss's thinking, this would be, in effect, to say that Nietzsche is, finally, not a philosopher, and we have another example of some sort of staging of a performative contradiction (of the "official" Nietzsche).

37. I can detect no argument for Reinhardt's assertion in his essay, and there is no satisfying gloss on what he means by *im wörtlichen Sinn.* The discussion of Otto and Hölderlin gives us some indication.

tween literary and figurative language and religious belief is much too complicated to single out the latter for that designation (*im wörtlichen Sinn*), at least as complicated as the issue of why a philosopher would *constantly* use figurative language to make his points.[38]

Strauss's imputation of such a genuine religiosity to Nietzsche seems to be based on a claim: essentially that the will to power (whatever its content turns out to be; Strauss moves very fast here too) could be the basis, as it appears to be, for a radical, *sub specie aeternitatis* affirmation *only if* the issues were already framed in a religious way, as a matter more of inspired insight than "justification," as we have come to know it since the Socratic enlightenment. And that turns our attention to the last major issue in the essay: the status of nature, if understood as will to power.[39]

## IV

In the "three waves" essay, Strauss does not emphasize this religious dimension. There he says that, without an appeal either to nature or to historical necessity, Nietzsche's hopes for a new future (one with the appropriate order of rank) must rest wholly on an act of will, an act so radical as to will nature itself and will a historical past. This, he says there, is the meaning of the doctrine of the Eternal Return, and this all seems in some obvious tension with a religious affirmation. Clearly we need a more extensive gloss on what this might mean. As it stands it sounds like an invocation to wishful thinking: obviously willing something to be so does not make it so. How could this be the basis of so much in Strauss's version of Nietzsche?

As he turns to the second half of *BGE*, on morals and politics, Strauss

38. Strauss, famous for his concern about this in Plato, does not raise this question (why Nietzsche does not write philosophical essays) about Nietzsche anywhere I am aware of. And, to reexpress a note of caution about concluding anything, we do not know much from this essay alone about what Strauss thinks "God" or "a god" refers to, especially for a "philosopher." It is quite possible that Strauss means to say: it is absurd to understand Nietzsche's religiosity as anything like submission to a higher power, and if Nietzsche's references to Dionysos and the will to power and the Eternal Return are understood as Reinhardt does, then I have nothing to say to that sort of Nietzsche either (with the implication that this of course could not be the right way to understand such references).

39. I should repeat here the obvious: all this discussion is, as it were, "inside" the Straussian operator, "I have no access to this." This suggests that Strauss is pointing us to the more genuinely religious interpretation as if to say: "I can't understand such an attribution to Nietzsche. It makes no sense to me."

comes more and more to associate Nietzsche with a characteristic dynamic of distinctively modern political thought: the mastery of chance by the conquest of nature. So "willing it to be so" in the previous paragraph has, at least to some degree, its more extensive gloss: *making* it so. Strauss does this while, now more explicitly, enacting the fact that such a control of nature still requires *natures* of a particular sort. "As we have observed, for Nietzsche nature has become a problem, yet he cannot do without nature."[40] Or, Nietzsche's philosophy appears to aspire to something it cannot achieve: absolute mastery of nature and human nature. But the existence of the few who are to count as the "highest" expression or the "most spiritual" expression of the will to power, those who legislate values, the philosophers of the future, are themselves wholly contingent manifestations of chance, or *fortuna*, or nature by another (modern) name. And so "belief" in the possibility of such dispensations again reintroduces at least some aspects of the religious dimension and decreases the tensions between the two aspects of the will-to-power doctrine according to Strauss.

So Nietzsche (understood in terms of this association) has more in common, Strauss suggests, with Marx than with, say, Aristotle. Strauss quotes those passages in what we now call Marx's "Economic and Philosophical Manuscripts" ("Nationalökonomie und Philosophie" in the edition of the *Frühschriften* that Strauss cites) which particularly emphasize the *complete* humanization of nature under communism ("the riddle of history solved and which knows itself as this solution"), or which stress the "resurrection of nature" in the naturalism of mankind and the "humanism of nature," as man produces himself as well as his products, or the true speculative identity of naturalism and humanism, materialism and idealism.[41] In Nietzsche, Strauss cites corresponding passages from Nietzsche's *Nachlaß* and *The Gay Science* that speak of the act of "naturalizing" man, *making* him a new nature; *Vernatürlichen* in the former and the reference to man as the "still undetermined animal" (*noch nicht festgestellte Tier*) in *BGE* §62.

But Strauss yet again "enacts" what he clearly thinks of as Nietzsche's unsolvable problem with nature or the unavailability of this complete humanization of nature, the return of the problem of human nature. In paragraph 35 Strauss does not revert to any suggestion of an affirmation made possible by some sort of religious inspiration. That would be very difficult any-

40. Strauss, "Note on the Plan," §35, 204.

41. Marx, "Nationalökonomie und Philosophie," at 235, 237, 273.

way, since we do not know much about what either Strauss or Nietzsche thinks of as "the religious essence." Instead, having introduced this radical willfulness (and these last remarks seem to me to reveal an unmistakable reference to Heidegger's interpretation of Nietzsche as the embodiment of the technological worldview), Strauss now invokes what is in fact his own framework—that any truly affirmable (that is to say, to speak like Strauss and not Nietzsche, righteous) human life can only be based on either reason or nature, and he argues that Nietzsche has not, in fact, explained why it is necessary to affirm the Eternal Return. Instead, "in the last analysis," such an achievement is "*not the work of reason but of nature.*"

In support of this claim he cites §231 and §8, and they are linked. It is another variation on the theme of the weakness of consciousness in directing a life, in founding commitments, now expressed as "something that will not learn," "a brick wall of spiritual fatum," the "great stupidity that we are," "the thing that will not learn."[42] In §8 he treats convictions as the stupidest-seeming of animals (*adventavit asinus*) but, in a way typical of Nietzsche, he also says that they come onstage as "beautiful and very strong" (*pulcher et fortissimus*). These positive adjectives might be connected to what §231 says about the value of the manifestations of such a natural fate, that such fixed convictions can be valuable "footsteps to self-knowledge, signposts to the problems that we are." And he indicates he means that in the sense of individual self-knowledge, knowing myself without self-deception. This at least suggests that these convictions are not permanently resistant to change or qualification, not a mere *fatum*. Self-knowledge might be possible, and their status as convictions might change.

Strauss does not focus on that hint, and instead proceeds for one last time to sketch Nietzsche's impossible position (and perhaps therewith the impossible modern position, post-third-wave) on nature. For while there seems to be this concession in Nietzsche to our dependency on the contingent dispensations of nature, providing the human natures capable of the strength necessary to will with ambitions of this magnitude, nature still remains a manifold "problem." In the first place, this is because "man is conquering nature and there are no assignable limits to that conquest."

42. This is one of the few places where Strauss comes close to dealing with what appears to be Nietzsche's position on the "weakness" of consciousness in reflecting on and "leading" a life, and so the importance, by contrast, of "instinct." But this just scratches the surface. As Strauss knows from the Platonic dialogues, there are many ways of characterizing what cannot be taught and why. (Cf. the issue of "virtue.")

This leads to a naïve and dangerous ambition to eliminate "suffering and inequality." This would be naïve and dangerous because, for Strauss's Nietzsche, these are the necessary conditions of any greatness. And apart from that, we are back with the problem of belief in something like nature's contingency and presumed beneficence. For if suffering and inequality are such conditions, we cannot trust to chance to produce them, but must will them. This is a very odd way of thinking, but Strauss seems convinced Nietzsche is caught up in it. It is odd because it is like thinking: *Overcoming great obstacles is what makes the attainment of an end worthwhile. This desirable one I am pursuing is coming too easily. I had better manufacture some great difficulties for myself.*[43] Or, *This society is becoming too prosperous and comfortable. I had better create some misery and inequality.*

So in the end neither a radical act of will nor a pious faith in nature's eternal affirmability can resolve Nietzsche's problem of nature. This is the context for the mysterious last sentence of the essay, *Die vornehme Natur ersetzt die göttliche Natur*. The game, as it were, of presenting and exploring aspects of the received Nietzsche and then qualifying, sometimes affirming, sometimes departing from what is standard (and a Nietzschean religiosity is far from standard), hinting at other possibilities, suggesting difficulties, all pointing to another Nietzsche, comes to a kind of culmination in that relatively unmotivated and so very surprising coinage. As noted, it embodies this double game. It is presented as if a quotation, but they are Strauss's words, not Nietzsche's, and in their shared native language. This means that one last time he calls attention to himself, to *his* aphorism, in effect, not to Nietzsche or the work.

To understand it, he refers us to a passage in the book whose title he translates as *The Dawn of Morning* (*Morgenröthe*).[44] That aphorism (199) is

43. I don't mean that such a way of thinking is impossible, absurd, or completely foreign to Nietzsche, just that it is odd and requires elaboration. For an interesting elaboration, see Reginster, *The Affirmation of Life: Nietzsche on Overcoming Nihilism*.

44. He also refers us to two passages in Goethe. The first, from *Wilhelm Meisters Lehrjahre,* is an explanation by Serlo to Wilhelm of the difference between *vornehm* and *edel,* which appears to be Strauss's distinction between *vornehm* and "noble," and an explanation of what *vornehm* consists in. For example: "Der edle Mensch kann sich in Momenten vernachlässigen, der vornehme nie" (Goethe, *Wilhelm Meisters Lehrjahre,* 87). In the description, he sounds very much like Aristotle's "great-souled" man, never lording it over the low, never calling undue attention to himself. And as in Aristotle, the component of moral luck is stressed, what Strauss calls "extraction, origin, birth," or, in general, "nature." The truly *Vornehm* cannot be imitated, is not a role one can adopt; one must be born to it and carefully educated over a long period. "Man sieht

an account of how what counts for us as noble is different from and superior to what was noble in the tragic age of the Greeks, who are characterized as proud but crafty and unprincipled, barely "decent." It is in this context that Strauss announces that the noble nature, *understood as this aphorism suggests*, or, in effect, Nietzsche himself, replaces the "divine" nature, or, unmistakably, Plato.

This first of all seems to suggest a resolution of the tension noted before between the absolute radicalization of will, on the one hand, and the dependence, for the possibility of such a radicalization, on the dispensations of nature, and so an eternally affirmable nature, on the other hand, as if the latter implies a new religiosity for the philosophers of the future.[45] It is enough that nature allows, and occasionally provides the resources for, such a will in order to be able to affirm the nobility of nature. That is religiosity (and gratitude) enough.[46] And at the same time, the sentence could simply announce the historical fact that Nietzsche has replaced Plato as the paternal source of any philosophy of the future, along with the expression of a hope (for those who can read the text in the original and so study it properly) that the "Nietzsche" who will emerge as such an ancestor will be the truly noble Nietzsche, not the "barely decent" blond beast of modern mythology.[47]

---

also, dass man, um vornehm zu scheinen, wirklich vornehm sein müßte" (ibid., 88). The *Dichtung und Wahrheit* passage briefly touches on the capacity of some for a "*Vorempfindung*" of sickness or death, and the uninheritability of such traits; thus again emphasizing our dependence on the arbitrary beneficence of nature. Quoting Goethe is perhaps a way of emphasizing what has always been known to those whom Nietzsche called simply in *The Anti-Christ* "*die Wenigsten,*" the few.

45. Another premise of this way of looking at things: the highest expression of the will to power is philosophy, understood as the nearly "insane" and nearly "divine" attempt to know the whole. The passages about everything being, in its intelligible nature, will to power would then be understood as imperfect strivings toward full self-consciousness and self-knowledge. I believe that this is how Strauss understood the will to power, but there are only suggestions of that here.

46. This hardly settles all the issues raised by the Eternal Return, in particular the problem of affirming, willing, *all* of the past and bearing the burden of *all* of the future.

47. The aphorism is titled "We are nobler," and Nietzsche distinguishes "our" more refined nobility when compared with the archaic Greeks, who believed in such things as "the perfect ruthlessness and devilry of the tyrant who sacrifices everyone and everything to his arrogance and pleasure."

# 10

# The Expressivist Nietzsche

## I

In a 2011 book, *Nietzsche, Psychology, and First Philosophy,* I argued for the importance of the French *moralistes* for any attempt to understand why Nietzsche should have said in *Beyond Good and Evil* that "psychology" might now (that is, because of him, Nietzsche) once again become the "queen of the sciences," and so once more the "path to the fundamental problems." Among other things, this led to a characterization of Nietzsche on agency that could be considered "expressivist." My intention here is to clarify that notion in more detail.

My purpose in invoking the tradition of Pascal, La Rochefoucauld, and above all Montaigne, aside from the fact that Nietzsche's frequent praise of that tradition and identification with it have gone relatively unnoticed, was twofold. First, the book is based on earlier lectures that were originally given in a *cours* at the Collège de France in 2004,[1] and anyone who knows anything about twentieth-century French philosophy and especially French appropriations of Nietzsche will know of the enormous influence of Heidegger on that tradition. My somewhat ironic intention was to remind my audience that from the point of view of Nietzsche, he is unquestionably better understood as a French *moraliste* than the German metaphysician of

1. Published as *Nietzsche, moraliste français: La conception nietzschéenne d'une psychologie philosophique.*

Heidegger's influential lectures from the 1930s and 1940s.[2] But this historical association raises the philosophical question. Granted, one might concede, Nietzsche admired these people and described what he was doing as psychology in a way that called them to mind, but what does that tell us? What, viewed this way, *is* psychology?

This is the question the book tries to answer from a number of different perspectives, but the core issue is the one that chiefly interested Nietzsche: the problem of self-knowledge and the relation between that problem and knowledge of others' actions and words, and especially the unique kind of difficulty one faces in attempting to know such things as why one (or anyone) did what one did, what it actually was that one (or anyone) did; what one (or some other) truly values; why one values what one does; could one come to know what sort of a life one might truly affirm, and if so how?[3] It is clear everywhere in his texts that Nietzsche did not think that this question could be answered by any manner of introspection, inner observation of any kind, anything like a natural science, and such self-knowledge is certainly not to be had by a priori philosophizing about *the* basic structure of the human soul, as in Plato's theory of the tripartite soul. It would at least be fair to say that the most prominent Nietzschean characterization of claims to self- and other-knowledge is that it is *extremely* difficult to arrive at such self- and other-knowledge, partly because it is neither empirical nor a priori knowledge, partly because the soul is not an object in the usual sense, but mostly because in his treatments such putative self- and other-knowledge is almost always an expression of some self-deception that must be overcome. (We should expect this to be the same problem, subject to the same nearly ubiquitous self-deception, even if we take Nietzsche to have some sort of "self-fashioning" theory of the self, as if an aesthetic product, a work of art. The question just becomes *what* "self" I have "fashioned" or "created." The questions of what it is I have fashioned in "fashioning myself" and whether

2. Heidegger, *Nietzsche, Vols. 1, 2, 3 and 4*, trans. Krell.

3. Why the pursuit of such questions should be understood not as a subfield or part of philosophy but as "first philosophy" or "queen of the sciences" (as opposed, say, to the conventional queen, metaphysics), is an even more difficult question. It turns on what appears to be Nietzsche's view on the role of some evaluative stance, mattering, or erotic attachment and commitment, in the possible intelligibility of anything at all, in any possible intentional relation to an object. This *does* tie him to Heidegger, but to the Heidegger of *Being and Time* and the role of "care," or *Sorge*, in any "horizon" of intelligibility, but that is a complicated separate topic. It will emerge a bit below with the issue of "depth commitments."

it was really *my* fashioning, whether it is as I take myself to have fashioned it, just begin with any aesthetic conception of a subject's relation to her activities and practices; that conception alone does not resolve them.)[4]

This is not to say that there is no such thing as self- or other-knowledge properly understood, but to suggest that the truth in such a realm does not have as its opposite falsity in the propositional sense but a kind of fraudulence in what one reports about oneself or claims about another.[5] Understanding this, the *moralistes,* for Nietzsche, offered observations on the sort of questions posed above, not by relying on a general theory that provided instances, but by finding ways to characterize how the human soul typically works (how such questions as those above are posed and pursued) in ways true to the unstable, variable, situation-dependent, self-interested contexts in which they arise. There is no way to summarize the "method" they used to do this because there is no such method, any more than there is any method that can be invoked to show how "I knew not only that she was lying but that she knew I knew she was lying and didn't care." We *do* know those things, and saying that we know them by "inferences from cues," say, gets us nowhere. One might as well ask what method Shakespeare (another of Nietzsche's heroes) used in coming to understand human beings like Macbeth or Othello (or ambition or jealousy) so well.

Here is a summary passage on the dangers of a philosophical psychology that, I argued in the book, should be adopted as some sort of publication hurdle: nothing can appear on Nietzsche unless consistent with the remarks. It is in the "Assorted Opinions and Maxims" section of *Human, All Too Human.* Nietzsche is describing what he calls the "original sin" of philosophers, who, he says, have always appropriated and ruined the views of the *Menschenprüfer,* the evaluators of the human and the *moralistes,* because "they have taken them for *unqualified* propositions and sought to demonstrate the absolute validity of what these moralists intended merely as approximate signposts or even as no more than truths possessing tenancy only for a decade—and through doing so thought to elevate themselves above the latter." The example of such an original sin he gives is Schopenhauer on the will. Nietzsche claims that Schopenhauer was in reality, without appre-

4. I raise several more objections to the self-fashioning view in chapter 6 of *Nietzsche, Psychology, First Philosophy,* 105 ff., several relevant to Alexander Nehamas's well-known interpretation.

5. See *Ecce Homo, Vorwort,* §3 (trans. Norman, 259): "Irrtum . . . is nicht Blindheit, Irrtum ist Feigheit."

ciating the fact himself, a "moralist," who rightly used the term "will" loosely, and in a way that referred broadly to a meaning common to many different human situations and merely filled a gap in language and so earned the right to "speak of the will as Pascal had spoken of it." Unfortunately, though, "the philosophical rage for universality" turned such a moraliste *façon de parler* into a metaphysical claim about the omnipresence of the will in all of nature. This is a claim some have attributed to Nietzsche, but that he calls a piece of "mystical mischief" (*mystische Unfüge*), and so ended up turning everything into "a false reification" (*zu einer falschen Verdinglichung*).[6]

## II

The crucial passage for the interpretation I present is *On the Genealogy of Morality*, I, §13:

> To demand of strength that it should not express itself as strength, that it should *not* be a desire to overcome, a desire to throw down, a desire to become master, a thirst for enemies and resistances and triumphs, is just as absurd as to demand of weakness that it should express itself as strength. A quantum of force is equivalent to a quantum of drive, will, effect—more, it is nothing other than precisely this very driving, willing, effecting, and only owing to the seduction of language (and of the fundamental errors of reason that are petrified in it) which conceives and misconceives all effects as conditioned by something that causes effects, by a "subject" can it appear otherwise. For just as the popular mind separates the lightning from its flash and takes the latter for an *action*, for the operation of a subject called lightning, so popular morality also separates strength from expressions of strength, as if there were a neutral substratum behind the strong man, which was free to express strength or not to do. But there is no such substratum; there is no "being" behind doing,

6. Nietzsche, *Human, All Too Human*, trans. Hollingdale, 215–16. In §14 of *The Anti-Christ*, Nietzsche continues to insist that in his view we have to understand the will in a new way, as a variety of different sorts of contradictory and coherent stimuli (*Reize*), and so that properly understood the will doesn't effect (*wirkt*) anything any longer, or "move" (*bewegt*) anything. And in many other passages he makes very clear that the "will to power" cannot be considered some sort of fixed instinct. It can fail, be absent, and even be transformed into something that is its exact opposite: *Der Wille zum Nichts*.

effecting, becoming: the "doer" is merely a fiction added to the deed—the deed is everything.[7]

The passage is highly literary, enigmatic, and not at all systematic. However fascinating, it does not give us a lot to work with, and much of the interpretive task consists in determining what Nietzsche could have meant, given what else he says (and manifests) about psychological explanation. The idea that Nietzsche is indirectly proposing here that the doer is "expressed" in the deed, and in that sense is not "behind" it as a separate cause, opens the door to very large issues prominent in Spinoza (on a substance's nontemporal, *nunc stans* expression in its attributes and modes), and similar issues in everyone from Leibniz to Schelling to Böhme, as Deleuze has argued.[8] But more directly and from the outset, one might entertain immediate doubts that, to explain the passage, we need to commit Nietzsche to that *different* relation between doer and deed than an ex ante causal origin, with the deed as a result. Why not, as the passage seems to suggest, "*no* relation"? No doer at all?

Admittedly, the most startling formulation in the *Genealogy* passage is an analogy: just as there is no lightning behind, and causing as a result, the flash (as might be suggested by "the lightning flashed"), so there is no doer behind the deed (as might be suggested by "John hit the ball"); such a substratum is a fiction added on; the deed is all there is, everything, *alles* (as if really we should say, I suppose, "there are just ball-hitting-events going on"). As noted, I argued that this passage should be understood as a quick sketch of an "expressivist" theory of action one can find throughout Nietzsche; that is, that he remains committed to the distinction between action and event, and is proposing a way to make the distinction different from voluntarism, spontaneity theories, intention-causal theories.[9] That difference involves noticing that Nietzsche is only denying that there is a doer "behind" and separate from the deed. The language of doer-deed is not dropped; a strong person's "strength" is *expressed* in "a desire to overcome, a desire to

7. *On the Genealogy of Morality*, I, §13, trans. Kaufmann, 45.

8. Deleuze, *Expressionism in Philosophy: Spinoza*, trans. Joughin.

9. Given the use of the notion of "expressivism" in logical positivism's characterization of value judgments, this is perhaps not the most felicitous of terms, but it is the term Nietzsche wants us to use to understand the relation between strength and its manifestation ("*sich äussern*") and I trust the difference with the positivist use is clear.

throw down, a desire to become master, a thirst for enemies and resistances and triumphs." The various bodily movements involved in each of these activities would be unintelligible, mere bodily movements in space and time, were we not able to understand them in their *psychological meaning*, as expressions of strength, as motivated by a strength that wants expressing. If deeds are reduced to mere bodily movements like natural events, we will have no way of distinguishing identical bodily movements that are differently motivated and so are different deeds. There would be many such problems. However, the "no substratum," nothing-"behind"-the-deed language prohibits us from thinking of psychological motives, or even their neurobiological counterparts, as causes of separate deeds, and we must keep this in mind when Nietzsche gives his own psychological explanations (and I wouldn't know how to characterize those explanations except as psychological) of pity, of humility, of the desire for equality, for the slave revolt in morality, and so forth. Hence my suggestion that Nietzsche is trying to get us to see the doer "in" the deed, rather than "behind it," and the point of that is to deflate our reliance on our own ex ante formulations of intention to account for what happens. Such formulations, while necessary (again, there wouldn't be deeds unless such mindedness could be attended to as such), are only *provisional*, are *realized* (or not) only in the deed that reveals what in fact we are committed to doing, what we "really" intended. Nietzsche does not go any further in the passage (or elsewhere), so, as noted, the task is filling out such a view in ways consistent with other things Nietzsche says (like the Schopenhauer/*moraliste* passage just quoted, or his own psychological explanations).

This is admittedly a complicated thought. It does not mean, as it might seem to, that in performing the deed I discover some ex ante, determinate intention that caused the deed without my being aware of it. Nietzsche's insistence that the doer is wholly in the deed must mean that "what I am willing to do," let us say, arises as the mindedness relevant to the deed, *as I actually act*, and only then. The model is something like an artist discovering what she wants only in the writing or the painting.

Now, I should say, there is a perfectly ordinary sense in which we want to call the intention that explains what the deed is and why it was done simply "what the agent had in mind to do," ex ante. Sometimes this intention is implicit and unformulated, but it is easily available at any point if I am asked what I am doing and why. We can certainly imagine this mental state occurring some time "before" the bodily movement begins, and so can say easily that such an intention and the agent who holds it can be understood as before and so behind the deed that is eventually performed. Likewise, there is nothing in what Nietzsche is suggesting to imply that there are not conditions that have to be met for the deed to qualify as mine alone. I have to be able to exercise some control over the events, not be coerced or duped and manipulated. I see no Nietzschean reason to deny that persons can come to understand themselves this way and can attempt to "live out" the implications of such a self-image. It is the correct analysis of this way of speaking that is at issue.

So the Nietzschean account need not deny that *there are* such ex ante formulations, as if they couldn't exist. His model just holds them to be *provisional*, most often, in ordinary doings, actually and unproblematically manifested in the deed, but it is only "there" that the provisional becomes actual. They *are* realized, made real in what we are willing actually to do. And they need to be considered provisional because in a surprisingly large number of significant cases, what we are willing to avow as our intention is a fantasy, largely self-deluded, and not consistent with what we do.[10]

In the passage, in other words, Nietzsche still refers to "deeds" and not events, and with that, as far as I can see, the question of how and why the deed was produced, and with *that* the problem of the "doer," is unavoidably raised. So I presume that everyone would agree that Nietzsche shows no tendency to treat a plant's phototropism or iron ore rusting as explicable in the same way as human activities. There is perhaps some analogous or metaphorical way to say that the plant's turning toward the sun "expresses" its need for light, but there is nothing in that that refers to *the plant's view of what it needs and why*, nothing "psychological." As indicated in the examples cited above—Nietzsche's explanation of such things as the slave revolt, pity, humility, egalitarianism—a reference to the mindedness inherent in such activities is essential to their individuation and explanation. If we simply try to do justice to the fact that Nietzsche's explanations of such phenomena

10. This raises a problem similar to one discussed recently in epistemology, called "disjunctivism." Here the issue would be: Why, in trying to understand the role of mindedness in some bodily movements, take one's bearing from odd or failed or infrequent instances, such as not actually doing what I sincerely avow I intend to do? That is too large an issue to address here, but at least in this case, the instances at issue, if unusual, are not thereby marginal or insignificant, especially given the prevalence of self-deception in Nietzsche's genealogies. We can be just as easily lulled into complacency about the form of action by the standard cases as we can be misled by unusual ones.

are everywhere psychological (an attempt to determine *what* mindedness is *really* expressed in the deed), the issue of how he understands the relation between the doer's mindedness and deed is unavoidable. He rejects "behind" and "before"; and I suggested he is thinking of "in" as a process of realization. Things get complicated quickly because Nietzsche is deeply suspicious of the avowed, self-ascribed motivations provided by agents, but he always suggests, as what truly motivates, other psychological phenomena, like ressentiment or fear or self-hatred.[11]

And although in this passage Nietzsche suggests that strength cannot but express itself as strength, that claim must be made consistent with a variety of things he says about such dispositions. There is the issue of what *counts* as the expression of strength, much easier to say in the case of birds of prey than human expressions. (The ascetic might regard his activities, refraining from expressions of strength, as the highest manifestation of strength.) Then there are contexts in which strength is not allowed its expression, and the strong can be said to rub themselves raw on the bars of self-imposed cages.[12] There is strength that can be said to turn against itself as strength. Distinguishing any of these will require the depth psychology Nietzsche is proposing.

Still, one might say, while agreeing that Nietzsche does not tie any notion of individual responsibility to a spontaneous causal power to initiate bodily movements, any talk of a doer, even in the deed, betrays a lingering reluctance to break more completely with the essentially moral notions of responsibility, agent, and accountability, a truly revolutionary break many suspect may be the sort Nietzsche intended. But it is not clear where such a radical break would land us. I made use of Nietzsche's invocation of Spinoza to show why, for him, agent regret is not regret that I could have done otherwise, but sadness that I turned out to be other than I had imagined. Such a suggestion requires much more filling out, but any such extension must be consistent with the fact that, first, Nietzsche clearly *wants* some sort of account of agent regret. That is why he turned to Spinoza. And, second, Nietzsche's rhetoric is everywhere hortatory and condemnatory. In some sense

11. There is no indication that Nietzsche thinks that ultimately such phenomena are to be explained by factors "outside" the psychological, as if ressentiment were some discrete sort of drive-quanta, pushing an agent into something. Ressentiment is what the slave feels, experiences (and denies to himself), and that requires that he understand the meaning of his situation in a way, all of which must be "inside" the psychological.

12. See, for example, *On the Genealogy of Morality*, I, §16, trans. Diethe, 32.

or other he expects or at least hopes that we can overcome nihilism, largely by listening to, being gripped by, him, a transformation that may produce what we now are not—sovereign individuals. All these notions continue and deepen the question of the right understanding between an agent and her deeds; it does not avoid or dismiss the question as if there is no such distinction.

And at this point, there are several things to be said about the "expressivist logic," let us say, of inner and outer, in, first, failed actions. They are the first sorts of cases often raised as objections, but they do not bear on Nietzsche's claims. Someone—Lanier, let us say—did everything he could to arrive on time for Joshua's party, but some intervening contingency prevented him. But surely he intended to arrive on time. Must an expressivist account say otherwise? No. Lanier took several steps toward the outer realization of the intention, there is plenty of evidence from other actions that he is always polite and conscientious about such things, that he values Joshua's friendship, and there is no way he could have *gotten himself* stuck in the traffic jam. He was well on the way, and there is plenty of "outer" manifesting his "inner," even if not completely. The situation would change if we imagine Lanier's wife saying, "Why do you always come this way to go to Joshua's? You know it *always* makes us late, and you know there is a better way." Or if we imagined Lanier at home, thinking, "There's plenty of time to get there, but I always have bad luck with traffic, so I might as well not even go since I'll arrive so late. But at least I intended to go until I remembered this."

Moreover, the fact that the doer must be understood to be expressed in the deed need not entail either that *everything* in the agent's ex ante mindedness must be expressed for the movement to count as a deed (that the doer is wholly identified with the deed in that sense; there can be degrees of expression that can be authentic expressions and not self-serving, or that that *expression* alone warrants the agent's *affirmation* of the deed.

On the former issue: the position I want to attribute to Nietzsche is not wildly indifferent to contingencies. I begin to sculpt, and a small insignificant chisel mark cracks the entire stone into pieces. One should not say that I must have intended this pile of rubble, that I must be identified with what happens. That is the key: *something happened*; the result was not a deed, an expression of any aspect of my mindedness. (Just as Lanier's getting stuck in traffic is not something, we assume, he did, but something that happened to him.) Again, the situation changes if we imagine someone warning our sculptor: "You take too many risks always chiseling like that; so many of your marbles crack." So on my account the relation between doer and deed is some form of identity. Something can count as a deed, even if not *the* deed I self-deceptively and self-servingly insist it is. The deed can be mine even if a lot remains undetermined for me and others about what I actually intended by doing it. We might have to wait and see what else I am willing to do in order to be more determinate. There can be a great deal of interpretive play and so indeterminacy (for me and for others affected) in what it is I have done. There can be a lot of imprecision in trying to draw a line between what happens because of me but is not something I did, and what I did.

On the latter issue, expression/affirmation, there are clearly two senses at work of "the deed being mine." The first might be called a merely forensic sense, an answer to the question "Whose deed is this?" This deed was brought about, but by whom? This is the sense in which the law wants to know "Whose deed?" "Whose murder?" The butler's; the mistress's (etc.)? Then there is another sense much more difficult to answer. The answer turns on the very elusive issue of the Nietzschean theory of freedom. Nietzsche was obviously concerned that the power of modern conformism would render *any* expression of anyone's mindedness some sort of distortion, and so some sort of social pathology. But a distortion of what? Of what the agent would have intended had he not been subject to these conforming powers? Would have intended if we imagine him free ab initio to be whoever he wants to be? That is clearly an idle fantasy for Nietzsche. No one could ever be in such a position. This latter sense of "genuinely" or "authentically" mine is extremely difficult and a long-standing problem (from the "happy slaves" issue to Rousseau and Kant on self-legislation to Emerson on self-reliance to Heidegger on *Eigentlichkeit*). And I don't think that some notion of one's "struggling to overcome some obstacle in the outer world" will get us very far on this issue. People can struggle very hard to express a canned and wholly inherited and manipulated sense of themselves. A few minutes observing American politics can make that point. I think that all the evidence is that Nietzsche thought *he* knew how to make this distinction between mine in the purely forensic or factual sense (not someone else's) and "truly" mine, all without a "true self" ontology, but he did not make it easy for commentators to state the nature of this distinction. So there is still much to be done.

## III

Here is another component any "psychological" reading of Nietzsche must face. Bernard Williams praised Nietzsche's "minimalist" psychology. He was aligning himself with what he took to be Nietzsche's suspicions of accounts of the human soul that were already committed to some moral or ethical ideal, and then postulated the faculties or capacities necessary to make the pursuit of such ideals look possible and coherent. The divided soul, the free will, conscience, and moral sense would all be examples of such a mistake. The relation, Nietzsche and Williams in effect argued, should go the other way. If we wanted to explain the possibility and coherence of the pursuit of such ideals, we ought to be constrained in doing so by an account of capacities and faculties available in nonmoral actions. In the book my emphasis on "the erotic Nietzsche" was meant to do justice to this constraint.[13]

Having introduced that notion, my aim was to associate it in its generality with the kinds of things the Platonic Socrates invokes eros to account for, from art to philosophy to love of good laws to friendship. The idea in such a generality was first to notice the signal importance of what Nietzsche sometimes called "esteeming," *schätzen*, valuing. Nietzsche considers asserting a claim or recommending an action, I argued, as expressions of some commitment to a value, something like promises to keep faith with and to be able to justify what was claimed, to remain committed to the implications of what one was recommending. (So the claim is *quite* general; it is that the domain of intentional intelligibility itself is the domain of value, self-subsumption under norms.) For Nietzsche, famously, these values are values because they are valued, not in themselves, although that intimation of a "projection" of value misleadingly suggests "acts" of projection at punctuated moments of time, "conferring" value. That is not the case. The claim is: there would not be such values were humans not to have come to value them, but that process is collective, sustained over time, mediated in many institutional, religious, and artistic practices, and inherited, *very rarely* open to revision. Nietzsche thinks we are living through such a potentially revolutionary time, comparable to the end of the "tragic age of the Greeks."

13. This is an invocation (*eros*) that begins early in Nietzsche's work and stays late, especially in the musings on himself as Dionysos in late works. See *Ecce Homo, Vorwort*, §2, or in frequent asides, as in the quotation from Ovid in §3. I note, but cannot now defend, the claim that I disagree with Williams on the larger issue. I think for Nietzsche all psychology is necessarily moral psychology. There is no purely psychological, and so "morally" neutral, point of view.

Making use of John Haugeland's "Truth and Rule-Following" article,[14] I went on to distinguish everyday commitments to various values, which are frequently subject to revision, expansion, or abandonment, and, by contrast, "depth" commitments, the loss of which would leave us near-literally lost, disoriented, so they are almost impossible to imagine giving up. In undertaking these depth commitments we are not fulfilling some *other* commitment, as if there could be a universal obligation to undertake some depth commitments. That would obviously start an infinite regress. But there must be a hierarchical relation between thin and depth commitments. In making a claim or recommending an action, we commit ourselves to a variety of obligations that cannot all be fulfilled, and we need some orienting concern, some general sense of what is more or less important to us, if we are to resolve such conflicts. We might say that this issue concerns what matters to us: which things matter because others do, and things that simply matter, that we could not imagine not mattering.[15] Since we do not *decide* what ought to matter, and thereby have it matter (even though we can do what we think ought to be significant to do, even without it actually mattering to us more than that), and since things can matter to us that we think ought not to matter, we have to call such commitments prereflective and prevolitional, or, I suggested, erotic attachments. (We do not decide whom or what to love, whom or what to care about.) This is all as mysterious in its way as the appearance and disappearance of an inspiring eros.

In our actions and inactions, we can be said to express what matters and what does not (much more reliably than by what we avow), and in certain rare "crisis" moments, a "depth commitment" can be at stake and the extent of such depth can be revealed. Now, this does not commit Nietzsche to any "inner self." He is a well-known critic of that notion. For one thing, there is no assumption about some underlying, permanent set of such commitments or bearer of such commitments. Things come to matter to someone in this critical way, and they can cease to matter, or matter in a different sense. The qualitative difference in the degree of the importance of the commitment, and the role of that commitment in ordering one's actions,

14. In Haugeland, *Having Thought: Essays in the Metaphysics of Mind*, 305–62.

15. This is much closer to the semantic field of "the erotic," and so less volitional than "valuing." One does not, cannot, will what ought to matter to one; one can come to have a belief that some goal is important, and yet still find it doesn't much matter to one; one can be ashamed of what does matter to one.

need not entail any inner-self ontology. Some critical deed may be critical because what is at stake is what matters the most, but only at that time, in that context. The spatial relation at issue is actually not rightly captured by notions like underlying or deep, but rather "highest," as in "highest values."

Now, I argued in the book and elsewhere that it was important to see things this way in order to understand that Nietzsche's diagnosis of nihilism was that it was not a crisis of credible belief or of strength of will, but the failure of desire, the failure of mattering. This, admittedly, immediately gives the impression that the signal manifestation of this problem is "failure" in the sense of collapse, nothing mattering enough to be worth any investment or sacrifice. Boredom would be an example. This *is* of course a clear manifestation, and Nietzsche does appeal to the failure of desire in this sense. But there are lots of things that "the last men," paradigmatic nihilists, *care about*, and they might even desire what they desire, however trivial, with passionate intensity. (Nietzsche's descriptions of "last men" and "pale atheists" do not suggest this, but he says nothing that would definitively rule it out.) The even more paradoxical thought is that Nietzsche seems to think that one particularly catastrophic manifestation of nihilism is *contentment*, bovine satisfaction in the low and base, caring about the wrong things, not "not caring."

Clearly we need a more general notion of "failure," more than just collapse or absence, if we are to understand nihilism as a failure of desire. We need something like: certain pathological *manifestations* of desire (not its absence) can also count as its "failure," as in obsessive and so forever unsatisfiable desire, desires for unreasonable, unattainable objects, and, an old standby in Nietzsche, self-deceived self-destructive desires.[16] (The self-deceit issue is very prominent in Nietzsche's accounts of what is going wrong. In §38 of *The Anti-Christ* especially, he marvels at the fact that, given what people do [*Nicht ein Glauben, sondern ein Thun*], it is clear that no one is committed to Christianity. ["There was only one Christian, and he died on the cross."] Yet they manage somehow to avow sincerely Christian principles. This is the cause for what Nietzsche often characterizes as his greatest danger, a thoroughgoing contempt for such a creature.)

16. I am much indebted to Ken Gemes for extensive correspondence about this issue. I don't regard myself as having provided yet an adequate answer to Gemes's questions about "failure" and pathology. These are only some suggestions.

One thought would be to pay attention to the fact that Nietzsche does not say that nihilism is the collapse of *anything* worth caring about, of all values. Nihilism is defined by the event: the *highest* values devalue themselves. We might have lost the distinction between highest and lowest, might cease to care about it, to care only for what we happen to want. So the last men might care about all sorts of ends but be without an orienting sense of the highest, that which matters most, worth sacrifice. This disorientation is treated by Nietzsche as a kind of failure. They drift instead from pleasure to pleasure, timid, unwilling to take any risks for the sake of something worth taking risks for. This would count as a pathology if we can imagine such a life, without begging any questions, as inevitably threatening some form of self-contempt, practical incoherence, conflicts that cannot be resolved, or as possible at all without these effects only by massive self-deceit. We could point to these *self*-defeating effects as a defense against the charge that we are inventing a capacity (for depth commitment) in order to defend an ethical ideal, contra Williams's minimalism. I don't suggest that it is obvious that Nietzsche thinks this, but just want to propose that this is the answer suggested by many of Nietzsche's formulations.

## IV

A final issue for the expressivist, psychological interpretation. It is how to understand the frequent Nietzschean emphasis on the value of "self-overcoming" (which he virtually equates with his understanding of freedom) and such remarks in *On the Genealogy of Morality* as his assertion that "every good thing on earth" eventually overcomes ("sublates") itself, or his proclamation of what he calls the "law of life," "the law of the necessity of self-overcoming in the nature of life" (where he uses both the Hegelian *Selbstaufhebung* and *Selbstüberwindung*);[17] and to do justice to the appearance of "constantly" (*beständig*) in remarks like:

> How is freedom measured in individuals and in peoples? It is measured by the resistance that needs to be overcome, by the effort that it costs to stay on *top*. Look for the highest type of free human beings where the highest resistance is *constantly being overcome*.[18]

17. Nietzsche, *On the Genealogy of Morality*, III, §27, trans. Diethe, 119.
18. Nietzsche, *Twilight of the Idols*, §38, trans. Norman, 213–14 (my emphasis).

Does this emphasis on Nietzsche's praise of self-overcoming skew the interpretation in favor of some sort of "priority" of self-dissatisfaction, as if only such endlessly unsatisfied individuals are worthy of Nietzsche's praise? I don't see why that should be the case. Here is my first attempt at a summary of what the self-overcoming passages show:

> One initial, still quite crude, summary of what Nietzsche is getting at in these passages would simply be that achieved freedom involves achieving a capacity both to sustain a wholehearted commitment to an ideal (an ideal that is worth sacrificing for, that provides the basis for a certain hierarchical unity among one's interests and passions) and what appears at first glance to be a capacity in some tension with such wholeheartedness—a willingness to overcome or abandon such a commitment in altered circumstances or as a result of some development. To be unable to endure the irresolvable dynamic of what Nietzsche calls an ideal's or a goal's or a value's constant self-overcoming, to remain dogmatically attached to an already overcome form of life . . . all these are treated as forms of unfreedom.[19]

If I am going to be upbraided for too "Hegelian" a reading of Nietzsche (as I frequently am), I might as well get the benefit too: a dialectical tension in the Nietzschean desiderata, not an unbalanced "priority."

Second, is it a consequence of this expressivism that it counts what should be, and is treated by Nietzsche as, a rare and very difficult achievement—seeing oneself expressed in one's deeds in a wholehearted affirmation—as a normal, everyday occurrence? As emphasized before, there are two separate questions here that must be kept distinct. "Expressivism" is a claim that shares an assumption with all accounts of actions as such—that there are bodily movements or mental happenings that stand in a relation to a subject's mindedness—and it argues for a kind of relation different from all causal, compatibilist and voluntarist, free-will accounts. There are then all sorts of *further* questions one can ask *about such expressed mindedness,* including whether the deed actually expresses what the agent avows, and whether the agent's mindedness can be said to reflect *her,* or is itself the product of a coercive conformism. So, to jump to another point, the "weak" types can certainly be said to express themselves in their, say,

19. Pippin, *Nietzsche, Psychology, and First Philosophy,* 112–13.

vengeful, moralistic acts of punishment. But what they avow as their intention is self-deceived, and because of that, they can be said to be engaged in a self-defeating pattern of valuation. Their acts express a motivation that they disavow (even to themselves, if they are self-deceived and not hypocrites), making holding together the deception, and the psychic satisfaction from realizing their real intentions, more and more difficult, especially in a religion that insists on honesty about intentions. Or, without self-deception, one could say: Teaching that course on "ethics for bureaucrats" is *what I did*, is my deed. My intention to teach the course is expressed in what I do; my preparation, my showing up on time, all express my intention to do a good job. But this job I found at East Podunk Technical Teachers College is the only one I could find after Princeton, and the activity is not an expression of my highest values, or what I would have chosen, or what I believe ought to be taught, etc. I can be said to see some aspect of myself in the deeds (say, my willingness to do whatever it takes to keep teaching some sort of philosophy), but certainly not the self I would wholeheartedly affirm. Nothing I attribute to Nietzsche is inconsistent with such a characterization.

# 11

# Alasdair MacIntyre's Modernity

## I

It has not gone unnoticed that Alasdair MacIntyre's rhetorically powerful, philosophically impressive and very influential book *After Virtue* (1981)[1] would be a bargain at twice the price. Buy one book and you actually get at least four, all of them full of challenging philosophy on every page.

There is first the display of and frequent remarks about MacIntyre's wholehearted embrace of what he calls his "historicism."[2] The premise is that philosophy cannot amount to anything very interesting in a historical vacuum. The terms under review, especially complex normative terms, will not even have been properly understood (we literally won't know what we are talking about) without some attention to their various historical uses in various communities at various times. And we are encouraged to recognize that the philosopher's own attention is guided by issues of salience and importance, which themselves require genealogical analysis to avoid self-deception, and indeed self-satisfaction and complacency. Philosophy must be historically self-conscious and historically oriented, and that orientation requires a historical diagnosis. Such a diagnosis requires in turn a develop-

1. All references will be to the second edition of *After Virtue: A Study in Moral Theory*.

2. This can be a misleading term, given its association with nineteenth-century historical relativists, which MacIntyre certainly is not. Perhaps a less misleading term would be the Diltheyean/Heideggerian term "historicity": broadly, having an essentially historical nature.

mental narrative of some sort, and MacIntyre has quite a sweeping declensionist account of the dire implications of our having rejected or lost the possibility of life with the notion of virtue at its core.

MacIntyre's now-famous diagnosis is bracing. Our invocation of moral norms is profoundly incoherent, and this in an extremely odd way. It is odd because, according to MacIntyre, the incoherence does not show up as such in our evaluative practices. (As in Nietzsche's account of the "last man," the most disturbing symptom of our crisis is its invisibility. No one thinks we are in any crisis. We "blink" in stupefaction at the very notion of such a crisis, like the last men, who "have invented happiness.") Even when this lack of coherence does in fact show up in hopelessly unresolvable ethical arguments, in interlocutors talking past one another, in the absence of any shared ground, we don't understand the reason for such unresolvability (that we don't really understand the terms we are invoking), and we simply argue blithely on. Interminable moral conflict is written off as due to the ignorance, depravity, irrationality, or confusion of whomever we are arguing with, and that favor is returned. In fact, our moral norms are actually just various strands of past uses, fragments, absent the context in which those uses would make sense.[3]

It is immediately important to stress the radicality of MacIntyre's claim. We are to imagine that in making moral claims on others, judging them, appealing to them for the sake of a moral cause, we have in fact "lost our comprehension" of what we are talking about *and we don't know that we have.* One could imagine, for example, an analogy: someone in the Roman Catholic faith standing up and sitting down at the right times in mass, advancing to the altar to receive communion, visiting a darkened cubicle once a week to tell intimate things to a stranger, without ever having understood or understood very well the point to such activities, performing them as an empty ritual, "because that's what a Catholic does," and unable to explain to herself why she was doing any of these things. It is even possible to imagine that the parishioner had *also* never noticed the emptiness or pointlessness, that it had never occurred to her that she didn't understand what she was doing, that all her life she had just watched other people and had done what

3. For example, MacIntyre is "indebted to" the most famous instance of this kind of analysis, Elizabeth Anscombe's 1958 argument that our notions of duty and obligation are derived from a theological context of divine command, and that absent such a context, the terms cannot mean what we take them to mean (*After Virtue*, 53).

they did. But by the "radicality" of MacIntyre's hypothesis, I mean that this last sort of example and MacIntyre's hypothesis about modern moral language are hard to imagine in the case of the parishioner, and *very* hard to imagine in our ordinary moral life.[4] I will return to this issue below.

In MacIntyre's own analogy, there is a culture that has lost its reservoir of shared natural-scientific knowledge, but it possesses enough fragments of the vocabulary of science to utter words like "molecule" or "cell" or "thermodynamics" in ways that "circulate" unproblematically—there are uses such that everyone thinks that they understand appropriate and inappropriate uses and combinations of terms[5]—but no one really understands what the terms mean, and there are no "crisis" occasions where someone (like Nietzsche, say) asks, "Do any of us really know what we are talking about?" Again, that, I suggest, is not impossible to imagine, but it is very hard.[6] This diagnosis comprises the first three chapters of *After Virtue* and reappears frequently throughout.

There is then an extraordinarily lucid and focused history of ethical thought, intertwined with world history itself and a sociological appreciation of the particular forms of life in which various moral notions would be

4. Another, and a real world example, of what MacIntyre is talking about could be the so-called hidden Jews of New Mexico, descendants of Spaniards fleeing the Inquisition who kept their Judaism a secret and pretended to be Catholic. Eventually many later generations grew up without knowing they were Jews, but still practiced, without genuinely understanding, religious rituals, and sang songs and ate foods that are Jewish in origin. Cf. this account:

> Far more common are descendants of hidden Jews who have forgotten, or almost forgotten their heritage. In many cases, families don't eat pork, or light candles or perform other rituals on Friday nights, which marks the beginning of the Jewish Sabbath, but they don't know why they carry on these traditions. In some families, children still play with handmade four sided tops identical to the Jewish toy called a "dreydl." The only difference is the letters on the sides of the top are written in Spanish instead of Hebrew. ("Search for the Buried Past: The Hidden Jews of New Mexico," http://www.nanrubin.net/uploads/2/8/5/5/28554143/transcript_-_search_buried_past.pdf, accessed October 6, 2014.)

5. This too is in itself an extreme assumption, that such successful circulation *could* occur. Even some sort of very modest holism about meaning would lead us to suspect that such a possibility is *extremely* unlikely, given the various exclusions, implications, assumptions, and inferences any one term would imply and the unlikelihood that no conflict would ever occur with what we *did* know and *could* demonstrate. It is, however, not an impossible scenario, and for the sake of argument, I'll assume that this bare sense of logical possibility is all we need. Of course, people use terms like "electricity" and "neurotransmitter" and "dark matter" all the time, and they couldn't define them if their lives depended on it. But they are rightly confident that they could find out if need be, that *someone* knows what they mean.

6. The few who notice the problem, like Nietzsche, are written off as cranks, Jeremiahs.

at home. This has two main parts (two more books, in other words), an account of what MacIntyre considers the utter failure of the Enlightenment project of justifying morality by appeal to nature, human nature, or reason (chapters 4 through 8),[7] and an account of what he calls the contrasting "classical tradition." He notes that this is not a monolithic tradition; there are serious differences, but similarity enough to group them together. The main figures are Homer, Sophocles, Aristotle, the New Testament, Aquinas, and medieval thinkers (chapters 10 through 13).

His book, or the fourth book, then concludes with a more thematic treatment of, in effect, what MacIntyre thinks we have lost, a proper appreciation of the centrality of the notion of virtue, its indispensability, in any form of life that makes sense, and so is worth living. His very bold (because so counterintuitive) view is that all the basic options in evaluative appraisal come down, finally, to "Aristotle or Nietzsche," *either* some sort of acceptable-to-modernity teleology[8] that can ground an assessment of whether a life or a collective life is lived well or poorly, *or* the pursuit of self-interest or personal preference (mere will to power), constrained, if at all, only by some collective maximizing formula (chapters 14 through 17). In these chapters, MacIntyre speculates about what conditions *could* supply some new tradition of virtue with the right context and coherence, since, MacIntyre admits, we cannot simply return to Aristotle's metaphysical biology.[9] Here the centrality of narrative forms of self-understanding, the achievement of goods "internal" to various practices (not an external good achieved by means of the practice, but achieving excellence *in* the practice as an end in itself), the structure of some local and living ethical community, and the inheritance (and collective embrace) of a common historical

7. One could count a fifth valuable book as part of the bargain. MacIntyre gets hold of Hume and the empiricist tradition in moral theory early on and never lets up. This thoughtful and compelling destruction of the credibility of that tradition could easily stand alone as a major accomplishment.

8. It is important to note, as Terry Pinkard has pointed out ("MacIntyre's Critique of Modernity"), that MacIntyre is not encouraging any "return" or indulging in any nostalgia. He rejects a good deal of Aristotle's specific politics as well as, most importantly, his "metaphysical biology." His "replacement" version of teleology will be discussed below.

9. This is a huge concession. I am not sure it is necessary or that, once made, there is anything much left of the notion of "teleology." For what is, in effect, an Aristotle without such a concession, see Michael Thompson's *Life and Action: Elementary Structures of Practice and Practical Thought*. More on these issues below.

tradition are to do this "replacing" job. These constitute what MacIntyre calls a "socially teleological account," not a biological one. And, given the plurality of practices, conflict will not merely be the result of flaws or mistakes or ignorance (as in Aristotle), but will be unavoidable.[10]

There is then in conclusion a pessimistic appraisal of the chances that some sort of a notion of virtue could again get a real grip on the lives of persons in the late-modern world. Those chances, aside from isolated communities serving as something like preservationist monasteries, are basically slim and none. The two main ideas in the book are then strikingly put in the book's penultimate sentence, after MacIntyre has compared our age with the dark ages.

> This time, however, the barbarians are not waiting beyond the frontiers; they have already been governing us for quite some time. And it is our lack of consciousness of this that constitutes part of our predicament.[11]

## II

I want to raise three questions about MacIntyre's account. First, in the next section, I want to introduce the possibility that the exclusive disjunction that is asserted around the middle and at the end of MacIntyre's book—"Aristotle or Nietzsche"—is not well formed and is too exclusive. It is not well formed because Nietzsche himself is a kind of virtue theorist, has nothing but contempt for the managers and therapists and aesthetes who make up MacIntyre's modern bestiary, and clearly regards the pursuit of self-interest as a craven, ignoble goal. It is hard to see him summarizing or standing for the philosophical underpinnings of one of the exclusive disjuncts. He certainly does not believe that the only serious question in assessing the worth of any life is whether one can subject others to one's will or is subject to the will of others. Christianity, for example, *succeeded* in achieving this "Master" position, and Nietzsche, while occasionally expressing grudging admi-

10. We can also count another book within the book: a fairly straightforward analytical assessment, running as if underneath the historical narrative, of the philosophical weaknesses of a variety of arguments and the positions of various philosophers: emotivism, rational egoism, Kierkegaard, Sartre, Goffman, Moore, Gewirth, Rawls, Nozick.

11. MacIntyre, *After Virtue*, 261.

ration (and wonder)[12] at that, is always clear that the uses to which Christian power were put were catastrophic. St. Paul's religion (which Nietzsche sometimes contrasts with Jesus's religion) produced a resentment-fueled, ascetic, life-denying, and dishonest (if also ruling, quite powerful) form of life, grossly distorting our possible appreciation of a finer, more beautiful, and more noble life. If her view of Nietzschean virtues weren't so extremely limited, it would be more correct to accept Philippa Foot's version of Nietzsche as, essentially, a virtue theorist, arguing on the same plane with Aristotle, just recommending very different virtues.[13]

In itself this, though, is mostly a textual or interpretive issue, and in this context a battle of citations would not be productive. I mean to make use of Nietzsche in this way only to begin to challenge the well-formedness and the exclusivity of the disjunction itself (or, rather, an exclusive disjunction and a controversial implication; that is, the disjunction: you are *either* some sort of virtue theorist *or* your moral philosophy is a failure, *and so* moral distinctions and evaluations will then have to look like the mere expression of preference or interest or will) and to introduce a larger issue in the next section.

MacIntyre's central question is, as he tells us, quite a simple one: "Can Aristotle's ethics, or something very like it, after all, be vindicated?"[14] It is in the light of that question that Nietzsche is so important to MacIntyre, because if the answer to the question is no, then, according to MacIntyre, Nietzsche is, has to be, right. MacIntyre understands this to mean

> that all rational vindications of morality manifestly fail and that *therefore* belief in the tenets of morality needs to be explained in terms of a set of rationalizations which conceal the fundamentally non-rational phenomena of the will.[15]

This is the assumption that leads to the claim mentioned in my title. When summarizing his "Aristotle or Nietzsche" claim, MacIntyre writes:

12. *Anti-Christ*, §§24–26, §43; *Beyond Good and Evil*, §195; *On the Genealogy of Morality*, §7, §8.

13. Foot, "Nietzsche: The Revaluation of Values."

14. MacIntyre, *After Virtue*, 118.

15. Ibid., 117. That "therefore" is quite a leap, or at least I don't understand it. Perhaps morality is a matter of local custom, has no rational defense, but is nevertheless taken quite seriously by its practitioners, inspires sacrifice, even of life itself. Why is "the will" the only explicans left?

> *There is no third alternative* and more particularly there is no alternative provided by those thinkers at the heart of the contemporary curriculum in moral philosophy, Hume, Kant, and Mill. It is no wonder that the teaching of ethics is so often destructive and skeptical in its effects upon the minds of those taught.[16]

But there *is* a third alternative, occasionally mentioned by MacIntyre, a philosopher to whom his whole historical approach is obviously deeply indebted because that philosopher was the first one to practice it: Hegel. With Hegel's option a bit more in view, we can offer an alternative account of the moral phenomenology provided by MacIntyre.

It will also allow us, in the last section, to assess the "post-Aristotelian" conditions sketched by MacIntyre as necessary and perhaps sufficient for a reanimation of the virtue tradition, at least in principle. My thesis there will be: MacIntyre's is a Hegelian approach, but it is impossible to be a half-hearted Hegelian, which I will argue MacIntyre is. One is either "all in," as they say in poker, or one doesn't play that game.

## III

I begin with MacIntyre's somewhat unusual reticence about Hegel in the book. I say unusual because, given the tenor, the tone, and the method of *After Virtue*, Hegel's is a name that ought to spring to mind immediately. This is because, on the one hand, modern philosophy at its core could rightly be summarized as "anti-Aristotelianism," especially in the foundational work of Descartes and Hobbes. Their contempt for the Aristotelian tradition is of course intertwined with the history of scholasticism, but the criticisms apply just as well to Aristotle himself, as they well knew. And, on the other hand, Hegel is the first modern philosopher to attempt a rehabilitation of Aristotle,[17] praising his metaphysics and philosophy of mind to the skies, appropriating Aristotle's terminology (*dynamis* and *energeia*) as his own (*an-sich-sein* and *für-sich-sein*) and citing him favorably when he is trying to make a point about his own position. In a way that aligns him with MacIntyre, this also means that Hegel does not believe that the metaphysi-

16. Ibid., my emphasis.

17. Leibniz should get some credit, but Hegel goes much further and is much more explicit.

cal assumptions of modern natural science have rendered Aristotle an impossible option, so standard a view in modern philosophy that it is treated as a truism.

Moreover, although it is often forgotten in the usual rush to condemn Hegel's triumphalism, reconciliationism, Prussian accommodationism, and so forth, all of his major works express varying degrees of MacIntyre-esque anxiety about the major norms and institutions, that basic form of life, emerging in Western Europe in the first third of the nineteenth century: "modernity," for want of a more precise word. In the 1812 Preface to his *Science of Logic*, Hegel describes *a way of thinking* as the most important characteristic of our age, a way he calls "the understanding," *Verstand* (especially as Locke and Kant understood it).[18] The dominance of this mode of account-giving has left us spiritually impoverished, like, he says, a richly adorned temple without a "holy of holies"; no metaphysics, no theology, and nothing to replace them.[19] We have just unreflective common sense and the fixity and rigidity of *Verstand*. In the Introduction to the work, he again notes that "the reflection of the understanding has seized hold of philosophy,"[20] leaving issues that cannot be solved empirically, the most important and pressing human issues, matters of mere private opinion.

Hegel's unease with all this, together with Rousseau's incalculable influence, and similar concerns in figures like Schiller and the early romantics, is what begat those familiar later claims about the "ideological" nature of bourgeois philosophy, the "one-dimensionality" of modern societies, the "totalization" of instrumental reasoning, the dominance of "identity thinking," the "crisis of the European sciences," the "colonization of the life-world," and so forth. Although *After Virtue* is not in the strictest sense "ideology critique,"[21] it can certainly be included in a list of these many gestures of great self-dissatisfaction.[22]

18. He means more by the term than MacIntyre does by claiming that modern reason has been reduced to the merely calculative, but there are nevertheless deep affinities.

19. Hegel, *The Science of Logic*, trans. di Giovanni, 8.

20. Ibid., 25.

21. Although see the "Nietzschean ideology critique," one would have to call it, in passages like "The major protagonists of the distinctively modern moral causes of the modern world . . . offer a rhetoric which serves to conceal behind the masks of morality what are in fact the preferences of arbitrary will and desire" (MacIntyre, *After Virtue*, 71) and the explicit acceptance of that label in some sense in the central paragraph on 110.

22. See my *Modernism as a Philosophical Problem: On the Dissatisfactions of European High Culture.*

While MacIntyre only mentions Hegel's name a few times (often in conjunction with either Collingwood or Vico, as a way of making a general point), it is certainly true that Hegelian ideas are everywhere in the book, and appreciating that will allow us to draw some contrasts with Hegel as well.

There is first what has already been mentioned, the historical method of philosophy. Ideas must be understood in their historical context, where that means not just in the light of their particular historical interlocutors, but as expressions of and responsive to the social struggles of a community at a time. MacIntyre wants to suggest something that could be read as a commentary on parts of the *Phenomenology of Spirit*:

> that the roots of some of the problems which now engage the specialized attention of academic philosophers and the roots of some of the problems central to our everyday social and practical lives are one and the same.[23]

And even more sweepingly:

> Every action is the bearer of more or less theory-laden beliefs and concepts, every piece of theorizing and every expression of belief is a political and moral action.[24]

Compare Hegel's remark that what he calls "thought determinations" (*Denkbestimmungen*) "instinctively and unconsciously pervade our spirit everywhere."[25] There are also striking, particular points of important agreement:

> For it is Pascal who recognized that the Protestant-cum-Jansenist conception of reason is in important respects at one with the conception of rea-

23. MacIntyre, *After Virtue*, 36.

24. Ibid., 61. This means exactly what it seems to imply for MacIntyre and is another example of his robust suspicion of empiricism and its epistemology and, by contrast, his deep sense of the historicity of every aspect of human life, a feature of his book that I have always found completely compelling every time I read it. So "the twentieth-century observer looks into the night sky and sees stars and planets; some earlier observers saw instead chinks in a sphere through which the light beyond could be observed" (79).

25. Hegel, *The Science of Logic*, 19.

> son at home in the most innovative seventeenth-century philosophy and science.[26]

This remarkable ironic association of theology and scientific conceptions of rationality calls to mind Hegel's account of the "Enlightenment's struggle with faith" in his *Phenomenology of Spirit,* where the same paradoxical point is made, that the Enlightenment's charge that faith represents unreason, and faith's charge that the Enlightenment is just another religion, are shown to be both correct.

And the following statement about historical temporality can fairly be called "pure Hegel":

> The past is never something merely to be discarded, but rather . . . the present is intelligible only as a commentary upon and response to the past in which the past, if necessary and if possible, is corrected and transcended, yet corrected and transcended in a way that leaves the present open to being in turn corrected and transcended by some yet more adequate point of view.[27]

Here again a citation battle will break out if we raise the question of whether Hegel not only agrees with this but goes much further, with a claim about knowledge of the Absolute, the end of history, a "pro-victors" or "victors' justice" conception of history. There are many more such issues. But we have enough agreement to raise a question that stems from a clear disagreement. (The largest issue of overlap and disagreement, the issue of narrative intelligibility, will be discussed in the last section.)

That disagreement concerns the use of terms like "incoherence," "lost comprehension," "fictions," "simulacra," and "mistaken rejections" or, most broadly, norms the uses of which indicate that the users do not understand what they mean. These undialectical or wholly negative notions could not be Hegelian thoughts, and not because he thinks everything that happens in history is just as it should be.

Indeed, even apart from Hegel, one already senses that something is going wrong with the extreme sharpness of the distinctions MacIntyre

26. MacIntyre, *After Virtue,* 54. MacIntyre means to point to how strict a limit is set for the scope of what reason can do by both enterprises. Reason ends up merely calculative for both.

27. Ibid., 146.

makes (any moral norm other than virtue-based must fail and reveal self-interest) when he writes briefly about Henry James's novel *The Portrait of a Lady*.[28] MacIntyre thinks that the novel helps him illustrate that in modern life "the distinction between manipulative and non-manipulative social relationships has been obliterated."[29] "Obliterated" is a red flag of sorts, a sign of something going wrong. In the novel there are certainly examples of grossly manipulative behavior. Gilbert Osmond and Madame Merle deceive, lie to, and manipulate the heiress Isabel Archer, and "trap" her in a marriage to Osmond, so that they can get their hands on her fortune for the daughter they have had, Pansy. MacIntyre also thinks that the novel and James's other novels as a whole show that James thinks that modern life has become a "whole milieu in which the manipulative mode of moral instrumentalism has triumphed,"[30] and that James wants to show us a society "that has become an arena for the active achievement of their [persons'] own satisfactions, who interpret reality as a series of opportunities for their enjoyment and for whom the last enemy is boredom."[31] But MacIntyre also ropes in Isabel's benefactor, Ralph Touchett, who clearly finds Isabel fascinating and so, he explains, wanted to "put a little wind" in Isabel's sails by giving her a vast fortune to see what such an interesting, brilliant, and fearless woman would do.

In the first place, this is not true of many, many other novels by James. Lambert Strether in *The Ambassadors* has as refined and acute a genuinely moral sensibility as any character in literature, and is perfectly capable of coming to see that the young man he is supposed to save from the clutches of an adulteress is not worth saving, so callow and selfish has he become, and that the adulteress, Madame de Vionnet, is a far worthier person, despite the adultery. (She is technically still married to someone she does not live with.) In fact it is the morally righteous Americans, the Henrietta Stackpoles of the world, who, while not manipulative or selfish, are morally stupid, a far, far greater sin in James than boredom.[32] There is no clearer example of unmanipulative and admirable behavior in the history of great novels than

28. MacIntyre is not only expressing his own views but, he reports, is following the lead in William Gass, *Fiction and the Figures of Life*.

29. MacIntyre, *After Virtue*, 24.

30. Ibid.

31. Ibid., 25.

32. James would certainly agree with MacIntyre's (not at all Christian) affirmation of Aristotle's view, contra Kant's, that "stupidity of a certain kind precludes goodness" (ibid., 155).

Milly Theale in *The Wings of the Dove*. Maggie Verver's complex maneuverings around and against the lover of her husband, Charlotte Stant, do not begin to be rightly described as simply manipulative. And poor Ralph Touchett! To be classified in the same category as Osmond is far too extreme a claim, when it is obvious that (a) he is dying and (b) he is profoundly in love with Isabel, and so (c) thinks of himself as having one great chance to help her to the kind of life with the kind of freedom that can make for the greatest realization of the best of human potentialities. He turns out to be wrong; but he is mistaken, not bad. Isabel is young and headstrong, and so committed to being different, unusual, that she deliberately does what she knows everyone she cares about will recoil from. But Ralph's generosity is not phony; he is not amusing himself at Isabel's expense. The ill-formed and too exclusive disjunction at the heart of MacIntyre's book, "Aristotle or Nietzsche," here manifests itself in the ill-formed and too exclusive disjunction of "nonmanipulative or manipulative," categories that do not begin to do justice to the world created in James's fiction.

But the basic problem lies even deeper. Consider a common moral issue, and then consider how MacIntyre's phenomenology could treat it. A husband betrays his wife by having a long love affair with her sister. The wife discovers it. She says such things as "Betraying and lying to me like that was just wrong." "We promised each other we would be faithful to each other, and you broke that promise. That is wrong." "You had no right to hurt me like that." "You are a very bad, vile person. What kind of a man sleeps with his wife's sister?" "What kind of world would it be if people couldn't count on each other? Not a good one, not one I would want to live in." "You owed me, you had a duty to me; I helped you when you needed help, and now I can never count on you."

If we imagine a response by the husband that amounts to "What do you mean, what could you possibly mean, by 'wrong,' 'right' (in the sense of entitlement, not the opposite of wrong), 'good,' 'duty'? We no longer have any sense of what those terms mean," we would be right to say that the husband is self-serving, sophistical, and changing the subject. What is it about those charges and that response to the husband that is in "serious disorder"? The successful use of these terms does not require either that the person using them be able to give a philosophical defense of them (I am not saying that MacIntyre believes that) or even that *someone* can give a philosophical defense of them. (I do think that MacIntyre probably believes something like that, but the main point is that his moral phenomenology should first convince us that the wife doesn't really understand what she is saying, and that the husband is basically right. He could be considered the "King Kamehameha II" of marital argument, sweeping away the taboos of the bourgeois institution of marriage.[33])

It is true that according to MacIntyre's hypothetical analogy, people *believe* they understand the terms they hurl at one another, but we should assume, for the sake of the analogy, that they do not. But how could we in this case? It is not difficult to imagine the wife in command of the usual implications and exclusions of the terms she uses, capable of drawing the right inferences, responding to challenges, presenting evidence, and so forth, all notwithstanding that she could not present a philosophically respectable argument about the ultimate foundation of such moral terms in a moral theory. Is it evidence of the "incoherence" of the notion of a human right that, probably, 90 percent or more of the people who use that term could not tell you what the basis of such a claim is, how many there are, and so forth?

Some sort of philosophical redemption of the claims of moral life does not seem to be the issue at all. It wasn't for Aristotle, for example, the hero of MacIntyre's book. The *phronimos* does not need to rely in any way, whether achieved by himself or by anybody, on some large-scale "metaphysical biology" and defense of teleology in order rightly to reason out what to do. Terms like "cowardice" and "magnanimity" for Aristotle "live" in concrete human practices (and die there sometimes), where their application requires discriminating judgment, not theory. Other terms, like "charity" and "humility," live in other sorts of practices, in other times. Given MacIntyre's sociological historicism, there should be nothing surprising or disturbing about this; nor should we be surprised if there is nevertheless some considerable overlap between heroic and classical and Christian and secular communities. It should be no more surprising than that students today can read Homer or Sophocles and not think of themselves as anthropologists confronting a deeply strange world.

Granted, they are not reading about *their* world, but as any teacher of these texts knows, that is in itself a fine topic for discussion: What remains, what doesn't; why; what has happened? For one thing it is possible to note that much of what has changed is not a wholesale revision in the basic principles of our moral lives, but a reduction of confidence that moral cate-

33. Ibid., 111–12.

gories can be easily *applied* (the rigidity and exclusivity issue in MacIntyre appears again; manipulative versus nonmanipulative won't get us very far in James's world); the hermeneutical complexity and self-consciousness of the modern social world, with its relatively new and immensely complicating notions of self-deceit and narcissism and the unconscious, creates problems in simply understanding what others are actually doing, even what I am doing. Diderot's famous Rameau's Nephew is not a self-indulgent, cynical aesthete, indifferent to the claims of others. That is what he *thinks* he is, but he is profoundly self-deceived, far more dependent on such others than he realizes. And the right moral stance toward someone genuinely self-deceived (someone who has genuinely succeeded in hiding who he is from himself) is hardly clear-cut. (There are hypocrites and frauds aplenty in the Jane Austen so beloved by Aristotelians, but there is nothing like the psychological complexity of Julien Sorel, Kate Croy, or Charlus, and accordingly there is in Stendhal, James, or Proust none of the firm judgmental confidence, and the bright clarity of the distinction between scoundrels and heroines, so on display in Austen.)

Indeed, even the philosopher who receives as much intense criticism as any in the book, Kant, certainly did not hold that *moral judgment itself* required universalization tests, with its concerns with "contradiction in conception" versus "contradiction in willing," false positives and alternate formulations of the Categorical Imperative. From his *Foundations of the Metaphysics of Morals*:

> But the most remarkable thing about ordinary human understanding in its practical concern is that it may have as much hope as any philosopher of hitting the mark. In fact it is almost more certain to do so than the philosopher, for while he has no principle which common understanding lacks, his judgment is easily confused by a mass of irrelevant considerations so that it easily turns aside from the correct way.[34]

MacIntyre wants to say that Kant was also wrong about the person of sound common sense, that, even if we accept that such a type has a better chance of figuring out properly what to do than befuddled philosophers, Kant still treated such a person as a kind of transhistorical touchstone for morality as such. He is not. He is the product of a stage of Christian, post-Reformation,

34. Kant, *Foundations of the Metaphysics of Morals*, trans. Beck, 20–21.

post–French Revolution civilization, and the theory that Kant builds up to defend his basic principles from skeptics is the pursuit of a fantasy, a putative universalism built on a contingent, particular perspective.

But this again seems to be built on too exclusive a disjunction, either particular, local, and contingent, or rational and universal. And it again ignores the possibility that the boundaries of these disjuncts are far fuzzier than admitted, with some considerable (and explicable) overlap—in itself, again, a Hegelian thought.

So, to return to the example: Is it credible that the wife does not really understand what she is saying? What is in profound disorder in her several charges? It seems likely that MacIntyre is thinking of the fact that the various charges represent different original sources of moral criticism, a kind of *jumble* (right, good, obligation), that he thinks the terms of this jumble are finally incommensurable (that is why they're a mere jumble and why they produce interminable and unresolvable conflicts) and that each has its own history, original context, and philosophical representative—and that it is fair to say that that historical moment and that context no longer obtain, no longer give the norms the successful circulation, power, use, they once had. They circulate now because everyone has tacitly agreed to use what have become "fictions" as if they were mutually understood. But they are not. The very diversity and variety of the accusations should, perhaps, give us some pause about, to use a distinction of Bernard Williams's, what we actually think (disorder, incoherence) and what we think we think (all in order; just a variety of wrongs). To address that issue, we need a bit more of the absent Hegel.

## IV

As noted, Hegel shares much of MacIntyre's phenomenology of modernity, although he never put things nearly as briskly and dramatically as MacIntyre, when the latter notes that much modern political theory seems to assume negotiations between strangers on a desert island, or that modern politics has simply become civil war by other means. But the analysis of historical forms of shared like-mindedness, what Hegel calls *Geist*, and especially the attempt to give an account of the breakdown of such shared mindedness, and the inseparability of such a diagnostic task and philosophy, unite them more as brothers in the same family than as distant cousins.

But the suspicions that arise for MacIntyre because of the jumble of different moral notions relevant in the example above do not arise for Hegel. Given that for Hegel (and, I would argue, in itself) we should expect considerable overlap, that a moral term could not survive, its force could not still be felt, unless we also still experienced in some sense the moral phenomena relevant to the term, unless we still shared some aspect of the form of life that is the necessary condition for the norm's meaningful use, the complexity of the situation is not surprising. Indeed why else would the term survive, even if a fragment? Some norms have not, as MacIntyre admits in his remarks on Aristotle ("You can't do that job; you are a woman"; "He is not one of us, is a barbarian, so he has no claims on us for proper treatment"). Why have those that have "survived" in fact survived unless something of the Hegelian account is true?

Here is a striking indication of the relevance of Hegel to these questions. MacIntyre uses the abolition of various "taboos" by King Kamehameha II in Hawaii to emphasize how fragile our hold on our moral notions likely is, as fragile as the hold of these taboos was when the king easily abolished them. He writes:

> Why should we think about our modern uses of *good, right,* and *obligatory* in any different way from that in which we think about late eighteenth-century Polynesian uses of *taboo*? And why should we not think of Nietzsche as the Kamehameha II of the European tradition.[35]

What is interesting about the examples, aside from the fact that it seems extremely hard just to *stop using* the terms in my example (*that* is why we should think differently about them), is that, written in exactly the order in which Hegel treats them, "right," "obligatory," and "good" are terms that characterize very well the structural parts of Hegel's *Elements of the Philosophy of Right.* That means of course that Hegel thinks he has a way to demonstrate the partiality but mutual interrelatedness of the notions, and so to deny any claim of incommensurablity or fragmented, unrelated shards of past traditions. This state of affairs does mean, as MacIntyre claims, that various conflicts will arise that will require quite a judgmental finesse, sometimes more than we are capable of. Someone can respect another's rights but act in other ways immorally (with great selfishness or wastefulness, for example); or various aspects of the pursuit of a good ethical life, like strong

35. Macintyre, *After Virtue,* 113.

nuclear family attachments, might conflict with universal obligations to treat all others equally; or someone with pure moral intentions can act unjustly, or even perform deeds that Hegel calls "evil."

Ultimately, Hegel's argument for this unusual unity does not only depend on the developmental deduction he goes through in that book. (By developmental deduction, I mean, for example, his showing that one way of making sense of Right, Abstract Right, is limited to the point of inconsistency; in Hegel's argument, by the need to distinguish punishment from revenge, a distinction that cannot be made, within that modality of that sense-making, without reference to a person's inner intention, or without the way "a moral point of view" makes sense of right.) It depends also on a very ambitious claim about, let us say, modalities of sense-making altogether, or his *Science of Logic*. That is far too large an issue to go into here, but the point is that MacIntyre is not entitled just to point to deep moral disagreements, unavoidable conflicts, and so forth, and claim incommensurability. What he calls disorder and incoherence could just as well be described as the results of human finitude: that we make claims on ourselves and others of a normative sort that are interrelated and complex, and we sometimes, perhaps often, do not know how to make it all work out. But then neither did poor Orestes, who faced only bad choices and no way out.

Moreover, there is a bit of a jumble in MacIntyre's own account. And how could there not be, given the complexity of this issue? The notion of virtue, doing well in a practice, is the core of the book, but MacIntyre admits that we cannot get along with just that notion. Despite his agreement with Anscombe, he also agrees with a bit of Aristotle and many of the Stoics that we need the notion of a binding law, and so a duty to that law. No matter what practice we are engaged in, there are, say, some things we may never do, no matter what, *unconditionally*. This is not, for MacIntyre, true only for those societies that have lost any sense of community, of communal ends. It is a necessity for any community.

> In discussing Aristotle's brief remarks on natural justice, I suggested that a community which envisages its life as directed toward a shared good which provides that community with its common tasks will need to articulate its moral life in terms both of the virtues and of law.[36]

36. Ibid., 169.

He does not raise as a problem how such a community could comfortably rely on such a notion of law. Whence such a law? Nature? God? Pure practical reason? How are we to understand potential conflicts between what virtue requires and what the law obliges? And that sort of question has to lead us back, I want to suggest, to some sort of dialectical approach like that pioneered by Hegel.

Finally we come to the issue of narrative, the key to MacIntyre's reanimation of an Aristotelian virtue theory without the "metaphysical biology."

## V

That reanimation depends on a number of interlocked notions, especially (i) a human practice, (ii) "the narrative order of a single human life," and (iii) a "moral tradition."[37] They are all ultimately necessary to understand this definition.

> A virtue is an acquired human quality the possession and exercise of which tends to enable us to achieve those goods which are internal to practices and the lack of which effectively prevents us from achieving any such goods.[38]

So a practice might be something like chess playing, an activity that does not count as a practice if engaged in merely for money or fame, but only if what one seeks is the good of chess playing itself, not some "external" good.[39] The practice has a teleological or "in order to" structure. One practices on the computer a few hours a day in order to be able to react faster when playing speed chess, moves to New York in order to study with the best teacher, exercises regularly in order to develop the endurance necessary to play long matches, and so forth. A practice, then, is something one can do well or poorly, as well as something one can get better or worse at.

37. Ibid., 187.

38. Ibid., 191.

39. The full definition of a practice: "By a 'practice' I am going to mean any coherent and complex form of socially established cooperative human activity through which goods internal to that form of activity are realized in the course of trying to achieve those standards of excellence which are appropriate to, and partially definitive of, that form of activity, with the result that human powers to achieve excellence, and human conceptions of the ends and goods involved, are systematically extended" (ibid., 187).

MacIntyre does not mean to say that virtues only show up in practices, just that practices are their natural home, or to say that practices as such, and the excellences required for them to be done well, all merit moral approval. But this is the basic structure.

We can now go on to say that such practices must be understood in that context within which the intelligibility of our actions as such is possible. For no one "just" engages in practices willy-nilly. The practices and their relation to one another must make sense to the agent, and this in the way we make sense of actions. That sense for MacIntyre, again in a way that is profoundly Hegelian, requires, first, as almost everyone agrees, reference to the intention of the agent. But that reference alone explains very little unless we can place the having of that intention in a context, a social setting, ultimately a social world, in which it would make sense to form and act on such an intention. But such social settings are themselves not isolatable; we won't have understood such a setting, it will rather appear strange and arbitrary, unless we can place that context itself in some historical narrative, unless we understand why it would have made sense in such a community that forming such an intention would make *that* kind of sense, the sense it does *at that time*. So, in summation, MacIntyre can say:

> Narrative history of a certain kind turns out to be the basic and essential genre for the characterization [what MacIntyre elsewhere calls the very intelligibility] of human actions.[40]

But of course narrative history is not really a narrative if it is just a "one damn thing after another" recitation of events. There must be a principle of unity, especially with respect to the question of the virtues, the unity of a human life. This can no longer be provided, MacIntyre argues, by the natural history of the life-form of some biological species. So if our lives are not intelligible to us except within a narrative structure (a structure that itself ultimately resides in a larger account of the intelligibility of such kinds of life-unities at a time), what could now, in our time, count as a credible sort of unified self-narration?

So MacIntyre has brought his account to the point where very sweeping and important questions must be posed.

40. Ibid., 208.

> In what does the unity of an individual life consist? The answer is that its unity is the unity of narrative embodied in a single human life. To ask "What is the good for me?" is to ask how best I might live out that unity and bring it to completion. To ask "What is the good for man?" is to ask what all answers to the former question must have in common.[41]

This does indeed bring everything, as if symphonically, to the point of resolution, or at least what one might expect as a resolution of themes. But we get something else:

> The virtues therefore are to be understood as those dispositions which will not only sustain practices and enable us to achieve the goods internal to practices, but which . . . will furnish us with increasing self-knowledge and increasing knowledge of the good.[42]

Or:

> We have then arrived at a provisional conclusion about the good life for man: the good life for man is the life spent in seeking for the good life for man, and the virtues necessary for the seeking are those which will enable us to understand what more and what else the good life for man is.[43]

This rather vague Socraticism is disappointing in several ways. If MacIntyre is right and Aristotle's own account of the basis for any possibility of answering such a question—the species-form of man, or "metaphysical biology"—then why should anyone commit to seeking "the" good life for man? It would seem to be Sisyphean. What basis, or what suggestion of a possible basis, is there in MacIntyre for expecting any principled resolution of the disagreements between those who believe that pious devotion to the revealed word of God, those who believe in endless experimentation with kinds of lives, and those who believe in endless philosophizing about the good life for man amount to the good life for man? And what does truly "*seeking*" amount to? Cracker-barrel or barroom reflection? Only the professional study of the giants of philosophy? *Any* earnest good faith at-

41. Ibid., 219.
42. Ibid.
43. Ibid.

tempt, no mater how clumsy? Why should we expect that any such notion of the human telos would be anything other than another confirmation of the incommensurable profusion of candidates that MacIntyre himself has presupposed? Given the buildup, the expectation was of something more substantive; not policy advice, of course, but perhaps something about the modern organization of labor, or the kind of politics such a conception of the human telos would require. Or: MacIntyre complains that there is no "coherent, rationally defensible statement of a liberal individualist point of view."[44] But MacIntyre's own terms suggest at least the possibility of a kind of Millian aspiration, one which holds that the best chance for collective progress in understanding the good life for man is a society with maximally free expression of individual points of view and a culture of healthy argumentation among individuals about the possibilities.

In his Postscript, MacIntyre notes that his notion of anything "rationally" superior to anything else is a historicist conception. He means rationally superior to a concrete prior alternative, superior in terms recognizable by the alternative itself. The proposed alternative can solve all the problems of the prior one and others that the prior one could not.

But this just emphasizes one last time Hegel's "third alternative" and the limitations of "half-hearted" Hegelianism. This sort of superiority is of no interest philosophically if the original position itself is not a substantive, serious alternative. That itself may be assertable only historically, in relation to its own predecessor, but then the point just gets pushed back, and we end up needing something far more weighty in a philosophy of history than MacIntyre has provided. Said another way, narratives have plots, and it is unsatisfying to hear that the best narration's plot concerns the search for the best plot.

Hegel's "plot," of course, concerns the "realization of freedom," something that will turn out to require certain institutional embodiments and certain practices of assigning responsibility and making claims on each other. The heart of it can be somewhat mysteriously summarized as "being one's self in another," and this is not the place to launch into an assessment of that claim.[45] But it is a substantive claim, and it is a far more nuanced

44. Ibid., 259.

45. The deeper issue presupposed in this formulation of the problem is one that must be faced by Hegel as well as MacIntyre. A contemporary account of Hegelian historicity, which eschews any sort of theodicy or a Cosmic Spirit puppeteer pulling the strings of world history, or any metaphysics of the necessary self-unfolding of the Divine Mind, or even any underlying

and historically extendable thesis than the traditional "knowledge of the Absolute" and "end of history" interpretations allow. And a Hegelian assessment of our current situation might be in many ways as pessimistic as MacIntyre's, but at least the Hegelians, awaiting the end of the new dark ages, will have a better sense of when it is safe to leave their monasteries.

---

appeal to human nature as the basis for the rational development of history, anyone who limits Hegel's ambition to "however much of the past development we can make rational sense of retrospectively" (with no guarantee that we will find any such order), accounts like Pinkard's and Honneth's and Brandom's and mine, must face an enormous question. It is this: Is it a matter of sheer contingency that history (or Western history) *can* be made sense of as some sort of progressive development? Could it just as easily have been otherwise, and are we, the inheritors, just fortunate? Even if we admit that "the Absolute" is not a thing, a *jenseits*, how can such a picture be squared with any sort of "absolute moment"? If it can't be, why would any sense we can make of what has happened before not manifest just another episode in the development, *how it looks now*, not a moment that allows us to claim even the little that MacIntyre does (that we now know that *the* best human life is the search for the best human life)? Hegel, without such an account of necessity and the absolute (or, in a formula, Hegel minus necessity), equals hermeneutics of various possible stripes, all the way up to and including Rortyean relativism.

# Acknowledgments

Earlier versions of the following chapters first appeared in the following places, and I am grateful to the editors and publishers for permission to reprint: chapter 1 in *Kant und die Berliner Aufklärung: Akten des IX. Internationalen Kant-Kongresses*, ed. V. Gerhardt, Rolf-Peter Horstmann, and Ralph Schumacher (New York: de Gruyter, 2001); chapter 2 in *European Journal of Philosophy* 13, no. 3 (2006); chapter 3 in *European Journal of Philosophy* 15, no. 3 (2007); chapter 4 in the online journal *Mediations* 26, no. 2 (Summer 2012) (www.mediationsjournal.org/); chapter 5 in *Philosophy and Social Criticism* 40, no. 9 (2014); chapter 6 in *Journal of Nietzsche Studies* 45, no. 2 (July 2014); chapter 7 in *Tragedy and the Idea of Modernity*, ed. J. Billings and M. Leonard (Oxford: Oxford University Press, 2015); chapter 8 in *Political Philosophy Cross-Examined: Perennial Challenges to the Philosophic Life*, ed. Thomas L. Pangle and J. Harvey Lomax (New York: Palgrave Macmillan, 2013); chapter 9 in *Principles and Prudence in the History of Political Thought*, ed. Jonathan Marks and Christopher Lynch (Albany: State University of New York Press, 2015); chapter 10 in *Journal of Nietzsche Studies* 44, no. 2 (July 2013); and chapter 11 in *Vermisste Tugend? Zur Philosophie Alasdair MacIntyres*, ed. Michael Kühnlein and Matthias Lutz-Bachmann (Berlin: Berlin University Press, 2013).

The discussion in chapter 3 grew out of three meetings, two in Chicago and one in Potsdam, organized under the auspices of an Alexander von Humboldt "TransCoop" grant held by Jim Conant and Sebastian Rödl. The subject of the meetings was "Transcendental Logic from Kant to Wittgenstein." I am grateful for the opportunity afforded by these occasions, the discussions they made possible, several exchanges and correspondence with John McDowell, and many conversations and seminar discussions with Jim Conant over the last several years.

I am particularly grateful to the Carl Friedrich von Siemens Stiftung and to its director, Heinrich Meier, for the fellowship that made possible work on many of these pieces while I was living in Munich during 2012–13. I am also grateful to Heinrich Meier for many very helpful conversations about the issues that arise in these chapters, especially for a long discussion about chapter 10.

# Bibliography

Allison, Henry. *Kant's Theory of Freedom*. Cambridge: Cambridge University Press, 1990.

Anscombe, G. E. M. *Intention*. Cambridge: Harvard University Press, 2000.

———. "Modern Moral Philosophy." *Philosophy* 33 (1958): 1–19.

Baron, Marcia. *Kantian Ethics Almost without Apology*. Ithaca: Cornell University Press, 1995. See esp. chap. 4, "Is Acting from Duty Morally Repugnant?"

Brandom, Robert. *Articulating Reasons: An Introduction to Inferentialism*. Cambridge: Harvard University Press, 2000.

———. "Facts, Norms, and Normative Facts: A Reply to Habermas." *European Journal of Philosophy* 8 (2000): 356–68.

———. "From a Critique of Cognitive Internalism to a Conception of Objective Spirit: Reflections on Descombes' Anthropological Holism." *Inquiry* 47 (2004): 236–53.

———. *Making It Explicit: Reasoning, Representing, and Discursive Commitment*. Cambridge: Harvard University Press, 1994.

———. "Reason, Expression, and the Philosophic Enterprise." In *What Is Philosophy?*, edited by C. P. Ragland and Sarah Heidt, 74–95. New Haven: Yale University Press, 2001.

———. "Replies." *Philosophy and Phenomenological Research* 57 (1997): 189–204.

———. "The Structure of Desire and Recognition: Self-Consciousness and Self-Constitution." *Philosophy and Social Criticism* 33 (2007): 127–50.

———. *Tales of the Mighty Dead: Historical Essays in the Metaphysics of Intentionality*. Cambridge: Harvard University Press, 2002.

Bubner, Rüdiger. "What Is Critical Theory?" In *Essays in Hermeneutics and Critical Theory*, 1–36. New York: Columbia University Press, 1988.

Cavell, Stanley. "The Avoidance of Love: A Reading of *King Lear*." In *Must We Mean What We Say? A Book of Essays*, 267–356. Cambridge: Cambridge University Press, 2008.

———. "Knowing and Acknowledging." In *Must We Mean What We Say? A Book of Essays*, 238–66. Cambridge: Cambridge University Press, 2008.

Chomsky, Noam. *New Horizons in the Study of Language and Mind.* Cambridge: Cambridge University Press, 2000.

Clark, Maudemarie. "On the Rejection of Morality: Bernard Williams's Debt to Nietzsche." In *Nietzsche's Postmoralism: Essays on Nietzsche's Prelude to Philosophy's Future,* edited by Richard Schacht, 100–122. Cambridge: Cambridge University Press, 2001.

Danto, Arthur. *Nietzsche as Philosopher.* New York: Columbia University Press, 1964.

Darwall, Stephen. "Abolishing Morality." *Synthese* 72 (1987): 71–89.

Deleuze, Gilles. *Expressionism in Philosophy: Spinoza.* Translated by Martin Joughin. New York: Zone Books, 1990.

Dickey, Laurence. *Hegel: Religion, Economics, and the Politics of Spirit, 1770–1807.* Cambridge: Cambridge University Press, 1987.

Fichte, J. G. "*Aenesidemus* review." In *Gesamtausgabe der Bayerischen Akademie der Wissenschaften,* edited by Reinhard Lauth and Hans Jacob, 11, 1, 287. Stuttgart: Frommann-Holzboog, 1965.

———. *Foundations of Transcendental Philosophy* (*Wissenschaftslehre nova methodo*). Translated and edited by Daniel Breazeale. Ithaca: Cornell University Press, 1992.

———. *Introductions to the "Wissenschaftslehre" and Other Writings.* Translated and edited by Daniel Breazeale. Indianapolis: Hackett, 1994.

———. "Second Introduction to the *Wissenschaftslehre.*" In *The Science of Knowledge: With the First and Second Introductions.* Translated and edited by P. Heath and J. Lachs. Cambridge: Cambridge University Press, 1970.

Foot, Philippa. "Nietzsche: The Revaluation of Values." In *Virtues and Vices and Other Essays in Moral Philosophy,* 81–95. Oxford: Oxford University Press, 2003.

Foster, Michael Beresford. *The Political Philosophies of Plato and Hegel.* Oxford: Clarendon Press, 1935.

Friedman, Michael. "Exorcising the Philosophical Tradition." In *Reading McDowell: Essays on Mind and World,* edited by Nicholas Smith, 25–57. New York and London: Routledge, 2002.

Gardner, Sebastian, and Matthew Grist, eds. *The Transcendental Turn.* Oxford: Oxford University Press, 2015.

Gass, William. *Fiction and the Figures of Life.* New York: Knopf, 1970.

Goethe, Johann Wolfgang von. *Wilhelm Meisters Lehrjahre.* Vol. 8 of *Goethes sämtliche Werke.* Berlin: Tempel, 2010.

Habermas, Jürgen. "From Kant to Hegel: On Robert Brandom's Pragmatic Philosophy of Language." *European Journal of Philosophy* 8 (2000): 322–46.

Harvey, David. *The Enigma of Capital and the Crises of Capitalism.* Oxford: Oxford University Press, 2010.

Haugeland, John. "Heidegger on Being a Person." *Noûs* 16 (1982): 15–26.

———. "Truth and Rule-Following." In *Having Thought: Essays in the Metaphysics of Mind,* 305–62. Cambridge: Harvard University Press, 2000.

Hegel, G. W. F. *Aesthetics: Lectures on Fine Arts.* Translated by T. M. Knox. Oxford: Oxford University Press, 1975.

———. *The Berlin Phenomenology.* Translated by Michael Petry. Dordrecht: Reidel, 1981.

———. *Die Phänomenologie des Geistes.* Hamburg: Felix Meiner, 1999.

———. *The Difference between Fichte's and Schelling's Systems of Philosophy*. Translated by H. S. Harris and Walter Cerf. Albany: State University of New York Press, 1977.

———. *Differenz des Fichte'schen und Scelling'schen Systems der Philosophie*. Vol. 4 of *Gesammelte Werke*. Edited by the Rheinisch-Westfaelischen Akademie der Wissenschaften. Hamburg: Felix Meiner, 1968.

———. *Elements of the Philosophy of Right*. Edited by Allen Wood. Translated by H. B. Nisbet. Cambridge: Cambridge University Press, 1991.

———. *The Encyclopaedia Logic*. Translated by T. F. Geraets, W. Suchting, and H. S. Harris. Indianapolis: Hackett, 1991.

———. *Faith and Knowledge*. Translated by Walter Cerf and H. S. Harris. Albany: State University of New York Press, 1977.

———. *Hegel's Logic: Being Part One of the Encyclopaedia of the Philosophical Sciences*. Translated by William Wallace. Oxford: Clarendon Press, 1975.

———. *Phenomenology of Spirit*. Translated by A. V. Miller. Oxford: Oxford University Press, 1977.

———. *The Phenomenology of Spirit*. Translated by Terry Pinkard. http://terrypinkard.weebly.com/phenomenology-of-spirit-page.html.

———. *Philosophy of Nature*. Translated by A. V. Miller. Oxford: Oxford University Press, 2004.

———. *Philosophy of Subjective Spirit*. Translated by M. Petry. Berlin: Springer, 1977.

———. *The Science of Logic*. Translated by George di Giovanni. Cambridge: Cambridge University Press, 2010.

———. *Science of Logic*. Translated by A. V. Miller. London: George Allen & Unwin, 1969.

———. *Wissenschaft der Logik*. 2 vols. Hamburg: Felix Meiner, 1969.

Heidegger, Martin. *Being and Time*. Translated by J. Macquarrie and E. Robinson. New York: Harper and Row, 1962.

———. *Nietzsche, Bd. I–II*. Pfullingen: Neske, 1961.

———. *Nietzsche, Volumes 1, 2, 3 and 4*. Translated by David Farrell Krell. New York: HarperOne, 1991.

———. *Sein und Zeit*. Tübingen: Niemeyer, 1972.

Henrich, Dieter. *Between Kant and Hegel*. Edited by David Pacini. Cambridge: Harvard University Press, 2008.

Henson, Richard. "What Kant Might Have Said: Moral Worth and the Over-Determination of Dutiful Actions." *Philosophical Review* 88 (1979): 39–54.

Herman, Barbara. "Leaving Deontology Behind." In *The Practice of Moral Judgment*, 208–40. Cambridge: Harvard University Press, 1993.

———. "Mutual Aid and Respect for Persons." In *The Practice of Moral Judgment*, 45–72. Cambridge: Harvard University Press, 1993.

———. "On the Motive of Acting from Duty." In *The Practice of Moral Judgment*, 1–22. Cambridge: Harvard University Press, 1993.

———. "The Practice of Moral Judgment." In *The Practice of Moral Judgment*, 73–93. Cambridge: Harvard, 1993.

Honneth, Axel. *Das Recht der Freiheit*. Berlin: Suhrkamp, 2011.

———. *Reification: A New Look at an Old Idea*. Oxford: Oxford University Press, 2008.

———. *The Struggle for Recognition: The Moral Grammar of Social Conflicts*. Cambridge: MIT Press, 1996.

Ishiguro, Kazuo. *The Remains of the Day*. 2nd ed. New York: Vintage, 1989.

James, Henry. *The Portrait of a Lady*. New York: Penguin, 1995.

Johnson, Adrian. "Slavoj Žižek's Hegelian Reformation: Giving a Hearing to *The Parallax View*." *Diacritics* 37, no. 1 (2007): 3–20.

Kant, Immanuel. *Critique of Practical Reason*. Translated by Lewis White Beck. Upper Saddle River, NJ: Prentice Hall, 1993.

———. *Critique of Pure Reason*. Translated and edited by Allan Wood and Paul Guyer. Cambridge: Cambridge University Press, 1998.

———. *Foundations of the Metaphysics of Morals*. Translated by L. W. Beck. New York: Macmillan, 1990.

———. *Grundlegung zur Metaphysik der Sitten*. In *Gesammelte Schriften*, Königlich Preussische Akademie der Wissenschaften, vol. 4. Berlin: de Gruyter, 1902–.

———. *Kritik der praktischen Vernunft*. In *Gesammelte Schriften*, vol. 5. Berlin: de Gruyter, 1902–.

———. *Die Religion innerhalb der Grenzen der bloßen Vernunft*. In *Gesammelte Schriften*, vol. 6. Berlin: de Gruyter, 1902–.

———. *Religion within the Limits of Reason Alone*. Translated by T. M. Greene and H. H. Hudson. New York: Harper, 1960.

Kaufmann, Walter. *Nietzsche: Philosopher, Psychologist, Antichrist*. Princeton: Princeton University Press, 1950.

Lacoue-Labarthe, Philippe, and Jean-Luc Nancy. *The Literary Absolute: The Theory of Literature in German Romanticism*. Translated by Philip Barnard and Cheryl Lester. Albany: State University of New York Press, 1988.

Lampert, Laurence. *Leo Strauss and Nietzsche*. Chicago: University of Chicago Press, 1996.

Landy, Joshua. *Philosophy as Fiction: Self, Deception, and Knowledge in Proust*. Oxford: Oxford University Press, 2009.

Lear, Jonathan. "The Disappearing 'We.' " *Proceedings of the Aristotelian Society*, supp. vol. 58 (1984): 219–42.

MacIntyre, Alasdair. *After Virtue: A Study in Moral Theory*. Notre Dame, IN: University of Notre Dame Press, 1981; 2nd ed. with Postscript, 1984; 3rd ed. with Prologue, 2007.

Marx, Karl. "Nationalökonomie und Philosophie." In *Frühschriften*, edited by S. Landshut, 225–316. Stuttgart: Alfred Körner Verlag, 1971.

McDowell, John. "Avoiding the Myth of the Given." In *Having the World in View*, 256–72. Cambridge: Harvard University Press, 2009.

———. "Brandom on Observation." In *Reading Brandom*, edited by Bernhard Weiss and Jeremy Wanderer, 129–44. Routledge: New York, 2010.

———. "Comment on Robert Brandom's 'Some Pragmatist Themes in Hegel's Idealism.' " *European Journal of Philosophy* 7 (1999): 90–93.

———. *Having the World in View*. Cambridge: Harvard University Press, 2009.

———. "Having the World in View: Sellars, Kant, and Intentionality." *Journal of Philosophy* 95 (1998): 431–91.

———. *Mind and World*. Cambridge: Harvard University Press, 1994.

———. "On Pippin's Postscript." *European Journal of Philosophy* 15 (2007): 395–410.
———. "Response to Dreyfus." *Inquiry* 50 (2007): 366–70.
———. "Selbstbestimmende Subjektivität und externer Zwang." In *Hegels Erbe*, edited by Christoph Halbig, Michael Quante, and Ludwig Siep, 184–208. Frankfurt am Main: Suhrkamp Verlag, 2004.
———. "Self-Determining Subjectivity and External Constraint." In *Having the World in View*, 90–107. Cambridge: Harvard University Press, 2009.
———. "What Myth?" In *The Engaged Intellect*, 308–23. Cambridge: Harvard University Press, 2009.
Moran, Richard. *Authority and Estrangement: An Essay on Self-Knowledge*. Princeton: Princeton University Press, 2001.
Muller, Marcel. *Les voix narratives dans la "Recherché du temps perdu."* Geneva: Droz, 1965.
Nehamas, Alexander. *Nietzsche: Life as Literature*. Cambridge: Harvard University Press, 1985.
———. "Nietzsche, Modernity, Aestheticism." In *The Cambridge Companion to Nietzsche*, edited by Bernd Magnus and Kathleen Higgins. Cambridge: Cambridge University Press, 1996.
Nietzsche, Friedrich. *Also Sprach Zarathustra*. Vol. 4 of *Kritische Studienausgabe*. Edited by G. Colli and M. Montinari. Berlin: de Gruyter, 1988.
———. *The Anti-Christ, Ecce Homo, Twilight of the Idols, and Other Writings*. Edited by Aaron Ridley and Judith Norman. Translated by Judith Norman. Cambridge: Cambridge University Press, 2005.
———. *Die fröhliche Wissenschaft*. Vol. 3 of *Kritische Studienausgabe*. Edited by G. Colli and M. Montinari. Berlin: de Gruyter, 1988.
———. *The Gay Science*. Translated by J. Nauckhoff. Cambridge: Cambridge University Press, 2001.
———. *Human, All Too Human*. Translated and edited by R. J. Hollingdale. Cambridge: Cambridge University Press, 1996.
———. *On the Genealogy of Morality*. Translated by Carol Diethe. Cambridge: Cambridge University Press, 2006.
———. *On the Genealogy of Morals and Ecce Homo*. Translated by W. Kaufmann. New York: Random House, 1967.
———. *Thus Spoke Zarathustra*. Translated by A. Del Caro. Cambridge: Cambridge University Press, 2006.
———. *Vom Nutzen und Nachteil der Historie für das Leben*. Frankfurt am Main: Insel, 1989.
———. *The Will to Power*. Translated by W. Kaufmann. New York: Vintage, 1968.
———. *Der Wille zur Macht*. Stuttgart: Alfred Kröner Verlag, 1964.
———. *Zur Genealogie der Moral*. Vol. 5 of *Kritische Studienausgabe*. Edited by G. Colli and M. Montinari. Berlin: de Gruyter, 1988.
O'Neill, Onora. "Kant after Virtue." In *Constructions of Reason: Explorations of Kant's Practical Philosophy*, 145–62. Cambridge: Cambridge University Press, 1990.
Pinkard, Terry. *German Philosophy, 1760–1860: The Legacy of Idealism*. Cambridge: Cambridge University Press, 2002.

———. *Hegel's Dialectic: The Explanation of Possibility*. Philadelphia: Temple University Press, 1988.

———. "MacIntyre's Critique of Modernity." In *Alasdair MacIntyre*, edited by M. Murphy, 176–200. Cambridge: Cambridge University Press, 2003.

Pippin, Robert. "Brandom's Hegel." *European Journal of Philosophy* 13 (2006): 381–408.

———. "Concept and Intuition: On Distinguishability and Separability." *Hegel-Studien* 39/40 (2004/2005): 25–40.

———. "The Conditions of Value." In Joseph Raz, *The Practice of Value*, edited by R. Jay Wallace, 86–105. Oxford: Oxford University Press, 2003.

———. "Die Begriffslogik als die Logik der Freiheit." In *Der Begriff als die Wahrheit: Zum Anspruch der Hegelschen Logik*, edited by Anton Koch, Alexander Oberauer, and Konrad Utz, 223–37. Paderborn/Munich: Ferdinand Schöningh, 2003.

———. "Fichte's Alleged Subjective, Psychological, One-Sided Idealism." In *The Reception of Kant's Critical Philosophy: Fichte, Schelling, and Hegel*, edited by Sally Sedgwick. Cambridge: Cambridge University Press, 2000.

———. "Hegel on Historical Meaning: For Example, the Enlightenment." *Bulletin of the Hegel Society of Great Britain* 35 (1997): 1–17.

———. "Hegel on Institutional Rationality." In *The Southern Journal of Philosophy* 39 (2001), supp., "The Contemporary Relevance of Hegel's Philosophy of Right," 1–25.

———. *Hegel on Self-Consciousness: Desire and Death in the "Phenomenology of Spirit."* Princeton: Princeton University Press, 2011.

———. *Hegel's Idealism: The Satisfactions of Self-Consciousness*. Cambridge: Cambridge University Press, 1989. See esp. chaps. 3 and 4.

———. *Hegel's Practical Philosophy: Rational Agency as Ethical Life*. Cambridge: Cambridge University Press, 2008. See esp. chaps. 2, 3, and 6.

———. *Idealism as Modernism: Hegelian Variations*. Cambridge: Cambridge University Press, 1997.

———. Introduction to *Thus Spoke Zarathustra*, edited with Adrian del Caro, viii–xxxv. Cambridge: Cambridge University Press, 2006.

———. "Kant on the Spontaneity of Mind." In *Idealism as Modernism: Hegelian Variations*, 29–55. Cambridge: Cambridge University Press, 1997.

———. *Kant's Theory of Form: An Essay on the "Critique of Pure Reason."* New Haven: Yale University Press, 1982. See esp. chap. 6.

———. "Kant's Theory of Value: On Allen Wood's *Kant's Ethical Thought*." *Inquiry* 43 (2000): 239–65.

———. "MacIntyre's Modernity: On the Third Alternative." In *Vermisste Tugend? Zur Philosophie Alasdair MacIntyres*, edited by Matthias Lutz-Bachmann and Michael Kühnlein. Berlin: Berlin University Press, 2013.

———. *Modernism as a Philosophical Problem: On the Dissatisfactions of European High Culture*. Oxford: Blackwell, 1991.

———. "Naturalness and Mindedness: Hegel's Compatibilism." *European Journal of Philosophy* 7 (1999): 194–212.

———. *Nietzsche, moraliste français: La conception nietzschéenne d'une psychologie philosophique*. Paris: Odile Jacob, 2005.

———. *Nietzsche, Psychology, and First Philosophy*. Chicago: University of Chicago Press, 2010.

———. "On Giving Oneself the Law." In *Freedom and the Human Person*, edited by Richard Velkley, 206–28. Washington, DC: Catholic University Press, 2007.

———. "Passive and Active Skepticism in Nicholas Ray's *In a Lonely Place*." *nonsite*, issue no. 5, March 18, 2012, http://nonsite.org/article/passive-and-active-skepticism-in-nicholas-ray's-in-a-lonely-place.

———. "Postscript: On McDowell's Response to 'Leaving Nature Behind,' " in *The Persistence of Subjectivity: On the Kantian Aftermath*. Cambridge: Cambridge University Press, 2005.

———. "The Psychological Problem of Self-Deception." In *Nietzsche, Psychology, and First Philosophy*, 85–104. Chicago: University of Chicago Press, 2010.

———. "The Realization of Freedom: Hegel's Practical Philosophy." In *The Cambridge Companion to German Idealism*, edited by Karl Ameriks. Cambridge: Cambridge University Press, 2000.

———. "Recognition and Reconciliation: Actualized Agency in Hegel's Jena *Phenomenology*." In *Recognition and Power: Axel Honneth and the Tradition of Critical Social Theory*, edited by Bert van den Brink and David Owen, 57–78. Cambridge: Cambridge University Press, 2007.

———. Review of *In the Beginning Was the Deed*, by Bernard Williams. *Journal of Philosophy* 104 (2007): 533–38.

———. "The Significance of Self-Consciousness in Idealist Theories of Logic." *Proceedings of the Aristotelian Society* 114 (2013–14): 145–66.

———. "Über Selbstgesetzgebung." In *Deutsche Zeitschrift für Philosophie* 6 (2003): 905–26.

———. " 'You Can't Get There from Here': Transition Problems in Hegel's *Phenomenology of Spirit*." In *The Cambridge Companion to Hegel*, edited by Frederick C. Beiser, 52–85. New York: Cambridge University Pres, 1993.

———. "What Is Conceptual Activity?" In *Mind, Reason, and Being-in-the-World: The McDowell-Dreyfus Debate*, edited by Joseph Schear, 91–109. London and New York: Routledge, 2013).

Reginster, Bernard. *The Affirmation of Life: Nietzsche on Overcoming Nihilism*. Cambridge: Harvard University Press, 2009.

Reinhardt, Karl. *Nietzsches Klage der Ariadne*. Frankfurt am Main: V. Klostermann, 1936.

Rödl, Sebastian. *Self-Consciousness*. Cambridge: Harvard University Press, 2007.

Rorty, Richard. "The Brain as Hardware, Culture as Software." *Inquiry* 47 (2004): 219–35.

Rosen, Gideon. "Who Makes the Rules around Here?" *Philosophy and Phenomenological Research* 57 (1997): 163–71.

Rousseau, Jean-Jacques. *The Social Contract and Other Later Political Writings*. Translated and edited by Victor Gourevitch. Cambridge: Cambridge University Press, 1997.

Royce, Josiah. *Lectures on Modern Idealism*. New Haven: Yale University Press, 1919.

Schacht, Richard. *Nietzsche*. London: Routledge, 1983.

Schlegel, Friedrich von. *Kritische Ausgabe seiner Werke: Charakteristiken und Kritiken I*

*(1796–1802)*, vol. 2, ed. Ernst Behler, Jean Anstett, and Hans Eichner. Paderborn: Schöningh, 1974.

Sellars, Wilfrid. *Science and Metaphysics.* Atascadero, CA: Ridgeview, 1992.

———. *Science and Metaphysics: Variations on Kantian Themes.* New York: Humanities Press, 1968.

———. "... this I or he or it (the thing) which thinks ...." *Proceedings of the American Philosophical Association* 44 (1971): 5–31.

Sluga, Hans. "Heidegger's Nietzsche." In *A Companion to Heidegger,* edited by H. L. Dreyfus and M. A. Wrathall, 102–20. Oxford: Blackwell, 2005.

Smith, Nicholas, ed. *Reading McDowell: On Mind and World.* New York and London: Routledge, 2002.

Smith, Zadie. "The North West London Blues." *NYR Blog,* June 2, 2012, http://www.nybooks.com/blogs/nyrblog/2012/jun/02/north-west-london-blues/.

Strauss, Leo. "Existentialism." *Interpretation* 22, no. 3 (1995): 303–20.

———. "Letter to Löwith." In Laurence Lampert, *Leo Strauss and Nietzsche.* Chicago: University of Chicago Press, 1996.

———. *Natural Right and History.* Chicago: University of Chicago Press, 1953.

———. "Note on the Plan of Nietzsche's *Beyond Good and Evil.*" In Laurence Lampert, *Leo Strauss and Nietzsche.* Chicago: University of Chicago Press, 1996.

———. "The Three Waves of Modernity." In *An Introduction to Political Philosophy: Ten Essays,* edited by Hilail Gildin. Detroit: Wayne State University Press, 1989.

———. "What Is Political Philosophy?" In *What Is Political Philosophy? And Other Studies,* 9–55. Chicago: University of Chicago Press, 1988.

Strong, Tracy. *Friedrich Nietzsche and the Politics of Transformation.* Berkeley and Los Angeles: University of California Press, 1975.

Taylor, Charles. "Dialektik heute, oder: Strukturen der Selbstnegation." In *Hegels Wissenschaft der Logik: Formation und Rekonstruktion,* edited by D. Henrich, 141–53. Stuttgart: Klett-Cotta, 1986.

Theunissen, Michael. *Sein und Schein: Die kritische Funktion der Hegelschen Logik.* Frankfurt am Main: Suhrkamp, 2008.

Thompson, Michael. *Life and Action: Elementary Structures of Practice and Practical Thought.* Cambridge: Harvard University Press, 2008.

———. "The Representation of Life." In *Virtues and Reasons: Philippa Foot and Moral Theory,* edited by Rosalind Hursthouse, Gavin Lawrence, and Warren Quinn. Oxford: Clarendon Press, 1995.

Wilamowitz-Moellendorff, Ulrich von. *Greek Historical Writing and Apollo: Two Lectures Delivered before the University of Oxford, June 8 and 4, 1908.* Translated by G. Murray. Oxford: Clarendon Press, 1908.

Wilcox, John. *Truth and Value in Nietzsche.* Ann Arbor: University of Michigan Press, 1974.

Williams, Bernard. *Ethics and the Limits of Philosophy.* Cambridge: Harvard University Press, 1986.

———. *In the Beginning Was the Deed: Realism and Moralism in Political Argument.* Princeton: Princeton University Press, 2005.

———. "Nietzsche's Minimalist Moral Psychology." In *Nietzsche, Genealogy, Morality,* edited by Richard Schacht, 237–50. Berkeley and Los Angeles: University of California Press, 1994.

———. "Persons, Character, and Morality." In *Moral Luck: Philosophical Papers, 1973–1980*, 1–19. Cambridge: Cambridge University Press, 1981.

———. *Shame and Necessity*. Berkeley and Los Angeles: University of California Press, 1993.

———. *Truth and Truthfulness*. Princeton: Princeton University Press, 2004.

———. "Wittgenstein and Idealism." In *Moral Luck: Philosophical Papers, 1973–1980*, 144–63. Cambridge: Cambridge University Press, 1981.

Witt, Charlotte. "Tragic Error and Agent Responsibility." *Annual Proceedings of the Center for Philosophic Exchange*, 1–22. Brockport: SUNY Brockport, 2005.

Wittgenstein, Ludwig. *Tractatus Logico-Philosophicus*. Translated by D. F. Pears and B. F. McGuinness. London: Routledge, 1966.

Wood, Allen. *Kant's Ethical Thought*. Cambridge: Cambridge University Press, 1999.

Žižek, Slavoj. *Less than Nothing: Hegel and the Shadow of Dialectical Materialism*. London: Verso, 2012.

# Index